The Presence of the Past

THE JOHNS HOPKINS SERIES IN CONSTITUTIONAL THOUGHT
Sotirios Barber and Jeffrey Tulis, Series Editors

Anne Norton
Reflections on Political Identity

Sheldon S. Wolin
The Presence of the Past: Essays on the State and the Constitution

Sheldon S. Wolin

The Presence of the Past

Essays on the State
and the
Constitution

The Johns Hopkins University Press
Baltimore and London

Hardcover edition originally published 1989
Johns Hopkins Paperbacks edition, 1990

The Johns Hopkins University Press, 701 West 40th Street, Baltimore,
Maryland 21211
The Johns Hopkins Press Ltd., London

The paper used in this book meets the minimum requirements of
American National Standard for Information Sciences—Permanence of Paper for Printed Library Materials, ANSI Z39.48-1984.

Library of Congress Cataloging-in-Publication Data

Wolin, Sheldon S.
    The presence of the past : essays on the state and the
Constitution / Sheldon S. Wolin.
        p.   cm.—(The Johns Hopkins series in constitutional
thought)
    Bibliography: p.
    Includes index
    ISBN 0-8018-3803-7 (alk. paper) ISBN 0-8018-4116-X (pbk.)
    1. United States—Constitutional history. 2. United States—
Politics and government. 3. State, The. 4. Democracy. I. Title.
II. Series.
JK261.W65   1989
320.973—dc19
                                                    89-2672
                                                    CIP

Contents

For Emily Purvis Wolin

Acknowledgments

I am greatly indebted to several institutions and individuals for their support and encouragement of the various endeavors represented by this volume. My thanks to Gary Bryner of Brigham Young University; William Appleman Williams of Oregon State University; Richard Ashcraft of the University of California at Los Angeles; William Connolly, editor of *Political Theory;* Fred Krinsky of Pomona College; Michael Roth of Scripps College; Joshua Miller of Lafayette College; Roger Boesche of Occidental College; and Dwight Anderson of San Diego State University. I am most grateful to the Department of Political Science and to the Clark Memorial Library, both of the University of California at Los Angeles, for a research appointment that enabled me to complete this volume.

Jeffrey Tulis and Sotirios Barber offered friendly encouragement, gentle pressure, and useful advice that contributed much to keeping me up to the mark. Special thanks to Arno Mayer, whose intellectual and political companionship helped to sustain these efforts during some bleak years; and, finally, to my former collaborator, John H. Schaar, whose friendship during our Berkeley years and whose profound grasp of American political culture did much to kindle my interest in many of the topics discussed in these pages.

Substantial portions of chapters 1, 4, 8, and 9 were previously published. I am grateful to the publishers for permission to reprint them here. "Collective Identity and Constitutional Power," in *The Constitution and the Regulation of Society,* ed. Gary C. Bryner and Dennis L. Thompson (Provo, Utah: Brigham Young University Press, 1988), pp. 93–122; "Toqueville: Archaism and Modernity," *Tocqueville Review* 7 (1985–86): 77–88; "Contract and Birthright," *Political Theory* 14 (May 1986): 179–93; "Democracy and the Welfare State," *Political Theory* 15 (November 1987): 467–500.

The Presence of the Past

Introduction

The writings that follow were composed for separate occasions, but they are offered in the hope that the reader will find in them a coherent political theory rather than an ill-assorted collection of essays. Political theory might be defined in general terms as a tradition of discourse concerned about the present being and well-being of collectivities. It is primarily a civic and secondarily an academic activity. In my understanding this means that political theory is a critical engagement with collective existence and with the political experiences of power to which it gives rise.

The present is neither a given nor an arbitrary designation of "now," that momentary experience of temporality which vanishes as soon as we name it. The present is another name for the political organization of existence. It is constituted by competing/cooperating structures of power that advance and secure the expectations and advantages of certain classes, individuals, groups, and organizations whose combination of authority and material resources enables them to concert power and thereby to exert a major influence over which of the possible presents a society is going to have or, at the least, which ones it will not have.

Collectivities take shape historically, that is, as a matter of fact; but they come into being mythically. Historians attempt to give evidentiary accounts of when, for example, the first settlements were established in North America or how the American presidency has changed. Myths have, however, more complex genealogies. They are stories that collectivities tell about themselves or have told to them. Their main purpose is to fix certain meanings about matters that are alleged to be fundamental because they pertain to the identity and flourishing of the whole society. Societies try to express what they are about as political collectivities by appealing to or constructing their pasts and connecting that past with present arrangements of power. The early American Puritans believed that their communities were favored by God and were the beginning of the fulfillment of certain biblical prophecies of a New Jerusalem. The myth thus supplied an ontological basis for the historical experience of the Puritan settlers, grounding it in the sacred truths of Scripture. Collectivity is an entanglement of historical and mythical elements which, to borrow a word, we might call mythistorical.

When the eighteenth-century American rebels tried to establish their independence from Great Britain, one of their first concerns was to define their collective identity as a "separate people" so that, as the Declaration of Independence put it, they might rightfully "assume among the powers of the earth, the separate and equal station to which the Laws of Nature and of Nature's God entitle them." An identity that is established by revolution is typically one that renounces the past and seeks liberation from it. A revolution, we might say, wants to begin history, not to continue it. And so the Declaration of Independence appealed to "self-evident truths" rather than to historical principles. The past was a reminder of their status as dependent colonials. About a decade later, when the erstwhile rebels turned once more to defining themselves collectively, they were no longer, so to speak, in British history. They now had their own history to interpret and to contend with.

The present is both fate and choice, history and politics. The pages that follow are all concerned with the present of the American collectivity and the presence of its past. They were written in response to the Bicentennial Era and to the phenomenon of bicentennialism itself. Beginning in the mid–1970s, Americans were invited to participate while government and corporate officials organized first the celebration of the Revolution of 1776 and then that of the Constitution of 1787, the two great events that, more than any others, are supposed to signify the decisive moments when the basic principles of American government and politics were established.

Bicentennials are by nature civic rather than scholarly events. They are rituals organized to promote a mythic history. They appear to be celebrating the past, but their most important function is to fix the collective identity in the present. A bicentennial might be thought of as an official story that narrates a past to support an image of collective identity that confirms a certain conception of the present. The narrative is designed to privilege a certain past in order to legitimate a particular present.

All of the essays revolve around the Constitution of 1787 in the sense that each adopts a somewhat different angle of survey in order to elicit further meanings from what is probably the richest source of American values, myths, ideologies, and theories. Each angle is chosen in the belief that it will illuminate the present political condition. Circling the Constitution is not offered as a way of establishing the "real" meaning of it or the "intent of the Founders," both of which strike me as incoherent notions induced by a misplaced biblicism. A constitution is not a revelation, and the Philadelphia Convention was not an epiphanic moment.

A constitution is simultaneously a political and a hermeneutical event. The Philadelphia Convention launched the Constitution in a heavily political way: those who attended were authorized to revise the Articles of Confederation, not discard it for an entirely new political scheme that radically shifted the emphasis of the system from the periphery to the center, from the states to a new national government. Even conventional historians have on occasion referred to the Constitution as a "coup." As a political event the Constitution represented a settlement about power on terms that the leaders of the dominant interests—"interests" defined here simply as amalgams of economic, class, sectional, and ideological elements—agreed upon and believed they could persuade the politically significant part of the population to accept. As a hermeneutical event it was a document whose content was agreed upon by the Founders, although its meaning was not. The Founders did not produce *a* particular meaning that was subsequently ratified. Rather, they set in motion a form of politics, a good part of which would be absorbed by contests to settle the meaning of the Constitution by unsettling some competing meaning.

There is a potential for controversy inherent in all constitutions and inevitable in a constitution that allows social forces to organize freely for political ends. Yet constitutions are not neutral or purely formal; they are prescriptive. This is because they deal with the highest of all political stakes. Constitutions and their politics are about power: about what power is to be used for, by whom, and according to what understandings and justifications, as well as to privilege certain public meanings and symbols. A constitution, even a liberal one, does not legitimate all types of politics, as the provisions of the original document regarding slavery and disregarding women demonstrate. A constitution is an attempt to constitute the conditions that will favor certain forms of politics over others.

Power struggles produce losses, and, as a consequence, things of value go out of the world. Constitutional struggles are no exception, although this wisdom runs counter to the American ideology of history, which wants to remember the past only for its monuments to progress. At the present moment, when a consciousness of the decline of American economic and political power has produced widespread anxieties, American public discourse is less hospitable than ever to languages of critical opposition. Like the dead whom we would rather honor than mourn, past losses are dissociated from present choices, and as a result the range of choice is circumscribed by the needs and wants of the victors. In one way or another, several of the chapters here are concerned with a particular kind of loss, the loss of democratic values, the constriction of democratic hopes, and the attenuation of the democratic element in institutions not otherwise conspicuous in their commitment to democratic ends (e.g., higher education). While what follows might justifiably be considered essays in retrieval, they are not intended as exercises in nostalgia. Rather, they express the conviction that the democratic way of life is the best for the vast majority of human beings and that a meritocracy with a human face and the existence of a few tokens supposedly representing the remarkable diversity of American society are not synonymous with democracy but a parody of equalitarianism.

Readers will find conceptions and emphases that are different from the ones favored by many historians and political theorists who prefer to interpret eighteenth-century American political ideas and institutions through the categories of "republicanism." In support of that interpretation, scholars have constructed a republican genealogy extending from eighteenth-century British publicists, such as Trenchard and Gordon, back through the "commonwealthmen" at the turn of the eighteenth century, and thence to Sidney, Milton, Harrington, Machiavelli, Cicero, and Aristotle. From that perspective, the most important categories for understanding the formative period in the American political tradition are virtue, civic participation, and liberty. The republican polity, it is claimed, depended upon the eagerness of its members to live by the prescriptions of "civic humanism" and to prefer civic over private life, sacrificing, when necessary, private to public interest.

This is not the place to dispute this interpretation. Suffice it to say that I believe that its significance is as much ideological as scholarly. Its categories serve to obscure questions of power and authority and to sever political activity from specific localities, thereby producing an abstract category, "participation," which can then be enlarged or attenuated, depending upon research needs. This strategy has the effect of muting the tensions between republicanism, with its strong historical attraction to elitism, and democracy, with its irreducibly populist strain. Although James Madison insisted that the Constitution posed a clear choice in favor of republicanism, most scholars have preferred the conciliatory view that the two were indistinguishable. The effect is to soften the antidemocratic tendencies of the Constitution as well as the ideological thrust of *The Federalist*. By this and similar maneuvers, democracy has acquired a paradoxical status in American public rhetoric: it is universally praised while dismissed in practice as irrelevant or embarrassing to a meritocratic society.

The use of the categories of republicanism and civic humanism also serves to obscure one of the most unique—and neglected—achievements of the Founders: they founded not only a constitution but the American version of the modern state. There are good political reasons why this accomplishment has not been praised or, until recently, made the object of historical and theoretical inquiry. Americans have been taught to view the state as an un-American invention, something that foreigners were burdened with, and something whose absence helped to define America's uniqueness. Those who drafted the Philadelphia constitution were clear-eyed about wanting to break out of what they viewed as the ineffectual system represented by the Articles of Confederation, and so they devised a different distribution of power and set about creating a different collective identity to sustain it. The Founders preferred the phrase *national government* rather than *state*. The end result of their labors at Philadelphia, however, was to launch America on the road toward greater centralized power and toward assigning the state a strategic role in the development of economic life, a road that had already been traveled a fair distance by European countries such as Britain, France, and Prussia. The uniqueness of the American political experience in the late eighteenth century was not that Americans chose a constitution instead of a state but rather that they chose both at the same moment.

Less than two hundred fifty years ago, "America" was primarily the name for the diffused powers represented by thirteen provincial societies and their scattered towns, villages, and settlements. Now it signifies an imperial system struggling to preserve its global influence while simultaneously launching its power into outer space. Once, America's economy was a decentralized system of small property owners, then one dominated by huge corporations; now it is that of a major player in an international political economy where all of the contestants desperately strive to reassure themselves and the nonplayers that it is really a system of orderly transactions and adjustments. Once, power had to operate in a context of a localized politics, emphasizing liberty, suspicion of concentrated power, and strict accountability of power holders to what was once called "the body of citizens." The politics of citizens has since been overwhelmed by an imperial system and rendered marginal and predictable, first by a politics of professional politicians and party bureaucracies, then by a politics of managers, and now by a politics consumed by low military and high technological "imperatives."

The irony of the Bicentennial Era is that it has been framed, so to speak, at each end by political scandal and constitutional crisis: the revolutionary bicentennial of 1976 followed not long after the Watergate investigations, which led to the resignation of President Nixon; the bicentennial of the Constitution overlapped with unconstitutional improprieties concerning the sale of arms to Iran and the diversion of funds to the Nicaraguan counter-revolutionaries. The woeful symmetry is, on the one side, between a celebration of revolution after the president had tried to subvert constitutional liberties and, on the other, a celebration of constitutionalism while the president was trying to evade constitutional limitations in order to finance the reversal of a revolution in a small country.

In light of these unhappy coincidences, one cannot but feel slightly apprehensive upon learning that bicentennialism is about to become a permanent fixture. Like all good bureaucratic institutions nurtured by public funds, the Commission on the Bicentennial of the American Constitution, which is headed by a former chief justice of the Supreme Court, has found that the obvious way to perpetuate its existence is to organize other bicentennial observations. So the bicentennial of Congress was to be celebrated in 1988; that of the executive will be observed in 1989; of the judiciary, in 1990; of the Bill of Rights, in 1991. That the commission is dedicated to preserving the past is undeniable. For when the chief justice was asked to justify his decision to continue holding the meetings of the commission in private, he replied that he was merely following the precedent of secrecy set by the Philadelphia convention.

These writings are intended as a contribution to a renewed democratic discourse, one that can be disentangled from the disillusions bred by recent neoconservative rhetoric and the cheap flattery of cynical demagogues of right-wing populism. That discourse must confront the meaning of the state and of its cohabitation with corporate power. Facing up to the state means recognizing that the dominant forms of power in the society, both public and private, are inherently antidemocratic in their structure and objectives and that if democracy is to be practiced and extended, the conditions of politics will have to be transformed.

One / Collective Identity and Constitutional Power

> Constitutionalism by dividing power, provides a system of effective restraints upon governmental action.
> — CARL FRIEDRICH

> The fabric of American Empire ought to rest on the solid basis of THE CONSENT OF THE PEOPLE. The streams of national power ought to flow immediately from that pure original fountain of all legitimate authority.
> — ALEXANDER HAMILTON

These two statements, one from a twentieth-century authority on constitutional government and the other from the most authoritative treatise ever written on the American Constitution,[1] set forward two principles that form the main paradox at the center of the American Constitution and perhaps of modern constitutionalism generally. One principle emphasizes restrained and divided power, the other an ultimate power, theoretically unified and unconstrained, the sovereign power of "the people."

This paradoxical conception of power is as old as the Constitution itself. On the one side, the Constitution provides for numerous arrangements, such as the separation of powers, and prohibitions, such as those embodied in the first ten amendments to the original document, designed to restrain and limit the exercise of power by public officials. On the other side, the Constitution provides for the positive exercise of power. In the form of authority to tax and spend, it makes possible the generation of power on a regular and assured basis. In the form of broad powers to regulate commerce and currency and to wage war, the Constitution encourages the use of power without specifying the ends of its use, provisions Hamilton seized upon in order to establish a high doctrine of state power early in the history of the Republic.

Collective Identity: Constituted and Disputed

There were stakes other than state power involved in establishing and operating a constitution, and these were suppressed by Hamilton's rhetoric. A constitution not only constitutes a structure of power and authority, it constitutes a people in a certain way. It proposes a distinctive identity and envisions a form of politicalness for individuals in their new collective capacity. The Preamble to the American Constitution, although it has no judicial standing, is a striking example of the assertion of a new collective identify to replace the one expressed in the Articles of Confederation: "WE THE PEOPLE of the United States, in Order to form a more perfect Union . . . " The Preamble also specified the values by which the new collectivity aspired to be known: justice, domestic peace, common defense, the general welfare, and liberty. Finally, the Preamble also suggests that a constitution is the result of collective action, that a people can act collectively: "WE THE PEOPLE . . . do ordain and establish this CONSTITUTION for the United States of America."

In large measure, collective identity is created by and perpetuated through public discourse. Public discourse consists of the vocabulary, ideologies, symbols, images, memories, and myths that have come to form the ways we think and talk about our political life.[2] How that discourse has come to be what it is is the history of American political and legal thinking and practices. Beginning with the controversy over the ratification of the Constitution itself, the basic terms of the discourse have been vigorously and repeatedly contested. The ratification controversy exposed a considerable body of opinion, loosely identified with the antifederalists, opinion that wanted to prevent political identity from becoming identified with centralized national power and a nationalized people. Identity, they argued, was in fact pluralistic and diffusive, centered primarily in the state and local governments, with only a minimal national loyalty and that owed to some loose confederational authority. In effect, the antifederalists denied the existence of "We the People" and rejected the mode of collective existence required for effecting the vision of an "American Empire."[3] With irritation (but for good reason), the British had described the colonists as a "fractious people."

This suggests that a certain problematic quality attaches to collective identity, that it is not just an inheritance but, perforce, an acquisition remade in the process of transmission. It is natural to assume that, with the ratification of the Constitution in 1789, America's collective identity was settled. It is easy to forget, particularly on celebratory occasions, that in the 1790s, the first decade of the Constitution, a fierce dispute raged over the constitutionality of the Alien and Sedition Laws. It culminated in the Virginia-Kentucky Resolutions that asserted the rights of the states to declare federal laws unconstitutional. During the next half-century preceding the Civil War, a number of equally intense debates erupted: the embargo controversy, the constitutionality of the national bank, the Hartford Convention, the nullification controversy, and "internal improvements." Each of these involved crucial questions about the meaning of such basic terms as power, authority, rights, consent, and federalism. The answers helped to define America's political identity and to legitimate certain ways of talking about it. Yet it is no exaggeration to claim that throughout much of American history the very idea of American collective identity has been a contested notion, contested not only by words but by force as well.

It may be, then, that American political identity lies essentially in its contested character, in the practical denial of metaphysical notions of "the people" or of "national unity." *E pluribus unum* has been more of an expression of faith, the political equivalent of trinitarianism, than a political fact. For the disputes over collective identity did not end with the Civil War. The dominant beliefs about it were challenged, in the name of anti-imperialism and American exceptionalism, at the time of the Spanish-American War and World Wars I and II. The most significant challenge since the Civil War came, however, during the 1960s when there was widespread resistance to the imperial image being cast for the society by its dominant groups.

Twentieth-century challenges have a surprising element of continuity with their historical antecedents. Antifederalists, nullificationists and secessionists, and Vietnam War resisters have been depicted as antiprogressive, literally reactionary, yearning for a pastoral America—Luddites resisting the march of industrialization and the responsibilities of power. Beginning with Ronald Reagan's election in 1980, there has been a special piquancy to the controversy over collective identity. Throughout most of the decade, the champions of technological progress and global expansion of American power were led by a president whose talent was to evoke the same anachronistic values cherished by the "reactionary" critics of unlimited technological innovation and global hegemony. For their part, the contemporary inheritors of the antifederalist tradition have seen themselves as radicals fighting against the centralization of power and the overproduction of it.

The question of what kind of collective identity has been at stake in contemporary debates can be clarified by reconsidering Hamilton's attempted resolution of the paradox of constitutional restraint and the theoretical claim of an unlimited power in the sovereign people. With typical panache, he would resolve the paradox by arguing for a dramatically expanded state power that was made possible because of the paradox rather than in spite of it.

Producing Power and Reducing Politicalness

No one appreciated more acutely than Hamilton that, although restraint on power was an important element of constitutionalism, it was not its essence. Rather, insofar as there was a constitutional essence, it was power itself. In Hamilton's expansive view, a constitution represented a way of organizing and generating power for the pursuit of great national objectives. The Constitution was to be the means of assuring a continuous generation of power. This would require a bold theoretical move that would transform the meaning of the power of the people while retaining the traditional meaning associated with contract theory. In contract theory, the power of the people was identified with a primal act of consent that legitimated the subsequent exercise of authority by officeholders. Thus, it stood for a formal principle rather than a material one. Hamilton transformed the power of the people to mean the substance of power, not simply its authorization. The sense in which the power of the people was sovereign or unlimited now assumed a different meaning: it referred to the material power of the entire collectivity, the aggregate of its social resources that consent now made potentially available to the state.

Hamilton: The Constitution of Power and People

According to Hamilton's formula, the "streams of power" ought to flow from the "fountain of legitimate authority," represented by the consent of the people, to those who govern. But precisely what kind of power is it that streams from the people, and how do they come to have it? Do they "have" power or would it be more accurate to say that they "compose" it? What does the introduction of a constitution do to that power—is it a way of composing consent to assure the flow of power and concurrently its legitimation? If so, what are the implications for the political status of the people? Are they being constituted so as to be watchers of how their powers are being used rather than participants in those uses?

Hamilton's account seems so formulaic to the contemporary reader, so similar to the pseudopopulist rhetoric packaged for today's political candidates, that the temptation is to see in Hamilton's metaphor only a ritualistic expression devised by a notorious antidemocrat who was compelled by political circumstances to give lip service to the noxious principle of popular sovereignty. Read differently, however, it is a formula for the constitution of power. The formula unlocks access to power, making it available to the state. Under its terms, consent does more than sanction or sanctify power. It opens up the possibility of an uninterrupted transfer of substance from the "fountain." Hamilton's imagery of a "stream" of power that flows to a government suggests that, by consenting, the people concede access to their power—power that the governors collect and regularize/channel. The power released by consent consists of resources such as money, skills, and bodily strength, which, in the form of taxation and conscription, government can draw upon because, ideally, its claims are recognized as legitimate. By the alchemy of authority, power is transmuted; it is embodied in public agents (e.g., bureaucratic and military personnel) and public policies and decisions. In this respect, Hamilton's imagery was a perfectly accurate representation of his intentions—and of most of the original Framers as well—of reducing popular influence and enhancing the power of the state.

One need not rehearse the familiar story of the numerous devices for restraining and reducing the power and participatory activity of the citizenry: indirect elections of senators and the president; staggered terms of office for senators and a long incumbency of six years; the reduction of the powers of local authorities. Thus, state power begins in the materialization of the activity of the people, that is, in what is produced by their labor and skill. What their consent signifies is their willingness to make over, in whole or in part, their powers and products to be used by the state. While their power is being made available to government, the loss is experienced by them as political passivity.

What is at stake here is an interpretation of the meaning of collective identity as expressed through the constitutionalization of power. Hamilton's interpretation was a theme on which there would be many later variations: it identified the collectivity with the exercise of power by state officials who would define, in policy terms, the meaning of national values or purposes, and who would be held accountable for their policies either by judicial decisions or by popular elections. At the same time, a constitution is an experiment in forging a collective identity. The identity of the collectivity, who it is and what it stands for politically, is made known through the constitutionally sanctioned actions of public officials and the response, or lack thereof, of the collectivity to those actions. Thus, a constitution has a circular nature: it is constituted by the collectivity ("We the People . . . do ordain and establish this Constitution . . ."), and the actions performed under it, in turn, constitute the collectivity. The inherent danger is that the identity given to the collectivity by those who exercise power will reflect the needs of power rather than the political possibilities of a complex collectivity; it will be a collectivity devoted to consolidating *unum* rather than to encouraging *plures*.

The power-generating nature of the American Constitution tends to be overlooked because so many constitutional controversies have been dramatized in tetms of alleged violations of constitutional limits. Important as these questions are, they should not obscure the various ways in which the Constitution has been used to legitimate the enormous structure of power created by later scientific and industrial changes. The peculiarity of the American way of legitimating power is that it tends, simultaneously, to disguise the actual expansion of state power under the category of pragmatic programs (from "internal improvements" in the nineteenth century to Chrysler bailouts in the twentieth) while welcoming the increasing power of "private" economic institutions and interpreting that increase as located "outside" the proper "sphere of government." These tendencies have their source in the narrow conception of a constitution which marked off the political thinking of the Framers from that of contemporaries such as Montesquieu and Hume.[4] Stated simply, American thinkers conceived a constitution primarily in terms of legal limits and procedural requirements for a selected set of institutions which were then identified as "government" and declared to be formally separated from social institutions of class, status, religion, and economy. Ideologically, the formal separation was justified on liberal grounds; that is, it promoted political equality, toleration, and private rights, especially those of property. In contrast, Montesquieu and Hume were constantly seeking to expose the interconnections between social and political practices and authorities. Indifference to these interconnections would later figure importantly in the Reagan administration's program for "returning" governmental power to local authorities and inviting corporate institutions to assume some of the functions of government.

In what follows I shall inquire into the two themes of collective identity and power. My thesis is that a crisis in collective identity began to crystallize in the 1980s and that it was interconnected with important changes in the form and substance of state power.

Collective Identity and Difference

Political rhetoric, even when artfully packaged, may yield important clues about changing understandings of collective identity and its relationship to political reality. Political rhetoric is public speech fashioned for public occasions. Typically, such moments are highly ritualized (e.g., the presidential State of the Union message) and marked by the recital of collective myths (e.g., the sovereignty of "the people"). The rhetoric of public occasions is often revealing for the promises that it makes, the political vision it unfurls, the metaphors it lingers over, the folk memories it appeals to. Public rhetoric is also concerned with educating the citizenry to perform a collective role in ways that will support and strengthen the powers of those who govern. Rulers are continually making judgments about what the real world is, and these judgments often run counter to the understandings and expectations that past rhetoric had encouraged. Recall in this connection President Carter's unsuccessful attempt to revise public perceptions of the Soviet Union. Political rhetoric is not synonymous with mere oratory. It is enveloped by a structure of expectations that limits what a political rhetorician may do and even dictates what he must do.

Presidential campaigns are particularly restricting precisely because of their ritualistic character. The efficacy of ritual depends upon its adherence to the formulas that govern the particular kind of ritual in question. Presidential campaigns serve as rituals of renewal. They prepare society for the reconfirmation of authority which will follow upon the ritual of combat reenacted by the two claimants. What the society expects from the two rivals is not only a demonstration of prowess but, equally important, a restatement of collective identity. The people want to be reassured of who they are, where they have come from historically, what they now stand for, and what is to be done about the perils and possibilities that lie ahead of them as a people.

Although presidential elections are often described as though they were military engagements in which campaigns are waged, strategies devised, and supporters mobilized, the struggle rarely pits sharply opposing conceptions of collective identity against each other. Rather, what is offered are nuances daubed over the same collective images. The apparent unanimity about common identity contrasts strikingly with the actuality of difference in American society. Although the sharpness of the lines may be disputed, there is no arguing that Americans are significantly marked off from each other by distinctions of class, region, race, ethnicity, religion, and gender, and by deep contrasts in education, wealth, literacy, health, and general life prospects.

In this context, collective identity appears as a superimposition, as a way of suppressing or containing difference. Differences can be especially painful among social groups in areas threatened by dislocative changes. They produce anxieties that are frequently expressed as a dogmatic demand that difference yield to unity. Groups whose identities are most threatened are often the most insistent champions of collective unity. During the 1960s, bumper stickers demanded "America: love it or leave it"; while the stickers could commonly be seen on pickups, they were rarely observed on sports cars or limousines.

The past two decades have seen the proliferation of varieties of differentiated consciousness. Blacks, feminists, Hispanics, Native Americans, homosexuals, and many others have challenged the images of homogeneity that have accompanied the dominant conceptions of collective identity. The images of homogeneity have been strained further by the global dislocation occasioned in part by American political and economic policies. These have caused thousands of human beings, many of them Asians and Hispanics, to flee their homelands for the United States, thereby helping to produce new differences and to accentuate existing ones.

In the course of American history, some differences have been celebrated, others suppressed; in some eras a difference that had previously been suspect, as in the case of the Nisei during World War II, has later been accepted, even admired. Acceptance into the collectivity or "mainstream" is predicated upon acceptance by aliens and immigrants of mainstream institutions and their prerequisites. This results in a paradoxical situation in which the newly arrived groups unintentionally connive at their own repression—and by repression here I mean no more than the inability to express difference freely. The mere fact of their presence signifies that they expect to find a freer life and a materially better one. Since the vast majority have come from countries that are poor and ruled oppressively, their condition in the new land is bound to be experienced as an improvement. For them the contrast is not between the promise of American democracy and the realities of corporate America, but between a life lived in fear and repression and a life in which one is left alone to compete furiously for economic survival and, occasionally, for large fortunes. In short, they become a force for conservatism, concerned mainly with economic opportunities and nondiscrimination.

The Narrowing of Collective Identity

From another perspective, however, the influx of potential citizens and resident aliens represents a population for which most of the symbols,

myths, and memories that compose the meaning of collective identity
are meaningless. There is, at the same time, not much confidence that
the public schools will be able to initiate the varied groups into the
common store of collective symbols, a task made all the more problematic by the pressures for increasing the number and variety of private schools and for promoting bilingualism. The implication is that
collective identity will survive in a sharply attenuated form, unable
either to give generous expression to differences or to assume a significant fund of shared symbols and representations.

The development toward a minimal collective identity is reflected
in the way that both of the major political parties have settled upon
ideologies that oscillate no farther than from right-center to center.
The center symbolizes a collective identity in which the only meaning-
ful differences are represented by taboos, that is, "the extremes of Left
and Right." Immigrant groups eager to learn the recipe of material
success in America thus complement a political system that finds it
relatively easy to reward difference when it is sublimated into entre-
preneurship (e.g., "black capitalism") but difficult to represent political differences when they challenge the status quo, even modestly
(e.g., the isolation of Jesse Jackson by the Democratic party).

There are pressures from a different source that work toward the
same result. American business, in its efforts to compete successfully
with its counterparts in Japan, Taiwan, and South Korea, has placed
special emphasis on the importance of a stable political base and of
supportive state policies. By a "stable political base," business spokes-
persons mean the absence of domestic unrest, that is, a politically passive population that is not likely to demand sharp departures in governmental policies or to take to the streets in the event of austerity
measures. By "supportive state policies" they mean nothing less than
an active state that will intervene to offset the advantages perceived to
be enjoyed by business in rival societies. The one thrust reinforces the
tendency toward constricting the expression and representation of difference, while the other presupposes an enlargement of state power
and thus produces a situation where, as state power enlarges, its base
becomes narrower.

The disparity between state power and its grounding in collective
identity is inherent in the dilemma confronting advanced capitalist societies generally. Compelled by the fierce demands of international
competition to innovate ceaselessly, capitalism resorts to measures that
prove socially unsettling and that hasten the very instability that capi-
talists fear. Plants are closed or relocated; workers find themselves
forced to pull up roots and follow the dictates of the labor market; and
social spending for programs to lessen the harm wrought by economic

"forces" is reduced so as not to imperil capital accumulation. Thus, the exigencies of competition undercut the settled identities of job, skill, and place and the traditional values of family and neighborhood which are normally the vital elements of the culture that sustains collective identity and, ultimately, state power itself.

Competing Myths: Archaism and Futurism

These developments are reflected in the opposing myths at the center of American self-understanding. One myth looks to the past for reassurance, the other to the future for hope. The first is a myth of fundamentalism. It wants to restore the system of free enterprise, recover the intentions of the Founding Fathers and the original Constitution of limited governmental powers, and revive religious faith. Fundamentalism wants schools "to go back to basics" and to teach the elements of morality; it wants to restore the traditional family and to keep sexual relations firmly within it.

If the one myth is archaic and restorationist, the other is futurist and innovative, caught up in the excitement of recurrent technological revolutions and convinced that only a rapidly changing, adaptive society, committed to superiority in the sciences, can preserve American hegemony. The futurist myth was expressed a few years ago by Reagan's secretary of state, George P. Shultz, on the occasion of the celebration of the three hundred fiftieth anniversary of the nation's oldest academic institution. "The advanced nations," he declared, "are already in the throes of a new scientific and technological revolution . . . an Informational Revolution [that] promises to transform the structure of our economies and the political life of the planet as thoroughly as did the Industrial Revolution of the 18th and 19th centuries."[5]

In keeping with his postmodern temper, the futurist is inclined toward agnosticism, preferring to emphasize national power rather than its constitutional limits, scientific inquiry rather than religious values, and schools that will prepare students for a high-tech economy rather than unduly worrying about their moral character. If he is like Secretary Shultz, the futurist will even warn against the "dangers" posed by the very values of the fundamentalist. The absorption in the American past and pride in America's uniqueness, Shultz warned, lie close to a "thoughtless escapism" and "isolationist throwback" that ignores America's global responsibilities and its interdependence and produces evils such as protectionism. He also attacked "self-righteous moralism" because it distorts political realities. He singled out "the fervor for punitive sanctions against South Africa" as an example. The image of collectivity which the futurist Shultz summoned up was far removed from the images evoked by the archaist Reagan in his appeals to the Declaration of Independence, the Constitution, and the morality of plain folks. It was, instead, an image whose basic elements were not political or moral, but economic and scientific: "So it is no coincidence that the free nations have once again been the source of technological innovation. Once again an economic system congenial to free scientific inquiry, entrepreneurial risk taking and consumer freedom has been the fount of creativity and the mechanism for spreading innovation far and wide."[6]

One of the striking features of Ronald Reagan's rhetoric in the past two presidential campaigns was his skill in combining the two myths of archaism and futurism. Sometimes he would identify American collective identity with the remote past, recalling the nation's founding myths, its favored self-images of freedom, progress, moral superiority, piety, chosenness, and free enterprise. He warned that collective identity had become blurred and compromised by the growth of governmental power, by the erosion of freedom and economic initiative, by the neglect of national security, and by the laxity that had come to characterize sexual conduct.

But he also spoke enthusiastically of new technology and of the importance of reshaping society and government to accord with the demands of the new age, all the while insisting that conservatism did not necessarily mean clinging to the past. His campaign speeches created a mood of expectancy that fundamental changes were in the offing, that regulatory power would be diminished while state power (foreign affairs, military, and police) would be increased, symbols of authority would be restored, and that, collectively, the society would be encouraged to think of itself in more assertive, hopeful terms. The ultimate reassurance was that the society could have it both ways: early modern fundamentalism and postmodern agnosticism.

The election of Ronald Reagan signaled a change that went beyond the simple transference of office from one political party to another or the replacement of a liberal centrist program by a self-proclaimed conservative ideology. The fact of the election should be interpreted in the context of national myth and ritual. For it was not only the fact of Reagan's victory that matters in the ritual of renewal but also what was signified by the incumbent's defeat after only one term, an event that had not occurred for almost half a century. It is far more traumatic, and because of that far more redefining of collective identity, when the highest symbol of authority is ritually sacrificed than when that authority fulfills the appointed term and hands over the regalia of office. Carter was dramatically stripped of office. It may be too strong to say that a ritual murder was performed, but it would not be to say that a ritual of rejection was acted out and that the decisiveness of the election had to do with the dissatisfactions felt by voters over the kind of collective political identity they had come to embody. The rejection of Carter was the expression of collective fear inspired by the hostage crisis, with its attendant feelings of frustration and anxiety about American "weakness," and by the gathering economic recession, with the doubts it inspired about the strength of the economy in the new era of international economic competition. Reagan's campaign first focused, then exploited, a widespread wish for an altered collective identity. As we shall see, that wish reflected deep-running changes in the nature of state power in America that raise the question of what kind of state or political order requires, or is congenial with, the newly emerging collective self-conception.

Finding a Vocabulary for the Redefinition of Collectivity

At the time of Reagan's striking electoral victory in 1980, numerous commentators sensed that a deep change in national orientation and consciousness had occurred. The notion that they felt best expressed it was "revolution." Even before the inauguration it was seized upon by defenders of Reaganism as well as by critics. There were some, for example, who contended that the actions of the Reagan administration were an attempt to reverse nearly five decades of enlightened social change by launching a counterrevolution against both civil rights and the doctrines of social equality associated with the welfare state founded by FDR's New Deal and completed by LBJ's Great Society. There were others who saw the Reagan record as a revolution manqué because, instead of restoring public piety and private morality, their leaders surrendered to the temptations of "pragmatism." And there were still others who were convinced that the campaign rhetoric about "a new beginning" was being realized in important ways and that everything would turn on whether the revolution would be consolidated and perpetuated. Despite these opposing views, it is clear, I think, that "revolution" was a surrogate for talking about a fundamental change, real or imagined, in collective identity.

We can make a start on the task of sorting out these interpretive efforts by posing the question, What kind of revolution was it that seemed bent upon breaking, not with the distant past, but with the recent present?

A plausible response to that question might be to say that it was a revolution of a limited sort: it brought a measure of efficiency and fiscal prudence into the operation of state and local governments while reducing the scope of some federal operations. It can, therefore, be described as a progressive change, perhaps even a modernizing one. It suggests further that the society may have reached a point in its history when administrative reform constitutes the meaning of progress or modernization and indicates their limits. In so doing, of course, this line of inquiry provokes the question of what all of this has to do with the self-proclaimed conservative character of the Reagan regime. That question presupposes, mistakenly, that Reagan conservatism can be reduced to nostalgia for the past. Perhaps, however, there are more complex, even contradictory tendencies reflected in Reaganism, and perhaps these reflect a larger change in American political identity.

The Contribution of the New Deal

Analysts arguing that Reaganism was a counterrevolution directed against the legacy of the New Deal have tended to focus primarily on the administration's animus toward government-sponsored social programs. Although many of today's historians discount the revolutionary nature of the changes introduced by the New Deal, a strong case can be made that the New Deal did produce profound changes in collective identity and that it did legitimate an enlarged conception of state power. The New Deal attempted to resolve a domestic economic emergency occurring within the international economy of capitalism by a variety of measures that signaled an unprecedented degree of state intervention into a peacetime economy and the beginnings of national social policy.

There was, of course, ample precedent for governmental action of a nonwelfare kind. Governmental intervention and regulation of the economy is as old as the Republic itself. Alexander Hamilton, the first secretary of the treasury, devised a program of state action that would lay the foundations for national economic power by subsidizing domestic producers and financiers and attaching the "affection" of the "propertied classes" to the new national government.[7] The difference between Hamilton's conceptions and those of later politicians was that, while he never faltered in his conviction that the economy was an instrument of state power, his successors tended to view the state as an instrument of private economic purposes.[8]

Although the period from roughly 1850 to 1880 was notable for regulatory legislation enacted by state governments,[9] federal regulation can be conveniently dated from the Interstate Commerce Act of 1887 and the Sherman Antitrust Act of 1890. The half-century following the Sherman Act saw a number of so-called independent regulatory commissions established to regulate various sectors of the economy, but with very few exceptions and rarely for very long were the commissions effective regulatory instruments. Other than an aptitude for survival the commissions have been notable mainly for the cozy relationships that they have cultivated with the economic interests they were supposed to oversee. That experience has testified less to the growth of independent state power than to the growth of a form of state authority that legitimated the economic strategies of powerful business corporations.[10] Thus, the New Deal inherited a tradition of what we might call the strong but heteronomous state. The one exception was the wartime state. During World War I the first experiment in government control over the economy as a whole was undertaken. Although the experience was too brief to be conclusive, it did plant the notion of a fully planned and regulated economy serving ends that were the projection of national power abroad, rather than of domestic policies, and were, at the same time, largely beyond the control of a mass electorate.[11]

The Regulatory/Welfare/Warfare State

As is well known, the New Deal evolved into a warfare state, bringing with it not only the regulatory traditions from the turn of the century but the newer welfare functions of the thirties. The evolution of the New Deal signified that a new synthesis of power was being consolidated, one that conjoined three distinct elements: regulation, welfare, and empire. The first two can be regarded as attempts to enlarge the meaning of rationality for a capitalistic society by tempering the pursuit of self-interest by more genial notions of the common good, social justice, and a socially guaranteed economic minimum for all. The third element, empire, was not new; but its previous forms—the practical implementation of the Monroe Doctrine in Central and Latin America, the Mexican War, the Indian wars, the Spanish-American War and the pacification of the Philippines, and World War I—were inhibited by the relatively undeveloped quality of America's economic and military power. World War II, however, marked the beginning of the American bid for supremacy among world powers and within the international economy. Henceforth the society would be encouraged to think of itself as having a special mission of defending the free world and combating communism and, therefore, of having to incorporate into its identity the economic and technological imperatives demanded by world hegemony. Thus, a new collectivity was being forged around the powers of the state as regulator, welfare dispenser, and a global suzerainty that depended less on the occupation or seizure of territories than on the penetrative power of American capital, productivity, technology, and a contagious culture of affluence.

To sum up: the New Deal falls into the typically American pattern of revolution; it was less a social than a political revolution. Its achievement was the extension and consolidation of state power and what might be called "the social legitimation of state power." [12] By means of programs such as social security, agricultural subsidies and marketing schemes, the Tennessee Valley Authority, the National Industrial Recovery Act, the National Labor Relations Act, and many others, vast numbers of Americans were tied into the system of state power, a system based on bureaucratic, military, and corporate institutions and operated by elites equally at home in any one of the components.

The New Deal State defined the American collective identity for roughly four decades. The pattern would be repeated later among its lineal descendants—the Truman Fair Deal, which ended in the Korean War; and the Johnson Great Society, which ended in the Vietnam War. These mimetic repetitions culminated in Lyndon Johnson's hubristic attempt to combine the vast social programs of the Great Society with the vast military expedition into Southeast Asia. That identity was profoundly shaken during the sixties by ghetto riots, military defeat, and the crisis of the presidency, which had first been intimated by Johnson's decision not to seek another term and was then intensified by the Watergate revelations of the early seventies. It was further undermined by a series of developments which signified the end of American world hegemony: OPEC's threat to deny access to petroleum supplies; the hostage crisis in Iran; and, above all, the successful challenge to American economic dominance, especially from Asian countries. "The decline of American power" became a standard topic in the mass media, while the sense of a "loss of control" in the face of a suddenly threatening environment became a familiar subject of discussion. And scholars composed disquisitions on "the vanishing presidency." [13]

Regressivism and the Backlash That Failed

That changes in the world were presented so as to persuade Americans of a threat to their autonomy, even to their national existence, was a measure of how deeply the collective identity had come to depend on power for its gratification. The elements were present for a strong, xenophobic reaction: foreign competition was beating America at its own game; multinational corporations were challenging the power of the state to control the national economy; foreign investors were becoming increasingly visible, in politics as well as in the economic life of the society; and, most threatening of all to a society whose history was marked by violent nativist reactions, huge waves of immigrants with different skins and cultures entered the country. The fact that many entered illegally seemed further evidence of weakness; the country was not even master of its own borders. That in some well-publicized instances some of the new immigrants displayed remarkable adaptability to American entrepreneurial ways, while others were willing to work for substandard wages, seemed merely to accentuate their un-American qualities. Suddenly there was a question of whether, in the face of this invasion by seemingly alien cultures and the disappearance of boundaries, there was anything "American," any distinctive collective identity, at all.

Ronald Reagan's election could easily have been the catalyst for a strong nativist backlash. This would have been in keeping with the regressivist tendencies in Reaganism noted earlier. During the campaign and his subsequent years in office, his public speeches continually appealed to the stuff of nativism: to patriotism, national superiority, the American past, colonial and frontier myths, traditional morality, fundamentalist conceptions of religion, and the parochial images of rural and small-town America. Even more ominous, as candidate and as president Ronald Reagan played to deep-seated resentments, especially among blue-collar citizens, by his coded references to "welfare cheats" and by his refusal even to acknowledge the existence of racial problems. Some of his cabinet officials made it clear that they were eager to discard many of the legal devices employed by previous administrations to combat discriminatory practices.

Regressivism and Modernization

This move to reinstate American identity around traditional symbols and myths could have led to a politics of *ressentiment*. It did not, however, and that fact reveals much about the political function of regressivism. The appeal to the past and its values was not meant to point the way back to the past. Such a notion is totally incongruous in an administration so completely beholden to corporate interests, the great modernizers of our age. Rather, it was meant to ease the path toward the future. Pseudotraditionalism mediates between the average citizen and the harsh reality that modernization imposes on even the most highly technologized societies. Pseudotraditionalism helps to mask the costs of adaptation to the intensely competitive political economy being ushered in by high technology, a political economy whose global boundaries are already being effaced by the outline of an interstellar economy. The dilemmas inherent in protectionism, declining industries versus sunset industries, industrial relocation versus the destruction of established communities, the priority of inflation over unemployment, the rationalization of agriculture, and a host of others all point to the hardships involved.

By describing this ideological element as "pseudotraditionalist" I am not suggesting that it was insincerely held by Ronald Reagan and the members of his administration, only that it stood in inherent contradiction to the outlook and aims of corporate interests, whose spokesman Reagan was from the beginning. George Bush, Donald Regan, James Baker, George Shultz, and Caspar Weinberger cannot be viewed as symbols of nineteenth-century rural America. This contradiction was not hidden but was embodied in the dualism located at the ideological center of Reaganism. Regressivism was paired with an explicit progressivism that distinguished Reaganism's conservatism from most other conservative orientations. It was a progressivism that not only placed itself squarely behind the drive for technological supremacy (Star Wars was merely a conspicuous example of this thrust)—that is, behind the modernizing forces eroding the remnants of an older America celebrated in the regressive side of Reaganism, but it also placed itself against another fundamental principle of Reaganism, the principle of reducing governmental power. "Government growing beyond our consent had become a lumbering giant," the president claimed, "slamming shut the gates of opportunity, threatening to crush the very roots of our freedom." [14]

Contrary to the impressions created by presidential rhetoric, however, the historical importance of the Reagan administration will not be the return of power to the people or the scaling down of centralized, bureaucratic power, but the continued modernization and strengthening of state power. Its vision was managerialist, not Jeffersonian. It was of "a leaner, more carefully focused Federal role" and "a leaner and more efficient Federal structure." [15]

The increase in state power during Reagan's terms in office was registered most spectacularly in the rise in military expenditures and in the strong efforts toward tightening centralized management within the government. But it was also bolstered by the strengthening of the agencies of law enforcement; the relative indifference to the rights of the accused; the steady development of surveillance techniques, especially those relying on centralized data collections; federal drug-testing programs; and tightened security procedures for federal employees. The Reagan administration was not, then, committed to the dismantling of state power but to its enhancement. Looked at in this way, the administration's efforts to prune social programs were an effort to strengthen the state by making it less unwieldy, more susceptible to managerial control. This does not mean hypocrisy but rather something far more important that was prefigured in the avowed aim of

Reaganism to change radically the boundaries between the so-called public and private sectors. Here I am referring to the well-publicized commitment of the Reagan administration to reducing state power by encouraging the voluntary assumption of governmental functions and responsibilities by the private sector. On the face of it, that aim would seem to violate an elementary axiom of politics, that no state voluntarily surrenders its powers. Why, then, was this regime apparently unlike any other? Why did it, as the guardian of state power and of public order, look so confidently to the private sector?

The Public/Private Inversion

President Reagan once said that "private values must be at the heart of public policies." [16] The distinction between "public" and "private" had traditionally occupied an important place in our political and legal notions. In the president's words cited above, however, the express aim was to challenge a traditional distinction older than the Republic itself. Among eighteenth-century liberals and progressives the public and private stood for two different realms, each with different ends and controlling ideals. The public denoted the "realm" or "domain" of proper governmental action. War, diplomacy, taxation, regulation of commerce, law enforcement, protection of life and property, education, and more recently, welfare have been recognized as functions that are peculiarly a matter of public interest in which the generality of citizens, regardless of class interest, has a stake. The notion of public functions publicly discharged also implied that there was a greater chance that these functions would be impartially performed if they were in the hands of accountable public officials sworn to serve the public than if they were controlled by entrepreneurs responding to the dictates of self-interest and the pressures of the marketplace. The underlying assumption was that public purposes and public officials were to be judged by different criteria. The public should be the realm of the common good, while public service should be conducted in the spirit of disinterestedness. The private realm, in contrast, was conceived as the domain where individuals were free to exercise the various rights guaranteed by the Constitution such as property and religious rights. It was the realm of discretionary behavior where individuals were expected to pursue their own ends, to follow their self-interest. Historically, the dominant belief has been that the private sphere is frequently threatened by the invasion of the public, that public authority tends to impose regulations on private behavior and reduce freedom of action. In the 1980s, however, there began to be signs that these metaphorical boundaries were being reshuffled. One of the main impetuses was the Reagan ideology of "voluntarism," which encouraged the private sector to undertake a variety of social services hitherto regarded as a public monopoly or as predominantly a public function.[17] For a long time, private nonprofit or charitable organizations have existed alongside and have supplemented public services, especially at the state and local levels. But in the early 1980s, in the words of a champion of this development, there began a concerted attempt to make "a profitable business out of social problems" previously thought to be in the public domain.[18] Hospitals, prisons, detention centers, welfare services, and education became the objects of voluntarism.

The privatization of public safety has proceeded rapidly. The number of private security guards was estimated in 1985 to be 1.1 million, of which 36,000 were employed by governmental agencies. There has also been a concerted effort to increase private or corporate responsibility and control in the domain of high culture; it already exists, of course, in the popular culture disseminated by the mass media. The same impulse was at work in the proposals by the Reagan administration to sell public power projects, railroad systems, and the assets of the FHA. Also in 1985, it was reported that the Reagan administration had slated some eleven thousand commercial activities of government to be taken over by private contractors whenever feasible.[19]

Thus, a radical inversion has appeared to be in the making: the private realm has invaded the public. Consider an especially striking example of privatization. It involves the projection of private initiatives into the domain of warfare and foreign policy, supposedly the classic preserve where state action has been accepted as an unchallengeable monopoly. Since the Bay of Pigs invasion, where private armies of anti–Castro Cubans were assisted by American intelligence and military advisers, that monopoly has been challenged. At the present time there are conservative foundations and individual donors who have recruited soldiers and furnished material to support anti-Marxist movements aimed at overthrowing governments with which the United States government has formal diplomatic relations. In Nicaragua, during the Reagan administration, these efforts were coordinated with official American policy aimed at toppling the government of that country. In El Salvador, on the other hand, American Protestant evangelical movements, which have made no secret of their anti-Marxism and of their determination to assist Reagan's policy of defeating the leftist enemies of the government, have made striking inroads into the traditionally Catholic population. According to a *New York Times* reporter, "The dramatic growth of the [evangelical] sects [in El Salvador] and elsewhere in Latin America is a result of an intense multimillion-dollar evangelical campaign by American-based churches and religious agencies." [20]

Clearly, these developments have blurred and confounded the distinctions between public and private. Public and private power are intermingled, and the result is not a net reduction of state power but its articulation through different forms. The appropriation of public goals by private enterprise means that state power is being decentered without being decentralized. State power is being expanded, but it does not necessarily flow from a common center as pictured in modern theories of state sovereignty. It excludes private agencies that work in an adjunctive relationship with state power. Contrary to the official interpretation, these tendencies do not signal a decrease in state power or in the state's apparatus but rather their literal transformation. What is "private" about these new forms of power is principally their location in a privatized rather than a public, political context. The new location helps to obscure their coerciveness by transferring formal accountability from traditional political processes, such as legislative oversight and elections, to the allegedly impersonal forces of the market.

The Revolutionary Transformation of Civil Society

At this point, a crucial question arises, and the answer takes us to the heart of the Reagan revolution. What happened in the private realm such that its institutions were deemed capable not only of taking over functions previously thought to be the unique preserve of the state but of appearing to favor functions—such as schools, prisons, and hospitals—that are particularly coercive and disciplinary?

The question points toward a change as fundamental as the change that has taken place in the power of the state—a change that is, in fact, its complement. It involves the transformation of the private domain, of that system of private relations and associations which the eighteenth and nineteenth centuries called "civil society." In most theoretical formulations, civil society comprised the family, various social relationships (e.g., friends and neighbors), churches, schools, professions and crafts, and economic organizations. These were perceived as private bodies and relationships, and they were thought to be importantly different from political institutions: they were freer, more spontaneous, less coercive, and more voluntaristic.

Whatever historical truth there may have been to this conception of civil society, it was radically changed by the rationalization of society effected by late modern capitalism. Civil society now presents itself as a structure of control and discipline rather than as a paradigm of freedom and spontaneity. The contemporary business organization is not

only a mechanism for economic decisions; it is also a carefully cultivated life-form that is deliberately imposed, with varying degrees of
severity, on its employees. In the same vein, recent demands for re-
schooling society have placed great emphasis upon restoring "discipline in the classroom" and modeling students for life in the era of high
technology. These same trends are evident in the rigors of Protestant
fundamentalism and in the reactionary pronouncements of the Vati-
can. In short, civil society now represents structures of power which
self-consciously exercise disciplinary functions that erase the differences between state and society, public and private. How far the evolution has gone may be gauged by the parallel efforts of private and
public employers to impose drug tests and lie-detector tests on their
employees and to insist on security clearances for numerous employees
in both sectors. As a consequence, it becomes increasingly more difficult to discern where the public sector begins and the private leaves
off. From this vantage point, "deregulation," with its faith in market
"discipline" and "free economic forces," appears less as a policy than
as a Freudian slip.

The transformation of civil society is strikingly registered in the
messages that are now regularly inscribed in television commercials.
Many of the most powerful advertisers no longer are content simply
to promote their products; they promote an ideology. One of the most
persistent themes invites the viewer to become dependent on a particular economic institution, which is then typically described in images
that emphasize its hugeness and its great power. The relationship is
conveyed in language and imagery that is strikingly paternalistic and
condescending. Thus, a couple is reduced to pygmy size and plucked
up by the huge hand of a bank while a friendly voice assures them that
the giant wants no more than to serve them. Or there is the assurance
tendered by Allstate Insurance that its customers will be in "good
hands"—and huge hands are then opened invitingly. Then there is
General Motors inviting its truck buyers to "lean" on that corporation
in the sure knowledge that it can be counted on.

The long-run implications of the double transformation, of state
and civil society, can be roughly summarized. But to do that we need
to locate them in the proper context of certain twentieth-century tendencies regarding power.

Modernizing societies of this century have displayed two contrasting yet interrelated responses to the rapidly changing environments
produced by their policies. One reflects a condition of severe social
dislocation that is commonly described by terms such as "anomie,"
"fragmentation," "class conflict," and "social disintegration." In this
case power tends to be centrifugal. The other response is to employ the

technology of modernity to amass and centralize power in magnitudes unavailable to previous ruling groups—then to use power to penetrate and change the social relationships, economy, and belief systems of civil society. The twentieth century is the century of totalizing power, of the concerted attempt to unify state and civil society.

Until now that attempt has taken the form of state domination of civil society, as in Nazi Germany, Fascist Italy, the USSR, and the People's Republic of China. What might be emerging in the United States is a new form of totalizing power that blurs the domination of the state by contracting its functions to the representation of civil society while at the same time the disciplinary procedures of society are being tightened. The new form is represented not as "the state" or "the dictatorship of the proletariat" but as "the system." In order to call attention to its tendencies toward totality, I call it the system of the Economic Polity.[21]

Collective Identity and the Loss of Collective Power

In light of the close integration of public and corporate policies and the cooperation that exists today between state officials and corporate representatives, the old dichotomies between the political state and the private economy are anachronistic. We live in an Economic Polity in which the state is merely the symbol of legitimate public authority, not the autonomous power suggested by early modern political theory. In the context of the Economic Polity, voluntarism, or the acquisition of public functions by private power, does not point toward the reduction of power but toward its decentering. Most contracts regulating private operators of hospitals or prisons, for example, enable public authorities to set standards and to enforce compliance. Thus, voluntarism does not presage a freer society but, on the contrary, a more controlled one in which the centers of control will appear decentralized and local, but in an administrative rather than a democratic or participatory sense. The confusion of privatization with voluntarism and of voluntarism with participation, which was such a conspicuous feature of the Reagan rhetoric, has reflected a turn toward different means of increasing social control at a time of diminishing confidence in the traditional state as the most reliable agency for supplying social control and coordinated direction. Let me consider this point by briefly describing the American response to its own centrifugal tendencies.

There are present in our public discourse profoundly contradictory notions and emotions about power. I exaggerate only slightly when I say that some forms of power are perceived and welcomed because they promise power without limits. Among these are the powers associated with the economy, the military, science, and technology. Yet there is also another, more uneasy feeling that as these forms of power become enlarged they render the society more rather than less vulnerable. Thus, industrial processes based on advanced technologies turn out to have seriously contaminated whole areas, rendering them unfit for human habitation. Or those processes may, by a mere human error, prove deadly to a whole region and harmful to a whole continent. These doubts have become so commonplace in discussions of nuclear arms that there is no need to cite the obvious fact that as nuclear power has grown so have nuclear fears. The suspicion is that the new forms of power have grown beyond the ability of traditional political institutions to manage them. One result is to seek solutions that seem to be able to dispense with forms of power that have become suspect.

Consider, for example, deregulation. Deregulation is widely regarded as a policy prompted by an ideological conviction that if economic actors were allowed freer rein, a more rational allocation of resources would result and more efficient practices would be introduced by producers and suppliers. But deregulation can also be interpreted as expressing a loss of confidence in the power of the state to deal rationally and effectively with economic activities. In order to compensate for the weakness of purposive action, as symbolized by the state, magical powers are attributed to the market: the market is said to reflect "forces" and to impose "discipline." Thus, there has to be faith in the workings of the market because there has been a loss of faith in the ordinary processes of government and politics. Meanwhile, very real forms of power, such as represented by large corporations, expand and evolve ever more complex ways of amassing power by playing the politics of markets—for example, in takeover strategies and arbitrage.

Deregulation is merely one of several signs of a pervasive belief that, as a collectivity, we lack the power to control our social environment. The national deficit seems beyond control. The Gramm-Rudman Act, which arbitrarily set dates for the reduction of deficits and then abdicated legislative power to allow the executive to dictate the cuts, was a desperate effort to assert control by decreeing what could not be accomplished by deliberative action. The same fears are reflected in the proposed constitutional amendment mandating a balanced budget. The distrust of the capability of normal processes of politics to achieve a desired goal produces an attempt to impose it upon the process. The rigidity of the solutions stands as a substitute for power.

The sense of powerlessness seems most acute when terrorism irrupts. It is the perfect symbol of frustrated will: the vast majority of

Americans want nothing more than to muster all of our vaunted power and use it to annihilate terrorists and the third-rate powers that subsidize them. And yet either it seems beyond our capability or the costs appear prohibitive. No matter how deadly our arsenal of weapons or how sophisticated our strike forces, we know that at bottom we are helpless. This was strikingly illustrated in the outburst of Secretary of State Shultz toward a Yugoslav official who tried to suggest that some terrorist causes were justified. In his anger, Shultz pounded the table and declared that a terrorist act has "no connection with any [genuine] cause. It's wrong [pounds the table twice]." [22]

These feelings of impotence often provoke an extreme demand for security. So Reagan proposed a shield to defend the society from any nuclear attack; and, until well into his second term, he resisted virtually all Soviet overtures for reducing nuclear build-ups. The highly publicized "window of vulnerability" was another perfect symbol: even the smallest opening was enough to justify escalation of the arms race in the hope that we can eventually spend the Soviet Union into exhaustion and thereby finally find security. Or, the Reagan administration supported any regime that appeared to be anti-Marxist, because while the administration was highly cautious toward large Marxist states, such as the USSR and China, and even helped to stabilize the economies of East European communist states, it was deeply threatened by the emergence of small Marxist states and responded by sponsoring another version of terrorism.

Thus, the condition that we have reached as a collectivity can best be described as a near-totality in which public and private distinctions are being steadily blurred. That the last administration pushed for the extension of state power into the most private areas imaginable (e.g., abortion, sexual conduct, and religion) and secretly wished to submit the whole society to urinalysis suggests that we are entering a moment in our history when it will become extremely difficult to find the terms for limiting power or for holding it politically accountable, much less for sharing it. The diffusion of power accompanying the emergence of our new constitution, the Economic Polity, portends a collective identity in which the collectivity—"We the People," in the brave words of the Constitution—becomes the passive object of power rather than the active political subject.

Two / Injustice and Collective Memory

The topic of collective memory has received relatively little attention from political scientists, political theorists, or social scientists generally. The major exceptions have been social or cultural anthropologists, especially those who have been influenced by the so-called *L'Année sociologique* school founded by Emile Durkheim and perpetuated by his nephew Marcel Mauss. This suggests that collective memory is part of a world we have lost, that as an analytical category or as an interpretative concept it is useful mainly for understanding or explaining primitive or traditional societies.

Another way of saying this would be that collective memory is a characteristic of societies in which custom or tradition plays a decisive role or in which change is assigned a negative value. Societies that place great value upon change and seek constantly for ways to promote it are most likely either to be indifferent to collective memory, even uncomprehending of its meaning, or to exhibit clear signs of a declining interest in the topic. We might call such societies post-mnemonic in the sense that collective memory is at best ritualistic and, more likely, treated as dysfunctional.

Hypothetically an anti-mnemonic society might seek to preserve a place for memory by cultivating historical knowledge to serve as a functional equivalent and according to history something like the respect and deference that mnemonic societies display to custom and tradition. History that understood itself to be in the service of collective memory and to be engaged in the exploration of traditions in a society that actively discounted the value of tradition would, unfortunately, find itself relegated to a marginal role. It would be reduced to justifying itself as an activity that sought simply to understand the past or to reconstruct it *wie es ist eigentlich gewesen*. Or, alternatively, it might accept the basic premise of its society and declare that history is knowledge of past change. In the first alternative, history would be caught in the bleak position of speaking to a society that had no strong interest in remembering its past; in the second, it would be simply redescribing and reaffirming society's self-understanding.

This last point might be summarized by saying that in a post-mnemonic society most of the intellectual disciplines that study society, such as economics, political science, social psychology, and (more ambivalently) sociology have become or always were antihistorical in outlook; when they were not, they were reductionist, that is, they sought to translate historical categories into social scientific ones and to replace narrative by demonstration. In response, historians have tried to find legitimacy in a post-mnemonic society by borrowing the methods and categories of the social sciences.

In what follows I want to explore the notion of collective memory in relation to a certain form of collective injustice. Collective memory has to do with the formation, interpretation, and retention of a public past. In a preliminary way collective memory might be said to refer to the public past preserved in public art and architecture, public rites, ceremonies or rituals, the rhetoric of public authorities, the educational curricula, and the ideological themes that pervade these. What is retrieved from the past is some event, person, institution, or artifact. An example would be the celebration of the bicentennial of the ratification of the American constitution. The bicentennial celebration could be described as an attempt at a ritual of remembrance or, as I prefer to put it, a post-mnemonic society's ritualistic attempt at a ritual of remembrance.

Societies tend to memorialize heroic deeds or shaping events rather than acts of justice. But they also tend to want to suppress memories of collective injustice. In order to establish connections between collective memory and a class of unjust acts which might properly be called "collective," a useful starting point is a remark of the French historian Ernest Renan. In *What Is a Nation?* (1881) he wrote: "But the essence of a nation is that all the individuals share a great many things in common and also that they have forgotten some things. Every French citizen should have forgotten the Saint-Bartholomew [massacre]."[1] As Benedict Anderson has noted, Renan's paradox is to claim that Frenchmen should have forgotten the massacre; yet the fact that Renan felt no need to explain what "the Saint-Bartholomew" referred to suggested that Frenchmen still remembered it.[2]

If we assume for the moment that Renan's advice was healthy; that it had been accepted by Frenchmen; and that a society which insisted upon periodically reviewing great historical wrongs it had committed would probably invite all the familiar metaphors about "obsessively picking at its own scabs," the acceptance of Renan's advice would also mean that the memory of a great wrong done to French Huguenots of the sixteenth century would have been suppressed.

A non-Frenchman might well be tempted to argue that over the centuries the fanaticism that produced Saint Bartholomew's Day had given way to widely shared social agreement upon the value of religious toleration. Therefore Renan need not have enjoined his countrymen to forget what had become a nonproblem. And although justice will forever be denied to the dead, it is rendered to the living in the form of religious toleration. So why should sharing be endangered; indeed, why wouldn't it be healthier for a society to remember its collective wrongs? Is there some fatal attraction toward likemindedness that led Renan to think that sharing is threatened by the experience of injustice recollected?

Collective memory seems thus to have some peculiarities that distinguish it from private or individual memory. In the *Confessions* Augustine likens memory to a trickster: I forget when I don't intend to and I cannot remember when I want to.[3] Renan's collective memory, however, seems more like an accomplice of injustice, forgetting or remembering—whichever is the more convenient.

Although the two notions are contradictory, they may not be mutually exclusive. What kind of memory is it that forgets though it still remembers? Renan seems to be saying that a society can ill afford to reexamine collectively a special class of political events in which the members of society feel tainted by a kind of corporate complicity in an act of injustice done in their name; and yet temporal distance and historical accommodations have so far removed them from it that they do not feel responsible, only uneasy. The event is not actually forgotten, only publicly unrecalled. We might call such events "collective wrongs" to mark their complicitous and historical character, their memorability as it were. Their wrongness seems to consist in singling out a particular group on the basis of its objective differences (Huguenots did hold different religious beliefs from Catholics); then drawing unjust conclusions from these differences (e.g., that all Huguenots were disloyal subjects of the king); and, finally, encouraging the group's slaughter as a patriotic act.

Coming closer to home, is the Civil War America's Saint Bartholomew's Day? Although Americans easily celebrated the bicentennial of their Constitution, most of them ignored the centennial of the Civil War and could not even bestir themselves to protest when, on Lincoln's birthday, television commercials presented their martyred president as an automobile salesman hawking Japanese cars. Thus, Renan's principle seems vindicated: by forgetting the experience of a divided nation at war with itself, the nation was able to restore its sense of shared destiny.

That war seems to have been forgotten, however, without one of its main issues, the status of black Americans, being resolved. Nevertheless, it is possible that collective amnesia was induced by the trauma of fratricide and that the attempt to right the wrong of slavery was responsible for the terrible bloodletting. Society will be reluctant henceforth to want to confront radically the grievances of those who still carry the marks of the original wrong. By its silence collective memory will have signified the limits of justice.

It is not difficult to understand, therefore, why the public memory of the conflict is suppressed and goes unrepresented in civic rituals, even though few would want to say, as was said in the example of Saint Bartholomew's Day, that there is nothing to remedy, no apparent injustice to correct. And since the institutions of slavery were abolished by the so-called Civil War amendments, we might say that although justice was rendered to the dead, it is being denied to the living. If the limits of justice are thus dictated by the limits of public memory, what are those limits?

Consider the story of the interned American citizens of Japanese descent. For nearly three decades the vast majority of Americans repressed the memory of the so-called Japanese relocation camps where American citizens were "detained" throughout World War II on the grounds that because of their national origin and the war against Japan they constituted a potentially disloyal population. Yet over the past decade various official measures for indemnifying the detainees for some portion of their losses and for extending a national apology have been passed or are pending. In addition, several court cases have been reopened with the result that the legality of the original government decrees now appears highly questionable.

What dictated this about-face? Was it less a question of injustice remembered than of a radical change in the American perceptions of Japan rather than of the Nisei, an official recognition on the part of

American policy makers, both governmental and corporate, of the extraordinary power now possessed by Japan and hence of its vital importance to global political and economic strategies? Is it part of a gradual downgrading of World War II, which, although sometimes said to be the last just war, never was celebrated as World War I was? And is the depreciation of World War II connected with the apparent fact that ever since the cold war began in earnest, American policy makers have been as concerned to repress the fact that the Soviet Union was once an ally as to forget that among America's present allies are three former enemies (although the bizarre episode of Bitburg stirred memory to reassert the historical dissatisfactions of justice)?

To ask why public memory works in this way is to ask how forgetfulness is established as a condition, perhaps even a precondition, of a certain form of society. By "form of society" I mean the characteristic ways in which its hegemonic powers are constituted. But first we must establish a richer understanding of forgetfulness than expediency or oversight or blocked recollection provides. I want to propose instead that we consider it in a context where the self must renounce some part of itself or of its own experience if it wants to be accepted into political society. In the act of reconstituting the self into a civic self, forgetting becomes a rite of passage and as such a condition of membership.

The most useful and possibly the most influential discussion of these matters is to be found in the early modern social contract theorists, specifically Hobbes, Locke, and Rousseau. I will focus my remarks solely upon Hobbes and Locke, and especially Hobbes, because of the continuities between some of their ideas and those of more recent writers such as Rawls and Nozick and because of some continuities with recent American practices. The excursion is of some value, not because social contract theories contain accurate descriptions of the actual constitution of contemporary society, but because they enable us to glimpse some of the inarticulate premises in the political practices and processes of our society.

Classical contract theory distinguishes between two states of affairs, one in which men live in civil society and under the legal rules of the state; the other in which men live in a pre-civil society, without a legal system, complex exchange relationships, a division of labor, settled domestic relations, or a system of political rulership. All social contract writers want to move men from the second condition to the first. The device that they use for that purpose, the social contract, is essentially an exchange in which individuals agree to obey political authority if authority will protect them. The differences among the three writers mentioned, however significant they may be, need not detain us for the moment because I want to focus not so much on what the self promises but on what the self has to forget about itself in order for the promise to be acceptable to the other promisers. Most commentary on contract theory has concentrated its attention upon the rights that are retained and those that are surrendered rather than upon the question of identities. Stated slightly differently, the individual of contract theory is a bearer of rights and a rational subject. His identity is thus derived from a universal status, as when the Declaration of Independence asserts that "all men are created equal" and "endowed by their Creator with certain unalienable Rights." He is not a bearer of particularized identities of, say, race, color, gender, community, or creed. His rights are, as the Fifteenth Amendment states, "regardless of race, color, and creed."

Each of the three great contractualists insisted upon equal conditions of entry for all of the parties to the contract: each made the same promise, which all contract writers put in the form of a surrender of certain kinds of freedom; each was offered the same guarantees; and each was to be subject to the same legal rules and under the same public authority.

But Hobbes was the one writer who insisted that men not only had to agree to a contract on "Equalle terms," but, if they wanted the proposed political system to work effectively, they also had to agree to forget some matters. He listed a series of "laws of nature," which he argued that men would have to observe if the social covenant were to be effective. The sixth of those laws requires that we should pardon past offenses if the offender sincerely repents and wishes to be pardoned. The seventh stipulates that we should lay aside the desire to avenge past evils but calculate instead "the greatness of the good to follow."[4] These laws were extensions of the crucial fifth law of nature, which Hobbes called "compleasance" and which dictated that "every man strive to accommodate himselfe to the rest." A society, he argued, was like a building being constructed of stones; some stones have an "asperity and irregularity of Figure [and hence] take more room from others" and so have to be discarded. Some men, by "the stubbornness of [their] Passion cannot be corrected" and so they must be "cast out of society."[5]

The Hobbesian imagery of building blocks is significant, not only for its thinly veiled impulse toward suppressing differences, but for the implied connections between the suppression of difference and the suppression of memories of past wrongs. The way that Hobbes formulated the requirement of forgetting past offenses made it appear that what was at stake was simply some individual acts of injustice committed in the past. This would be in keeping with the radically individualistic, even atomistic character of the Hobbesian subject.

But what Hobbes was suppressing by his laws of nature was not the memory of personal grievances but recollections by his contemporaries of historical and collective actions, the actions of kings, parliaments, judges, and armies, of Lord Protectors and Puritan zealots during the civil war and Interregnum, which had produced the upheavals that Hobbes rendered abstractly as "the poor, nasty, brutish, and short" condition of a "state of nature." The succession of different regimes with sharply contrasting visions of society and of policy seemed to Hobbes to have contributed to the accumulation of resentments without settling sharp disputes over basic principles of politics and religion. His covenant was a device to incorporate social amnesia into the foundation of society. If men could forget, mutual absolution was possible, allowing society to start afresh without inherited resentments. A necessary condition of social amnesia was, therefore, that men dehistoricize themselves.

The Hobbesian individual steps forward as the first of a long series of blank individuals who fake their nature by denying historically acquired and multiple identities. Every contract theorist posits a person who is initially defined without reference to gender, family, local community, social class, religious commitment, or vocation. Twentieth-century writers are not much better. They may stipulate "veils of ignorance" as a condition of contract, but in the presence of distinctions of color and gender that stipulation strikes one as incoherent. What can it mean to say that for the moment I must forget that I am a person of color or a woman so that I may think about the basic conditions of a just society, when for me what matters most is how that difference will be treated?

The individual who contracts or covenants is thus an artifact, a constructed being whose attributes appear as unconditioned by the kind of resentments at past offenses which were and are the notorious accompaniments to the categories of gender, etc. referred to a moment ago. All social categories are power-laden; some are complacent, some apologetic, others protestant. Hobbesian and Lockean men have passions, interests, even experiences, but they seem not to have, or only barely to have had, the searing experiences of those for whom social categories have symbolized social wounds.

The trade-off is equality for remembrance, or rather a certain kind of equality—not equality as an ideal that is necessarily at war with power (because power presupposes inequality) but equality as a fiction that serves to legitimate power. Societies that understand themselves in large measure through the categories of contract theories are committed to inequality because they value a conception of justice that justifies individual acquisitions if these can be shown to be due to merit. Even so strong a critic of liberal meritocracy as John Rawls conceded that "the basic structure contains social and economic inequalities" that "are necessary and highly advantageous."[6]

Justice will therefore mean equal protection of inequalities. As Madison put it in the tenth *Federalist,* "the protection of different and unequal faculties of acquiring property . . . is the first object of government." It means that covenanters must forget notions of natural equality. The question of who is "the better man," Hobbes wrote, has no meaning in the state of nature.[7] But as Hobbes was quick to insist, that question takes on a ferocious quality in society: in the competition for power, wealth, and status it is virtually the only question.

The trick for the contract theorist was to get equality to serve the ends of inequality. To accomplish this, memory was enlisted and told that it had to forget the social categories that were the marks, in some cases ineradicable marks, of inequality. By divesting the person of his or her multiple identities and replacing them with the single identity of "the individual," then declaring that each individual would enter society on the same terms as every other individual, the way was prepared for the modern liberal solution to the problem of justice. In Locke's proviso: "That all Men by Nature are Equal, I cannot be supposed to understand all sorts of Equality. . . . Excellency of Parts and Merit may place [some] above the Common level."[8] Neither Hobbes nor Locke argued that the social categories had been abolished by the state of nature and would no longer operate when civil society was established. Rather, they were only temporarily suspended. Thus social classes were not abolished, much less distinctions between rich and poor; family and gender relations resumed. But there was an important change, for now these social categories could be judged by the equal justice requirement implicit in the terms of the covenant. What this means, however, is that the burden of rectifying injustice was now placed squarely and solely on the shoulders of the state. Hobbes asserted this in the most unequivocal fashion: justice does not even exist outside the state's law and authority. In the absence of state authority, and power there are only private versions, which have no objective standing.[9]

Hobbes's formulation may seem extreme, but even for those writers who are identified with more liberal conceptions of limited government, the main instrument of justice remains the state. This seems a straightforward matter until we ask whether the individual of contract theory has been so reconstituted as to make him conformable to a society in which all look to the state for justice. What has he been asked to forget?

Interestingly, for Hobbes the emphasis falls upon recollection rather than forgetting. If the individual can remember the fear and terror of life when there is no effective authority to protect him, then he will be more apt to treasure the security brought by the covenant and be all the more ready to observe his promise to obey the sovereign. At the same time, for Hobbesian man there can be no recollection of injustice in the state of nature. For in that condition every man has the right to do whatever he thinks will advance his own security and protect his life. He cannot, therefore, commit injustice; in the state of nature, no one can.

For Locke, however, there is justice in the state of nature, and hence there is potentially available a recollection of justice and of a prior practice of it which, by definition, did not depend upon the existence of the state. In the Lockean state of nature, every individual is responsible not only for observing the law of nature but for enforcing it.[10] Thus, individual responsibility for justice preceded the responsibility of the state. What, then, happens to this experience with justice? Is it forgotten? Suppressed?

For Locke, it was the inadequacies inherent in individual dispensation of justice that made the state necessary. Men judge subjectively, especially in cases where their own interests are involved. Justice demands objectivity, detachment, and dispassion—or in Locke's formulation, "a known law," "an indifferent judge," and an executive who will enforce the law impartially. Ideally, justice is best served by the suppression of the self. The reason for this is not simply that the self is self-interested. That is part of it. The deeper reason is multiplicity, the sheer variety of selves. According to Hobbes, "Divers men differ not onely in their Judgement, on the senses of what is pleasant, and unpleasant to the taste, smell, hearing, touch and sight; but also of what is conformable, or disagreeable to Reason, in the actions of common life. Nay, the same man in divers times, differs from himself."[11]

Memory, we might say, is the guardian of difference. The individual acquires and accumulates his or her different selves, and memory allows for re-collection. Difference within the self and between selves is not merely received; we may not choose our genders or our skin color, but we do choose in some measure how we are going to interpret that difference, how we are going to live it along with the other differences we receive or acquire in the course of our lives. But, as the excursion through contract theory suggests, memory is being enlisted as a suppressant of multiplicity because the kind of society of which contract theory is and was the expression seeks a different kind of self, a self that has to operate under what one might call conditions of pure power. The classic statement of it comes from Hobbes: "The Value, or WORTH of a man, as of all other things, his Price; that is to say, so much as would be given for the use of his Power; and therefore is not absolute; but a thing dependant on the need and judgement of another. . . . And as in other things, so in men, not the seller, but the buyer determines the Price." [12]

The radical character of Hobbes's formulation lies partly in the transvaluation of value into economic value and hence in the reduction of all forms of individual identity to one saleable power, and partly in the incoherence that the formulation introduces into Hobbes's laborious attempt to erect an awesome sovereign power. On the first point, the transvaluation of all value into economic value means, among other things, that the diverse identities of the person could be discarded because all that mattered was his or her usable power. The buyer did not ask for a narrative of "who are you?" and "where did you come from?" but simply "what can you offer me that I can use?" As Paul Hazard pointed out, the capitalist never looks at people to see who they are; he is willing to sell regardless of personal biography. [13]

On the second point, the incoherence that begins to undercut this "greatest of human Powers," as Hobbes called his construction, comes from a rival form of power which Hobbes's sovereign is committed to encouraging. It has its basis in another kind of contract of exchange, between buyers and sellers. What Hobbes had done inadvertently was to expose a different system of power, one in which the concept of equality was never mentioned and could not be without making nonsense of the new system. The novelty of that system is its hybrid character, partly economic in its reference to "buyer" and "seller" and partly political in that the fundamental transaction consists of a power relationship. We can call that new system a "political economy" and Hobbes its founding father.

Although Locke introduced significantly different political emphases from Hobbes, he enlarged rather than rejected the idea of a political economy. "Government," Locke declared, "has no other end but the preservation of Property." [14] One of the basic arguments used by Locke in defending the rightness of private property is that it contributes to greater productivity. Indeed, the limits to the amount of property one can accumulate are set either by consumption or by productivity. Thus, while property was a right for Locke and was intimately connected with personhood, it also had a deep economic structure. How deep was suggested by Locke's deliberate attempt to widen the meaning of property to include life and liberty as well as estate. [15] Lockean government was thus to be concerned primarily with the political economy of property, not only with the institution of property in its narrow sense of material acquisitions but also with human life and liberty in their economic involvements.

Defined in a preliminary way, the concept of a political economy is a mode of life in which society is conceived primarily as "the economy." Further, instead of economic relationships being viewed as embedded in and conditioned by a complex of social and political relationships and moral norms, they are treated as forming a distinct system of power that is at once autonomous and determinative of all other social and political relationships. The limits of justice are dictated by the condition of the economy as interpreted by those who are the authorities of political economy.

The system of political economy was to have profound effects upon collective memory and notions of collective injustice. These effects have been overlooked by critics of capitalism, who have concentrated primarily upon the institution of private property and the distinction between the propertied and the propertyless. In so doing they have missed the effects that the system of political economy had upon the status of membership in contractualist societies. From roughly the nineteenth century onward, the political economy was rapidly established as the defining structure of membership. For Hobbes and Locke the contract had established equal political membership, in the form of the citizen, as the fundamental category of society. At its best, it was a political vision of individuals freely binding themselves into a new collective relationship. That relationship had one radically democratic element: it was a vision of society in which all were included, in which everyone was in. No one was excluded, and all who accepted the terms were permanently incorporated.

The political economy, not the institution of private property, cut short the political possibilities of contractualist societies. The first development was sketched by Karl Polanyi in his classic, *The Great Transformation*. There he traced the emergence of the economy as an autonomous entity independent of history, religious values, moral constraints, and political regulation. In its early form, the political element in the political economy appeared as "administration." This marked a significant evolution away from the participatory implications of Locke's state of nature, where each person was responsible for interpreting and enforcing the law of nature. Adam Smith provides a convenient measure of how much political experience has been forgotten as attention is now focused upon the state, not as the locus of political life but as the servant of a higher order: "Commerce and manufacture can seldom flourish in any state which does not enjoy a regular administration of justice, in which the people do not feel themselves

secure in the possession of their property, in which the faith of contracts is not supported by law, and in which the authority of the state
is not supposed to be regularly employed in enforcing the payment of
debts from all those who are able to pay." [16]

As careful readers of Adam Smith have long recognized, he advocated a state with well-defined functions, not a negative state. Certainly the dominant economic interests and social classes of early modern capitalism consistently sought as much state power as they thought
was needed to promote and defend their interests. In the early years of
the Republic, owing primarily to the genius of Alexander Hamilton, a
powerful state was established. Public policies quickly laid the basis
for a neomercantilist program through which the state actively nurtured and promoted capitalism while cultivating a distinct state interest in the form of a bureaucracy, a military establishment, and a vigorous foreign policy. The United States, it might be said, was fairly
launched as a political economy. Although the most spectacular
growth of state power occurred only with the Civil War and afterward,
the most profound effects upon collective memory and notions of collective injustice were the result initially of economic developments.

Stated in a highly schematic way, the close collaboration between
science, industry, and the state, which began in the seventeenth century, was perfected by the end of the nineteenth. It resulted in forms of
power which produced a series of technological revolutions that dramatically altered the human capacity for collective memory. The system of production drew men, women, and children from the country-
side and gathered them into cities of strangers; old skills and crafts had
to be forgotten and new ones acquired; the rhythms of the factory
replaced those of the natural seasons; tradition and custom as arbiters
of existence gave way to rational calculation of utility. The pace of
change grew ever more intense, and survival came to depend upon
rapid adaptation. Those who traveled fastest and farthest were those
who traveled with the least baggage inherited from the past. Memory
was transformed into nostalgia, the longing for that which had once
been but could be no more. Ronald Reagan would prove to be the
consummate master of that genre. Stated differently, late modern economic development was on the way to accomplishing the social amnesia that the seventeenth-century contractualists had only glimpsed.

What does justice look like in the era of the political economy? The
answer is that although for Locke and Hobbes justice meant first and
foremost that political authority should protect each person in his or
her rightful possessions, this is no longer a primary concern. Instead,
the principal preoccupation of the state is to protect and nurture the
economy. This takes the form of policies for money supply and credit,

taxation, investment, and trade. Justice means guarding that which forms the basis of national power, security, and prosperity.

But in the political economy justice has also come to mean distributive justice. Distributive justice is most commonly associated with various programs designed to assist individuals who are unemployed, disabled, retired, or prevented from working by virtue of parental responsibilities. The political economy mentality sees the problem of distributive justice in terms of payments derived from the incomes of those who work and transferred to those who mostly do not. The currently favored rationale for distributive justice is supplied by John Rawls: "The higher expectations of those better situated are just if and only if they work as part of a scheme which improves the expectations of the least advantaged members of society." [17]

Distributive justice owes less perhaps to principles of justice than it does to the workings of the political economy. The need for distributive justice arises not because the system, or some agent of it, behaves aberrantly and departs from accepted norms. The ills that distributive justice seeks to remedy are the result of the normal operation of a healthy political economy. No one predicts that full employment will be achieved, for in the normal workings of the American political economy a superfluous population is produced. The reasons for this are numerous and complex, as are the forms of unemployment. But the fact of at least fifteen million unemployed is not disputable. Nor is the fact that in certain sectors of the population the cycle of unemployment thus far resists solution. The significance of this is that the old contractualist understanding of membership has tacitly been redefined. To be a member or citizen in the political economy is to be employed. To be unemployed is to be in the political economy but not of it; it is to be denied participation in the central civic activity.

Thus, membership in the political economy is constantly in jeopardy. Technological innovation is continually rendering large numbers of citizens obsolescent and superfluous—noncitizens, in effect. Further, recurrent cycles of recession, depression, and recovery introduce an uncertainty into the notion of citizenship that was unknown to the contractualist. By the contractualist's terms, "once a citizen, always a citizen"; but in the political economy, full citizenship is a temporary state of affairs because the economy is in the business of periodically producing and reproducing noncitizens.

The political economy does commit acts of injustice, but there seems to be no conception of collective injustice of the kind we saw in mnemonic societies. This is most poignantly evident in the case of factory closures and relocations. A worker may have invested much of his adult life in a particular job and in a particular community. Even the most modest conception of justice might seem forced to acknowledge that he has earned a claim, but that claim is overridden by political economy's version of "reason of state," namely, that in the interests of efficiency a firm is justified in closing down a plant and relocating it or eliminating it altogether. At the same time, there is mirrored in this controversy a vision of the good citizen in the political economy: he or she is one who is mobile, who is willing to tear up all roots and follow the promptings of the job market. What is being denied is the narrative structure of justice: the worker had come to possess a claim to a way of life which he had helped to found and nurture over time and perhaps even over generations. That claim thus has a story. It is, however, denied, not by a counternarrative but by a demonstration of the costs and benefits involved in the decision to relocate.

In a political economy justice is replaced by a concern for social discipline.[18] This is natural, because the political economy produces a surplus population of economically useless people; however, under the notions of electoral democracy inherited by the political economy there is always the danger that the poor might mobilize politically and use their ballots to extract benefits that might endanger the economic priorities of a society threatened by fierce competition from abroad. Disciplining the poor becomes a major function in the political economy, and social theorists respond obligingly by rediscovering the need for strong authority. According to one recent writer, government needs "to set norms for the public functioning of citizens," because previous social programs for the "disadvantaged and unemployed" have not been sufficiently "authoritative." The poor, he continues, lack a proper sense of social obligations, preferring handouts rather than work, and so "they must be made less free in certain senses rather than more." A "paternalist kind of program" should be used to force them into "'dirty' low wage jobs" rather than allowing them to follow their "self-interest," and "employment must become a duty, enforced by public authority."[19]

If a political economy signifies that notions of political community and collective memory have been rendered anachronistic, it may well be the case that we are entering an era in which justice no longer figures as the main category of collective existence. Perhaps accident and risk are the proper terms for analyzing existence in the post-mnemonic polity. Perhaps insurance is, as the eminent legal theorist Ronald Dworkin has already suggested, the appropriate substitute, distributing risks rather than justice. It would be appropriate because collective wrongs are not so much perpetrated as inherent in the system, or represented as such. Pollution, toxic wastes, choosing low inflation over employment, making education a scarce value, and a score of other problems testify, however, that wrongs exist in abundance and that many of them have aroused widespread indignation. One can even say that numerous publics have emerged in response to these wrongs. Publics do not, unfortunately, a collectivity make; they do, however, point in the right direction, that of the need to subordinate economy to polity.

Three / Elitism and the Rage
against Postmodernity

At a time when professors of literature find "politics" abounding in the most obscure seventeenth-century poems and assume without argument that politics existing outside texts can nonetheless be read as though it is a text, it is difficult to gain a hearing to protest that some matters really *are* political and others not, and that if the distinction is systematically neglected it is possible to trivialize politics even beyond the dreams of media advisers and political consultants.

Education is one of those truly political matters and has been recognized as such for a long time. Since antiquity many philosophers, including twentieth-century figures such as James, Dewey, Whitehead, and Russell, have insisted that the level of public life and the wisdom of public actions depend primarily upon the quality of education in society and its ready availability. Most of them defined education as a principal, even *the* principal, public responsibility.

The connection between education and politics has seemed of special importance to political societies that think of themselves as democratic or liberal. For more than two centuries, countless commentators have pointed out that education was *the* necessary condition for the intelligent practice of self-government and for the exercise and defense of the individual rights which democratic and liberal governments are pledged to extend and protect. Even putting aside considerations of justice, simple prudence would seem to dictate that if a society were committed to the liberal idea of representative government and to the democratic idea of the sovereignty of the people, education should be as widely and equally diffused as the right to vote, while its value should be as unquestionable as the right of freedom of speech. This amounts to a claim that the successful operation of the political system depends as much upon education as it does upon the Constitution.

However plausible this line of thinking might appear, the actual political status of education has been different. This is because education has been shaped, not only to rebut critics who have charged that popular government installs popular ignorance in power, but to accommodate them by having education attend more to producing future elites than to encouraging a democratic citizenry. In this respect, the history of education recapitulates the dualism of the original Constitution. The Founders hoped to combine the principle of rule by a republican elite with the principle of popular consent: real politics for the few, formal participation by the many. Education followed the same pattern. Just as the Constitution made no reference to equality and tacitly legitimated slavery, the inferior condition of women, and unequal suffrage, so it was silent about education.

By the early nineteenth century, the republican-democratic dualism was clearly established. Free public education of the elementary kind struggled to become established while higher education for the few flourished in private seminaries, academies, and colleges. Although public education grew steadily during the century, especially as businessmen came to appreciate the value of a literate work force, it was badly disrupted by the Civil War and Reconstruction. There was fierce resistance in both North and South to attempts at providing equal education for the freed blacks. Then, as now, many communities were willing to sacrifice public education in order to prevent blacks from gaining access to it.

Higher education was changed dramatically by the development of state universities and colleges, which began in the last decades of the nineteenth century. This system has become the heart and soul of popular education in the United States, and it probably represents the last, best hope for the survival of democratic values. Yet, public higher education did not produce a general democratization of higher education; it merely sharpened the dualism. Just as the original Constitution was supposed to enable a national elite to control national politics, so it has been that certain private universities and colleges have sought—and successfully—to assume the role of national or public universities, "in the nation's service," as the motto of one of the most exclusive universities proudly declares. The so-called selective institutions have provided "the best and brightest" of political leaders, bureaucratic managers, and corporate executives, fitting examplars of the concept of "meritocracy" which these institutions have defined in their own images. Meritocracy is republican elitism in the age of the Educational Testing Service.

Following World War II, education in general and higher education in particular experienced a period of accelerated growth in numbers of students, faculty, and material resources. Public monies were generously distributed to both public and private institutions of higher learning. Education was mobilized for the expansion of American economic, political, and military power that took place after the war. Soon education would come to resemble a benign conscription as racial minorities and working- and lower-middle-class Americans were allowed to experience higher education, particularly in the form of overcrowded community colleges.

The democratization of education owed much to the pressures and fears generated by the civil rights movement of the late fifties and early sixties. However, the role played by colleges and universities, especially public universities such as Berkeley, in fostering public opposition to the Vietnam War during the sixties produced a reaction. The lowered barriers to higher education became identified as a causal factor in the intense political activism occurring on the campuses. Beginning in the late seventies and continuing into the eighties, the response in governing circles was to cut back support for education at all levels. Lower-income and minority students were hardest hit. The democratization of education was halted. Politicians justified the cutbacks by pointing to the economic recession of 1978–83.

Retrenchment was, of course, a general phenomenon; but, morally and politically, much turned on how the sacrifices were to be distributed, who could best absorb them, and whose grip on a decent existence was most precarious. Not surprisingly, the social classes and groups that suffered most from retrenchment were the least powerful or, what amounts to the same thing, the least prosperous. The point was given further emphasis by the cutbacks in financial aid initiated by the Reagan administration. And while the astronomical costs of higher education could be attributed simply to inflation, as educational administrators have claimed, they could also be said to reflect a conception of education geared to the yearnings and earnings of the upper classes.

During the early eighties, however, education was rediscovered, not as the crucial means of political education for self-government and a democratic way of life, but as a vital resource in the struggle for international hegemony. The Reagan administration supplied the rhetoric but without pledging any significant financial support. Education, too, was to be privatized. What that would mean was signified by the dramatic increase of collaborative research between university and corporate scientists, the amounts of monies given to higher education by corporate donors, and the creation of a university culture that has increasingly become a glittering world of superstars, supersalaries, and technical competence and what goes with it, increasing doubts about the meaning and value of the enterprise.

This is the context in which candidate Bush declared his intention of becoming the "education president." That context included another element, a sputtering, disoriented debate about the nature of education, especially of higher education. It was symptomatic that the terms of that debate should have been importantly influenced by a book that was as archaic in its inspirations as in its deceptions.

The remarkable popularity of Allan Bloom's *The Closing of the American Mind*[1] presents an intriguing puzzle. It is wrong about many of its facts, often bizarre in its interpretations of ideas and theories, consistently inconsistent, underargued and overstated. It is a dogmatic book guarded by monumental prejudices, though it professes to be about opening closed minds. One reviewer, Robert Paul Wolff, has mercilessly satirized it, implying that its intellectual claims are not to be taken seriously.[2]

It may be, however, that Wolff has disposed of Bloom too quickly. After all, the book has been highly acclaimed and recommended by luminaries such as Saul Bellow and Leszek Kolakowski; it has sold hundreds of thousands of copies; it has been widely discussed and some critics have credited Bloom with at least raising an important topic, namely, the condition of the contemporary university, what it is and what it should be.

Most important of all, the book is a triumph and an event. It is a triumph of *haute vulgarisation* and, what may be the same thing, it marks the first exposure of "Straussism" to a mass audience and vice versa. Straussism is a self-styled "philosophy" that is well known in some academic circles but unknown to the larger reading public and, apparently, to most reviewers and talk-show hosts. It has been a singular presence in the field of political theory for nearly four decades. Now it has come out of the closet. Before the advent of *The Closing of the American Mind*, Straussians would have regarded mass popularity as a sign of their own degeneration. Before the advent of Reaganism, Straussism was regarded as erudition gone slightly bonkers. Readers of *The Closing of the American Mind* probably assumed that they were reading Bloom when, in fact, they were being treated to a jazzy version of the works of Leo Strauss, an erudite scholar whose retiring nature was in inverse proportion to his dreams of glory.

Straussism is remarkable for being the only academic ideology to organize its adherents into a compact, intensely loyal, doctrinally fastidious sect that carefully selects its members, shepherds them through their novitiate, supports them by fellowships and teaching positions, and alerts the faithful to any changes in the doctrine. It is a major force in the field of political theory, and several of its followers occupy important governmental positions. It bears a certain resemblance to religious fundamentalism in its reverence for a few written texts, which are believed to contain the truth; in its theory of interpretation, which emphasizes esoteric meanings available only to the initiated; in its concern to keep internal differences private in order to present a facade of unity to the outside world; in its insistence that truth and virtue are inseparable; in the male-dominated character of the sect, which makes it a *Bruderschaft* rather than a simple sodality; in its sensational rise from apostolic poverty to endowed plenty; and in the apotheosis of its founder to a pedestal where he is beyond criticism.

In this context, the title of the book appears, as Bloom helpfully suggests, ironical. Its real purpose is the opposite of its stated one. It is not to open the student mind; as we shall see, Bloom believes the student mind is too open, and he wants to close it to all but the truth of which philosophy alone is the bearer. It also alerts us to the political agenda hidden in the subtitle ("How Higher Education Has Failed Democracy"); for, as we shall see, that failure is not a failure of insufficient democracy in education, but the reverse: Bloom will claim that higher education has failed because it has been insufficiently antidemocratic.

The Closing of the American Mind is reactionary in a literal sense. One of its recurrent phases is "once there was . . . ," followed by an assertion about some utopian state of affairs in a past that never existed (e.g., "Philosophy has been dethroned . . ."). Although at times Bloom sounds like he wants to return to fifth-century Athens, he is really a modern romantic who thinks he is a rationalist. He professes concern only for those students at "the twenty or thirty best universities . . . who are most likely . . . to have the greatest moral and intellectual effect on the nation," not with those who "lack the freedom to pursue a liberal education" (p. 22); but he claims to be against racial discrimination and for equality of opportunity. He is wary of religion and dislikes Southerners and radicals in the same degree. He adores the Constitution, the Founding Fathers, and freedom, but he also deplores the apparent loss of interest in Europe (by which essentially he means

Paris) as an intellectual home. He clearly believes that the only culture worth having is French, and he despises and distrusts democracy as a species of boobism.

He claims that the contemporary university is in "crisis" because of a moral, philosophical, and erotic degeneration—yes, "erotic." Bloom points to a mixed bag of symptoms. It includes easy sex, feminism, Freud, Nietzsche, Heidegger, the natural sciences, rock music, relativism, historicism, social science, divorce, the culture and politics of ethnicity, reverse discrimination, and the abolition of core curricula. He laments the prevalence of divorce; two-career families (because they diminish male aggressiveness and protectiveness toward females); feminism, because it causes women to abandon their "natural" function of child-bearing; the decline of romantic love ("love suggests something wonderful, exciting. . . . Love presents illusions of perfection" (pp. 124, 125); and the preoccupation with rape, which he sees as hypocrisy on the part of middle-class women, who are rarely raped. Most of the things Bloom despises are standard items in what can be called "postmodern culture." For the moment, I shall define the postmodern simply as various ways of being skeptical about truth-claims, foundational myths, privileged narratives, moral absolutism, and claims of a social crisis owing to widespread resistance to strong authority. The flavor of Bloom's anti-postmodernism is best sampled in his discussion of education.

For Bloom, true eroticism is "the longing for education." He asks: "Are we lovers anymore? This is my way of putting the educational question of our times" (p. 133). Faculty no longer love the truth but teach the relativity of beliefs, the value of non-Western cultures, the primacy of scientific methods, and the historically contingent character of human understanding and social forms. Students are slack, ignorant, tormented by sex, their "taste for the orgiastic state" of eros corrupted by the music they admire (p. 72), their "souls" turned into automata by Freudian "therapy" (p. 120), tolerant of different opinions, respectful of other cultures, deeply egalitarian, unmoved by models of heroic action, and content to be careerists. Universities are no longer confident that there is a "common core" of classic texts which all educated persons should read and share. Faculties, instead of teaching the true doctrine about "the nature" of man and the world or about "the order of the whole"—terms whose meanings are never disclosed by Bloom although, apparently, perfectly clear to "philosophers," i.e., Straussians—corrupt the deepest questions by treating them in the language of "values," a method that subverts the true hierarchy of superior/inferior and replaces it with "preferences" (p. 143); or they treat man as the plastic creature of "culture" instead of a being with a permanent nature. The result is a general aimlessness relieved only by the confidence of natural scientists who exploit the university for their own ends, buying off the demos by practical applications of scientific knowledge but never addressing the truly important questions of ultimate beliefs and the highest good. Administrators are castigated for compromising standards of admission by bending to minority pressures and faculty for lowering performance levels that allow blacks, for example, to secure "tainted" degrees. "Democratic society," Bloom warns, "cannot accept any principle of achievement other than merit" (p. 96). This last, I might add, signals that what Bloom means by "democracy" is equality of opportunity in a society ruled by a meritocratic elite.

For Bloom the university should not only be insulated from the world; he assumes that, except for the sixties, it usually has been. Like the modernist conception of art as autonomous and unsullied by the marketplace or the needs of ordinary humanity, Bloom offers a modernist view of the university, immaculately conceived and unbeholden to any principalities or powers, the embodiment of pure reason, devoted to unchanging questions and permanent essences, and to a set of masterpieces whose identity is known to every Straussian. Society, Bloom pronounces, "is ministerial to the university" rather than vice versa. Society should support "an eternal childhood" for faculties because of the "blessings" that universities bestow on society. Without the university, society would return to a "primal slime" (p. 245).

Bloom, who presides over the John M. Olin Center for Inquiry into the Theory and Practice of Democracy,[3] regards it as a major mission of the university to serve as a corrective to democracy's deficiencies, specifically its lack of deference to its betters. Because the university is virtually the only sanctuary of reason in society, it must be protected from the ever-threatening "tyranny of the majority" and from "native populism and vulgarity" (p. 324). It must be kept free to pursue its task of criticizing the "emergent, the changing, and the ephemeral" (p. 253). Thus, Bloom wants a society which he describes as democratic to subsidize a group of men who, by his formula, are not only properly contemptuous of democracy but would prefer a different political system. A university dominated by this understanding of philosophy would be devoted to producing antidemocratic values and antidemocratic men.

The philosopher is the avant garde in Bloom's modernism, but his philosopher expresses that role not by daring to experiment with new forms of understanding but by making the defense of Great Books seem an enterprise fraught with risks. This is what motivates Bloom's frequent appeals for risk-taking and heroism. It is the avant garde as saving remnant. The threat to the "high culture" of Great Books is represented by "populism," as though the demos organized, financed, and advertised what passes for "mass culture."

Although Bloom's strongest ire is, predictably, directed against targets such as student radicalism of the sixties and feminist and minority students of the eighties, he is also critical of, and uncomfortable with, some of the values of the dominant economic and political elites. This points to the nub of the book and the clue to its peculiar brand of reaction.

I want to suggest that *The Closing of the American Mind* is not primarily about the universities, or about education, or even about the alleged miseducation of young American men. It is not even primarily about the political order. All of these topics are discussed and some general positions are established but—and this is what reviewers have not understood—each is ultimately subordinate to a higher end. If everything were in its proper or "natural" place, the end that education, university, students, and political order would serve is philosophy. Democracy and philosophy are enemies; indeed, Bloom considers philosophy to have been "dethroned by political and theoretical democracy" (p. 377). By "theoretical democracy" Bloom means a principle that denies the existence of absolute truth and objective standards and reduces beliefs to "values" that are determined by the particular culture to which the individual belongs.

Although Bloom is, in my experience, wildly wrong about students being critical of the meritocratic principle and deeply egalitarian, he is roughly correct in suggesting that relativism and historicism are important, even predominant, assumptions in the research, writing, and teaching of many, even the majority, of faculty and probably in the belief systems of students as well. Bloom means to argue that these intellectual positions discourage certain moral, social, and political beliefs and attitudes which, he suggests, are crucial to the well-being of what he calls the "American regime." These social myths are essential because the vast majority of people need "help on a vast number of issues." They need authority, tradition, but above all the reason of "wise men." In short, they need to be dependent. However, relativism undercuts all of this and paves the way for majority rule (pp. 246–47). It leaves the masses undisciplined because undeferential to their natural superiors and unawed by transcendent norms.

In this light it is easy to see what the function of the university is: to protect philosophy against democracy. Now, philosophy means something very special to Bloom. It does not refer to what the vast majority of philosophers in all societies do. Rather, it refers solely to what the epigones of Leo Strauss call philosophy. And what that means is an intricate narrative about how the truth of philosophy was first discovered by Plato, then mostly preserved by Aristotle, only to be corrupted by modern philosophers, beginning with Machiavelli and ending with Nietzsche and Heidegger, but saved by the restorative revelations of Strauss. Straussian philosophy is seen as the only true form of philosophy in the world. Philosophy also means a conception of the philosopher modeled after the form in which Plato, according to Bloom's version, put the basic political problem: what are the political and social conditions that would assure the safety and flourishing of philosophy? Plato's formula is familiar to all: let philosophers rule the polity, that is, shape the polity so as to secure the well-being of philosophy.

In the modern world, philosophers have had to "switch parties" from aristocratic regimes to liberal democratic ones (p. 288). So for the Straussian the question becomes, How to preserve philosophy in a political regime not ruled by philosopher kings? The answer is, philosophers must practice deception. They trick the "gentlemen," that is, those of wealth and power who have some fondness for ideas but who do not suspect the guile hidden in the breast of earnest philosophy instructors. A university of true philosophers would only pretend to serve the powerful (pp. 279–82). Their trickery extends to sending secret messages about what their "real" teaching is (p. 283).

Throughout his book Bloom assumes that the moral and educational failings of faculty and students have produced a crisis in political life. It does not occur to him that the equation might also run the other way, that a crisis in political life is being reflected into universities and that the usual flow chart is not from university to political system, from relative powerlessness to power, but vice versa. Bloom has long discussions of student protests at Cornell, none about Watergate or about the intrusion of corporate models into public life and education. He commends the rich and powerful for their "toleration" of the university during its travails; he ignores their exploitation of it.

At no point does Bloom raise the possibility that the condition of higher education has been importantly shaped by the needs of the economy, the pressures of corporations, or the policies of the state. He is absolutely insistent that the sixties caused universities to be dominated by "populism," which he likens to Nazism; but he seems, for example, totally unaware of the troubling extent to which university science and corporate science have become intertwined. Bloom never once contemplates the possibility that physicists don't decide spontaneously to invent atomic bombs or that engineering departments don't conclude one day that it might be an amusing idea if they were to concentrate upon developing technologies in which corporations happen to have a tangible stake. It is not that Bloom favors practical science; he does not. Rather, like Nancy Reagan, he believes that scientists need only say "no." Similarly, he criticizes the social sciences for teaching the primacy of "culture" over "nature," but his attention is never taken up with the question of the "service" function of departments of economics, political science, and public administration or their consultative roles with business and government. Bloom simply averts his eyes from the entire historical record of corporate and state influence over the internal life of universities because the university is for him the last and only hope, the haven of "permanent questions" (p. 252), the place where the "emergent, the changing, and the ephemeral" are to be fought against, and where there are men "contemptuous of public opinion" (pp. 253, 254).

Instead of analyzing the incorporation of academic science and social science into the structure of power, which might then enable him to give a political account of the condition of higher education, he turns away and blames the alleged moral crisis of universities on the weakest elements in American society: feminists, student radicals, humanities professors, black activists, reverse discrimination, Woody Allen, and Mick Jagger. It is a strange example he gives of the philosopher he claims to be: he coquettes with, even fawns upon, the powerful, yet he relentlessly pursues the powerless. "Law," he declares to the feminist, "may prescribe that the male nipples be made equal to the female ones, but they will still not give milk." Or, after bemoaning the decline of "male protectiveness" Bloom demands, "These days, why should a man risk his life protecting a [female] karate champion who knows just what part of the male anatomy to go after in defending herself?" (p. 131)

I suggest that there is a displacement effect at work that leads Bloom to side with the social and political powers which have brought universities to the condition he laments, a condition that is the natural consequence of the dynamics of the system of power which the dominant groups are trying desperately to direct and exploit. The very things that outrage Bloom—relativism, passivity, lack of passion for the noble, the true, and the good, the corruption of academic standards, the primacy of the sciences, the decline of the humanities, media-manufactured culture for the young—all of these are traceable to and many of them help to sustain the very system of economic, political, and cultural power which Bloom sides with because he fears "populism." The movements Bloom despises most are feminism, minority demands for greater access to educational opportunities, and rock music. Yet it is fair to say that while each of these arose as protests against inequality and liberal hypocrisy, that is against the system of power and rewards shaped by capitalism and administered/policed by the state, the dominant elites have responded by giving ground, accommodating, coopting, and marginalizing the more radical elements. But the main point is that elites are staring at the consequences of the system which they have largely shaped and from which they have extracted the larger share of advantages and benefits. It is their creature.

That Bloom insists on talking about "aristocrats" when he should be considering technocrats is a sign of a condition where things cannot be called by their right names for fear some dreadful truth may be exposed. What is being represented by Bloom is the displaced rage of elite groups as they survey the implications and consequences of their power and influence over society, politics, and culture, including the culture of education, especially higher education. That kind of rage can be described as the antimodernist rage of modernizing elites which have discovered that they have created a self-subverting society when they intended their project to be simply progressive. "Creative destruction," which the great economist Schumpeter declared was the secret driving force of capitalism, seems to have gotten out of hand.

It should be apparent to anyone that what destroys traditions and absolute values is not, as Bloom would have us believe, philosophers like Nietzsche and Heidegger; the fortunes of societies are influenced rather less by philosophical proofs than by the visible consequences of social and political practices. The destruction of old practices, customs, beliefs, myths, and rituals was the work of modern industrialization, urbanization, imperialism, and the spread of secular and pragmatic attitudes congenial to those developments. The peculiar problem of ruling elites in an advanced society like our own is that the institutional practices which are essential to the kind of power they are trying to acquire and exercise subvert the legitimating beliefs to which, historically, elites have appealed. The institutional practices by which our society promotes science and educates scientists; by which it develops technological innovations; and by which it idealizes certain forms of behavior (competitive, aggressive, opportunity-seeking, acquisitive, self-interested) deemed necessary if our economic system is to be continually renewed promote and demand attitudes that are experimental, flexible, skeptical, pragmatic, and secular. These are inconsistent with attitudes that need religious or moral dogmas and myths about Founding Fathers. What this means is that, ineluctably and unintentionally, elites have been producing a world they did not intend. Consequently, as the technocrat becomes more technocratic, he longs for absolute values and high culture. "Ancient Greece" is the metaphorical expression of a need for absolute superiority—and a cultural weapon.

In the sense that I have been using the term, "elite" refers not only to those whose power or influence predominates in the sectors of American society just mentioned but who, above all, have been and remain the self-conscious agents of modernization. In what follows I shall associate "modernization" with the following set of interrelated beliefs: that the main business of society and its government is to promote and exploit scientific research on a systematic basis; to be committed to continual technological innovation insofar as it contributes to more efficient or cost-effective production; to encourage a more rational organization of society, with rationality primarily understood by reference to economic and managerial criteria; to accept as both normal and ideal that change will be continuous, rapid, far-reaching, and often disruptive of traditions, expectations, and close relationships; to rely upon a structure of incentives that holds out the prospect of high rewards of wealth, power, and status; and to accept as legitimate vast differentials in income, education, power, culture, and health as long as these seem to be justified by the merit principles recognized by our society.

There are, however, certain new developments in higher education, indeed, in education generally, which provide, I think, a better context for understanding the crisis in higher education, especially as it relates to my theme concerning the problem of postmodernity. I want to suggest that the main outlines for a postmodern education have already been drawn, but this requires that both education and postmodernism be understood in more specific terms than Bloom will allow.

The crucial development in American higher education is less than a half-century old. It is the nationalization of higher education with the accompanying conception of education as forming one complete "system" which could be progressively rationalized by public policies that would regulate education to serve national goals. This ideology first emerged toward the end of World War II in the legislation which provided the educational benefits in what became known as the G.I. Bill of Rights. Prior to that moment education had been a highly diversified, and certainly uneven, matter which was in the hands of the several states and local governments. From that point on, the federal government became the dominant influence in setting educational policy and objectives. But for roughly three decades, from 1944 to 1976, most policies were directed at encouraging specific programs or specializations without much effort to rationalize the system or to redistribute emphases within the various fields that made up the curricula of higher education. Policies were "added on" rather than reshaped, and higher education rapidly expanded, especially under the impetus of various scholarship programs. Save for the sputnik program, whatever specific targeting occurred was primarily the work of private foundations. As a result, a loose pluralism was allowed to persist; no particular educational ideal was imposed and no serious homogenization of education took place. Equally important, substantial efforts were undertaken to make higher education more accessible, especially to students from lower-income families and racial minorities, than ever before. These were the years when a liberal, modernist conception of education prevailed.

But toward the end of the 1970s a change began to take place that would be accelerated as a matter of policy during the Reagan administration. For the first time a distinctively national conception of education began to emerge. Its formulation has been the work of government officials and educational administrators working in close cooperation with foundation executives and leaders from the corporate world. A specific agenda has been defined and promoted. It is to assure a sufficient supply of well-trained workers with scientific, technical, and managerial skills. At the same time, the modern, expansive, egalitarian view of education was replaced by a restrictive conception that brought a radical redefinition of the relationship between education and society, between education and the state, and education and the individual. The political background was the growing perception of a relative decline in American economic and political power. The victim of the change would be the liberal version of modernity with its moderate meritocracy, its relatively generous philosophy of welfare, and its all-important assumption that it was possible to have defense and welfare, meritocracy and limited egalitarianism, because of the unlimited capability of the American economy for accommodating all manner of claims upon it.

The new view can be described as the official version of postmodernity. It rejects the liberal version of modernity, especially in its emphasis upon equality as more than equal opportunity and upon the economy as a cornucopia capable of subsidizing the poor as well as the rich. Official postmodernism is unabashedly elitist, anti-egalitarian, and insistent about priorities and rather clear about what they should be. But it accepts in a purer form the modernist faith in science and technology because it knows that these forms of power have been wholly incorporated into the larger system of state and corporate power. Its ideal person is competent, tough, aggressive, calculating, and exploitive.

The purpose of education in this view is political and concrete. It is to enable American capitalism to compete successfully in an increasingly competitive international economy in which American superiority is seriously threatened and, in many cases, even overcome by foreign rivals. Increasingly the model of education is drawn from Japan, that is from a society notable for its relative indifference to individual needs and for its fetish of group solidarity. This new educational vision also importantly serves the end of the state. For so closely interwoven are corporate and state power today and so increasingly similar are their personnel needs that the new vision also serves the ends of state power, most notably in space research, weapons development, and medical research, not to mention in providing a steady supply of technicians of power, that is, lawyers and administrators.

The new vision of education is the acquisition of the specific job skills needed in a high-tech society. There are some striking consequences of this definition of education or, rather, the redefinition of it.

One is that the principal purpose of education is no longer conceived primarily in terms of the development of the person. In the past, the person was understood in complex terms of diverse potentialities. The academic subjects to be studied represented not only different methods of understanding but elements of a different sensibility. Becoming a person meant embarking on a quest for the harmonizing of diverse sensibilities.

The rejection of that conception of person can be measured by the disappearance of the older rhetoric about "personal discovery," "the exploration of diverse possibilities," or "initiation into a rich cultural heritage." In its place is an anti-sixties rhetoric which is really an attack on education as the representation of human diversity. Or it is the rhetoric of "core courses" which work to dismiss the very subjects they profess to be defending. The new education is severely functional, proto-professional, and priority-conscious in an economic sense. It is also notable for the conspicuous place given to achieving social discipline through education.

It is as though social planners, both public and private, had suddenly realized that education forms a system in which persons of an impressionable age are "stuff" that can be molded to the desired social form because for several years they are under the supervision of public and private authorities. (Parenthetically, it is in this light that private religious schools have found great favor in the eyes of public and private policy makers: these are perceived as superior means for imposing social discipline, although that discipline is usually described as moral or religious education and as anti-drugs and -sexual permissiveness. Such schools represent the privatization of public virtue.) Third, and closely related, the new conception is tacitly a way of legitimating a policy of social triage. High-tech societies are showing themselves to be economic systems in which a substantial part of the population is superfluous, and so is the skill-potential of perhaps a majority of the working population. Such economies tend to dislocate workers, replace them by automation, or relegate them to inferior, less demanding, and less remunerative types of work. If such a population is not to be a menace, its plight must be perceived as its just deserts, that is, the failure must be theirs, not the system's. More prisons, not social and educational programs, must be seen as the rational response. The schools should operate, therefore, to sort out people, to impose strict but impersonal standards so that responsibility for one's fate is clear and unavoidable.

A landmark in the development of this new vision was the Report of the National Commission on Excellence in Education (the so-called Bell Commission) of 1983 dealing with the state of secondary schools. It was set out in the opening sentences: "Our nation is at risk. Our once unchallenged preeminence in commerce, industry, science, and technological innovation is being overtaken by competitors throughout the world."

Although the Bell Report never suggested how it had come about that the nation was at risk, its remedy was remarkable for its pared-down vision of education, its emphasis upon the disciplinary role of schools, and its martial rhetoric. It warned of "a rising tide of mediocrity" in educational performance, and it likened that prospect to "an act of war." It compared current educational practices to "an act of unthinking, unilateral educational disarmament." While one might dismiss this as mere hype, the uncomfortable fact is that that rhetoric was chosen in order to establish the context in which the problem of education was to be resolved. Military language is inherently uncongenial to thinking about individual growth but not about adapting individuals to organizational functions. Its barracks language of pseudo-democracy is also a way of brushing off problems of minorities and of the poor. Indeed, the coercive language of war, crisis, and mobilization is so antithetical to what education has traditionally symbolized that it should alert us to the radical recontextualization being proposed for education.

The curriculum proposed for the secondary schools was called the "New Basics." Its purpose was to impose a greater emphasis upon English, mathematics, social studies, computer sciences, and proficiency in foreign languages. Except for the suggestion that social studies ought to focus upon the differences between "free" and unfree societies, the curriculum was remarkable only for its bleakness, its silence about stimulating curiosity, its indifference to the rich cultural heritages of a society as diverse as ours, and its clear hostility to any suggestion of the importance of critical thinking. Students were looked upon as "the essential raw materials . . . waiting to be mobilized." The society for which they were to be prepared was not defined by any democratic or even traditional liberal conception but rather a society whose identity was imposed by the imperatives of international competition. How that society was being conceived was reflected in the habits and values which the schools were supposed to instill. Schooling reduces to work habits in a controlled environment. Thus, the report recommended more homework, a longer school day, a mandatory curriculum, a tightening of discipline through "better classroom management," "firm and fair codes of student conduct," "segregation of continually disruptive students," stricter enforcement of attendance, greater emphasis upon standardized achievement tests, stricter standards of admission to colleges and universities, higher standards for teachers, more effective means for evaluating teachers for salary increases and tenure, and the extension of the teaching contract to eleven months.

The report also drew the parent into the system of discipline. Parents were urged to be "vigilant" in "monitor[ing] your child's study" and to keep the pressure on. Then it addressed a final "word," as it called it, to the students, warning them that unless they acquired the requisite knowledge and skills, they would be left powerless and "your future" will be "thrust upon you by others." Now *there* is a context for learning: fear.

The Bell Commission was quickly joined by a number of other groups, such as the Hunt Commission and the Business-Higher Education Forum, and a presidential task force on "Chaos in the Classroom," which, incidentally, recommended the reversal of certain Supreme Court decisions for allegedly tying the hands of school administrators. Each of these reiterated the main theme of the Bell Report, no-nonsense education for an intensely competitive world being continuously changed by technological innovations.

The Bell Report can be fairly described as an official attempt at defining postmodern education. It is postmodern because it substitutes a narrow conception of competence for an integrative conception of rationality and because it elevates discipline to such a central place that it all but eliminates the notion of education as the development of individuals who will be able to practice the life of free citizens—which, among other things, does not mean mindless loyalty or uncritical acceptance of things as they are.

The postmodern preference for a minimalist education is deceptive because in emphasizing practical education it gives the appearance of promoting the power of the individual. The individual who is "trained" for a job will stand a better chance of becoming employed and will, therefore, be in a position to use the income to make personal choices. But in a rapidly changing high-tech society it is not at all clear that individuals can be assured of that kind of power, because a job is not a career and jobs are what "basic education" is about. Careers, in contrast, are what lawyers, doctors, managers, and comparable professionals can look forward to. Professionals are not, however, usually produced by a minimalist education; if they are, it generally carries the stigma of the second-rate. The prospects for a career, we could say, increase when preparation for it occurs at one of Bloom's elite institutions.

What is true of the kind of empowerment careers bring is true also at a subtler level. The pressures for a narrowly practical, vocational, and preprofessional education are usually aimed most often at public higher education, at junior colleges and public universities and colleges, in other words at those institutions in which most citizens are educated. When curricula are shaped overwhelmingly by job considerations, students are being denied significant forms of power. They are being culturally deprived in a deep sense; but this is not understood, because literature, philosophy, history, and art are assumed to be essentially frivolous, however amusing or ornamental they may be. They are, in other words, conceived as being completely unrelated to power. They don't pay off, they don't produce anything tangible, and they clutter résumés. Yet the very subjects being dismissed are precisely the ones from which one's inevitably narrow personal experience can be deepened, broadened, and diversified. These subjects tell us what it means to be a person, and they tell us important things about power in all of its forms—intimate as well as impersonal, social as well as political, material as well as intellectual and spiritual; power arising from class, sex, race; power in its aesthetic forms. They tell us too about the extraordinarily diverse ways that human beings have organized their lives, individually and collectively, or that they have confronted their lot, measured their mortality, protested their fate, and expressed their solidarity. To be deprived of this range of experience is to be ignorant, not practical; to be made more powerless, not more competent.

Unwittingly, what has happened is that the interpretive modes of inquiry, the modes that explore the diverse expressions of human being in the world, have acquired a greater rather than a lesser importance because of the remarkable advances in scientific knowledge and technological power. Examples of the interpretive mode would be: historical studies of various forms of ideas (history of philosophy, theology, political theory), artifacts (history of art and architecture and music, archaeology), and practices (anthropology, church history, political, social, and economic institutions).

Unlike the scientific modes whose ideal discourse is parsimonious, propositional, abstract, and universal, interpretive accounts tend to be rich in historical innuendo. Such accounts typically assume that regardless of whether the object of the account is a person, a place, or a practice, whether it is an individual, an artifact, or a collectivity, the object will be, in Husserl's phrase, "sedimented" yet singular, even unique. It will be an accretion of different layers or strata representing different epochs, experiences, understandings, and values all intersecting around or in one object.

Scientific modes tend to be reductive; their patron saint is William of Ockham; their icon is the razor. Such modes are constituted by what Popper called "the logic of discovery." A logic of discovery adds new items as it uncovers new realms, entities, and relationships. But typically it tends to reduce the theoretical population. The condition of discovery is that previous theoretical objects must be abandoned or subsumed in drastically diminished form. The logic of discovery stands for an eternally modernizing mentality; it is the theoretical counterpart to the ever-expanding economy and what I have elsewhere called the "megastate." All three reduce or incorporate their world of objects: the first talks of more comprehensive theories, the second of corporate takeovers and buy-outs, the third of global power.

Interpretive modes, in contrast, proliferate theoretical objects, and while some abandonment occurs, it is substantially less. Think of the theoretical object called "Shakespearian studies," how it has accumulated, and how much of eighteenth-and nineteenth-century scholarship is still read. Interpretive modes, we might say, are the guardians of plurality and difference, even sometimes to the point of preciosity. Their patron saint is Hegel. The idea is to keep things in the world, including memories of monstrous historical acts.

The interpretive mode is crucial to education because postmodern forms of power are capable of so much more rapid and total devastation than all previous forms of human power. It is not only postmodern weaponry that is devastating, but also the effects of postmodern productivity upon natural environments, urban habitats, human skills, and social and political practices (as in the family, sexual relationships, practices of self-government and responsibility). With such extraordinary power available to human minds, it becomes crucial to the survival of the species not only that minds be instructed in the arts of handling power but that sensibilities be cultivated about the mishandling of it. This sensibility is precisely what is special about the interpretive modes because it is a sensibility about human differences and the inestimable treasure and endless source of delight they represent.

And this nurturing sensibility is what a postmodern education has to incorporate if it is to educate human beings for a world threatened by a surfeit of power (think of nuclear proliferation or of Stinger missiles) and the paradoxical powerlessness to which it gives rise: think of the difficulty of controlling, let along eradicating, terrorism. In the light of these considerations the cultivation of interpreting faculties is not an elective subject but an indispensable prerequisite to the most urgent of all vocations, of being human.

Four / Archaism, Modernity, and Democracy in America

The text that serves as the basis for the reflections that follow is a familiar sentence from Tocqueville's *Democracy in America:*

A new science of politics is needed for a wholly new world. [1]

In a letter written to his English translator, Tocqueville attempted to explain how it had been possible for him to see the American democracy in a different light than previous observers and thereby to grasp why a new science was needed and what its basic outlines were. Unlike some of his contemporaries who attributed their insights to possession of a method of inquiry that was, in principle, accessible to anyone, Tocqueville traced his to the accidents of biography. He had, Tocqueville noted, been born between two worlds: "I came into the world at the end of a long revolution which, after having destroyed the old order, created nothing that could last. When I began my life aristocracy was already dead and democracy was still unborn. Therefore my instinct could not lead me blindly toward one or the other. . . . I was so nicely balanced between the past and the future that I did not feel instinctively drawn toward the one or the other." [2]

Tocqueville's theoretical life was devoted to adumbrating the two worlds between which he professed to be balanced. *Democracy in*

America described the new world of democracy, *The Old Regime and the French Revolution* the old world of prerevolutionary France. Before turning to consider the newness of the one world and the oldness of the other, we need to pause and consider the curious quality of Tocqueville's self-description quoted above. For I have omitted from the passage the reasons that Tocqueville gave for being detached from both democracy and aristocracy. No family or personal interest, he explained, "gave me a natural and necessary affection toward democracy. I have no particular motive to love or hate it." Similarly, he professed to have "no natural hatred or jealousy of the aristocracy" nor any natural affection toward it, "for one can only be strongly attached to the living."[3]

This inversion startles the reader's natural expectations. In the aftermath of the French Revolution, the question for one of Tocqueville's social class was not whether he had "a natural and necessary affection for democracy," much less a "natural hatred or jealousy of the aristocracy," but whether he had a natural hatred for democracy and a natural affection for aristocracy. Once on guard, a reader might be skeptical of Tocqueville's pronouncement that it was pointless to consider restoring aristocratic institutions "because one can only be strongly attached to the living." There are many forms in which aristocracy might be perpetuated without seeking to restore the Old Regime, just as there are many ways of coming to terms with democracy without really embracing it. "I confess that in America I saw more than America; I sought an image of democracy itself."[4]

Democracy in America was Tocqueville's attempt to create in theory the new world of democracy and to preserve in practice a certain specific political truth that had been embodied in the old world of aristocracy. There is an important sense, therefore, in which *The Old Regime and the French Revolution* both precedes and completes *Democracy in America,* even though it was actually written later. In the earlier work he argued that democracy might be saved from itself provided it were restrained by a proper admixture of elements, some of the more important of which were in *esprit,* if not in form, redolent of the Old Regime. The latter work, *The Old Regime and the French Revolution,* was written more than a decade after the publication of the final volume of *Democracy* (1840).[5] Despite his disclaimer that one can only be attached to the living, it was to the dead, that is, to a vanished political world, that he returned to compose his last masterpiece. *The Old Regime* recounts how the aristocracy had been destroyed by a combination of state centralization and revolution. It is the story of the destruction of a political culture and in particular of those elements of plurality, difference, communalism, and mediated power which had been crucial in making America not just a new form of government but a political civilization. *The Old Regime* was thus a *memento mori,* a commemoration of the living and the dead as well as a warning about the future.

There is, then, a complex relationship between Tocqueville's two worlds and the two theoretical works corresponding to them. The later work represented a return to a historical as well as a personal past. Its subject concerned .the French past, which was also the past of Tocqueville's aristocratic ancestors. It was, as well, a return to Tocqueville's theoretical past. The old regime, as I have suggested, had been prefigured in *Democracy in America.*[6] When Tocqueville came to write his foreword to *The Old Regime,* Louis Napoleon's dictatorship was being consolidated. Pointedly Tocqueville recalled *Democracy in America* and proceeded to quote "almost verbatim" from what he had written "more than twenty years ago about another society."[7]

The connecting link, in his mind, was despotism. In *Democracy* he had warned of the dangers of "democratic despotism": the parallel with the France of his own day was too obvious to need further elaboration. But the root cause of despotism in both France and America was the same: "the destruction of the aristocracy."[8]

The complex relationship mentioned earlier involves, then, a relationship between different texts with their different orders of time as well as their different worlds. The two worlds were, of course, the Old World of Europe and the New World of America. More precisely, Tocqueville's Old World was a representation of the prerevolutionary world of eighteenth-century France. That the imagery of "new" and "old" should have been chosen to epitomize and contrast two political cultures was a tribute to the startling effect of American life and the country's physical landscape upon the young traveler from France.[9] America seemed to violate every expectation a European might have about the requirements of political and social order. Americans had constructed a different civilization, and they had done it in a natural setting that was at once savage and bountiful. They had developed a political society in which the state was practically invisible. To call America a new world was understatement rather than hyperbole.

For us, a century and a half after the publication of the first volume of *Democracy in America,* its Old and New World terms of reference seem strange. This is not because we are less accustomed to thinking in terms of "worlds," for clearly we are not. "Third" world, "communist" world, and "free" world are part of our everyday political vocabulary. Rather, what has become strange is the category of the "old" when every world seems determined to become new. Few if any old "worlds" exist except in isolated backwaters that (in the revealing cliché) "time has passed by." Fewer still want to remain old. Such societies are of greater interest to the anthropologist than to the political sociologist, the political scientist, or the political theorist. The "political" and the "old" don't seem to have much to say to each other.

Although for a brief moment during the 1950s the concept of "traditional society" enjoyed a vogue among social scientists, that, too, proved as evanescent as the social conditions which that concept was attempting to capture. The pace of change being experienced today by almost all societies seems to demand some category, partly temporal and partly cultural, that will furnish, if only illusorily, a point of reference, an illuminating contrast, that will enable us to comprehend what is happening to us individually and collectively beyond the fact of change. But even the categories for describing change are themselves quickly overtaken. Change is perhaps to our historical moment what "ce premier fait" of equality was to Tocqueville's: "universel . . . durable . . . tous les événements, comme tous les hommes, servent à son développement."[10]

During the last decade the term "modern," together with its cognates "premodern," "modernizing," and "modernization," promised to provide a purchase on the cultural meaning of our peculiarly rapid mode of temporality and to give us some clues about from what and into what we were changing. The several variations on the theme of the modern were stabs at stabilizing, if not existence, then at least its meaning. The presupposition that underlay the variations on the theme of modernity was that modern science and advanced technology represented what is quintessentially and uniquely modern, the discovery of how progress and growth could be rendered perpetual, produced and reproduced at will. That guarantee gave a distinct meaning to the modern. It appeared as an ultima Thule, a historical stage with no beyond, no further or postscientific stage. Although it was conceivable that a nonrational society, such as a primitive tribe or a countercultural commune of hippies, might choose to remain in or revert to a premodern condition, it seemed incomprehensible that a rational society would aspire to venture beyond modern science.

At least that seemed to be the situation until, suddenly, the modern was pronounced passé and the era of the postmodern announced. The rapidity with which the postmodern was welcomed and the signs of its real presence in many areas of contemporary life suggest that the modern is in the process of disintegration. Admittedly, it is not easy to pin down the meaning of "postmodern," and it may well be useless to try. It means something different to the art historian than to the literary critic, to the social historian than to the music critic. One thing, however, can be said with some assurance about postmodernism in most of its various guises, that it insinuates a question mark after "modern" as a way of registering skepticism, even suspicion, about the primary icons of modernity.

Although the postmodern mind, as yet, hesitates to provoke a head-on confrontation with modern science, which has served as the principal icon of modernity, the subversion of the supporting culture of science is clearly under way. The postmodern individual has pretty much renounced the objectivist view of scientific knowledge, indeed of all forms of knowledge. S/he accepts cultural and moral relativism while barely acknowledging solipsism to be a problem. S/he tends to regard most academic disciplines as merely representing different ways of telling tales, with no mode of discourse occupying a privileged status. Preoccupied with language and indifferent to substance or, rather, inclined to believe that language *is* substance, the postmodern mind displays an alarming number of advanced symptoms typical of an addiction to morphemes. If we were to accept these temporal-cultural signs as marking a division between modernity and postmodernity, and if, *pace* Tocqueville, we were to imagine ourselves situated between the modern and the postmodern worlds, between a world that is/has been and one that is/is becoming, would we want also to urge that a new science of politics is needed for a wholly new world?

As a way of considering that question I shall return to Tocqueville and explore his understanding of the "new" and the "old." Two additional questions will be involved; neither of them will make much sense at this point, but I trust that they will appear less opaque as my themes emerge. The first is, in *Democracy in America* what functions as the modern and what is the premodern? The second is, in contemporary American political society what signifies the premodern and the postmodern, and how do these stand in relation to their counterparts in Tocqueville's work on America?

AT FIRST GLANCE, there is nothing surprising about Tocqueville's juxtaposition of a "new science of politics" with a "new world." From the time of the first settlers to the most recent installment in the interminable debate over American "exceptionalism," Americans and foreigners alike have taken to calling the United States a "new world" as though that characterization were yet another self-evident truth. This convention has encouraged readers of Tocqueville to assume that his new science was about America and for Americans. That assumption does not square with Tocqueville's professed intentions. *Democracy in America* is not about America in a direct sense but about "a great democratic revolution that is at work among us." [11] The work is directed at the general phenomenon of democracy, which, according to Tocqueville, had been gathering force for several centuries and had now revealed itself to be what he called "a providential fact," a universal and irresistible tendency whose progress was frequently promoted by actors whose conscious intentions were opposed to or ignorant of democracy.[12] Rather than being composed for the intellectual and political edification of Americans, the work was conceived both as a contribution to the political education of Frenchmen and as an intervention in French politics. "I wanted to find there some lessons from which we [Frenchmen] could profit."[13] He confided to a friend, "Although I have rarely mentioned France in this book, I have not written a page without thinking about her and without having her, as it were, before my eyes."[14] Thus, *Democracy in America* may have been about the new world, but it was for the old.

Although, ironically, in France *Democracy* never became the classic it did in America and did not become the subject of a large scholarly literature until fairly recently,[15] the fact that it was conceived and shaped for a French audience must have conditioned the way in which he conceived the old and new worlds and juxtaposed them. How did his new science seek to understand political newness, and what role did the old play in that understanding?

The brief answer to the first part of the question is: with severe reservations. Certainly Tocqueville did not urge his readers to embrace democracy but rather to reconcile themselves to the inevitable. This general advice was accompanied by a set of ideological assumptions about which social groups and interests were in need of reassurance concerning democracy and which were not. Tocqueville seemed to assume that one important aspect of the new world of democracy was that the workers, elements of the petit bourgeoisie, and the peasantry would be more closely identified with the political system, that it was, in an important sense, their system. Yet his new science of politics did not speak to them or attempt to educate them politically. In contrast, for the bourgeoisie and the still significant aristocracy *Democracy in America* was a cautionary tale, full of warnings about the dangers of democracy, its leveling impulses, the tyranny of majority opinion, the atomization produced by the equality of "social condition," and the obsession with individual self-interest. *Democracy* was also a book of remedies, of practices that would curb democratic excesses and blunt the drive toward uniformity.

Thus, the new science was conceived, at least in part, as a book of counsel on how to combat the new.[16] It was intended as an antidemocratic science and disposed to be antimodern in spirit. It was by no means, however, meant to be a reactionary science. Tocqueville once described himself as "a liberal of a new kind." [17] He meant that, unlike many contemporary liberals, he was not committed to perpetuating the antireligious and anticlerical attitudes of the Enlightenment; and, unlike some continental liberals, he was inclined toward an accommodation with democracy, although not at the expense of individual freedom or property rights. One could say that he was, in the strict sense, committed more to the liberalization of democracy than to the democratization of liberalism.

The association of a new science with antidemocracy was not an original idea of Tocqueville's. He had borrowed liberally from the authors of *The Federalist Papers*, who had been among the first to argue for a "new science of politics" suited to the needs of a new world in which republics were to be designed to occupy huge land masses and democracies were, for that reason, anachronistic. [18] Thanks to the careful scholarship of J. T. Schleifer, we are better able to specify the influential role of *The Federalist Papers* in shaping Tocqueville's understanding of the American constitutional system. [19] Tocqueville drew heavily on the antimajoritarianism of *The Federalist* and reiterated its distrust of the state legislatures, which, at the time of the ratification controversy over the Constitution, had often been controlled by popular forces. [20]

There were, however, some substantial differences between *The Federalist* conception of "new science" and Tocqueville's. Both described the American political system as an experiment, but they differed over the nature of the experiment. For Madison, writing in *Federalist* 14, the new constitution represented the "experiment of an extended republic." A large-scale republic, he claimed, could remedy the inherent deficiency of democracies. A democracy was unworkable if it had to govern a big land mass and a large but scattered population. A part of the strategy of this argument was to historicize democracy by suggesting that it was the creature of classical antiquity and hence limited by the special conditions of its origins. Thus, democracy was, in effect, tarred with being premodern. [21]

Tocqueville, however, regarded America as an experiment in democracy rather than as a republican alternative to it. He described it as "the great experiment . . . in the attempt to construct society upon a new basis. . . . Theories hitherto unknown, or deemed impracticable, were to exhibit a spectacle for which the world had not been prepared by the history of the past." [22]

For *The Federalist* the new science was embodied in the proposed constitution, while for Tocqueville the new science would show that the Constitution was only one element in American political society and that the success of the experiment depended on elements such as *moeurs,* or traditions of conduct, whose nature was such that they could not have been designed by constitutional provisions.

The nub of the matter was that *The Federalist* had been concerned to establish a strong national government, which meant, *inter alia,* a more centralized system and a powerful executive. Tocqueville, however, had a certain political kinship with the arch-enemies of *The Federalist,* the antifederalists. He believed that the states were the prime source of America's political principles and that America possessed "a municipal spirit" reminiscent of ancient Athens.[23] His famous discussion of voluntary associations was indicative of an outlook that was sympathetic to precisely what *The Federalist* had distrusted, an active citizenry and local institutions by which they could govern their common affairs independent of centralized authority.

It has long been recognized that Tocqueville was deeply influenced by Montesquieu,[24] but to my knowledge no one has connected that influence to Tocqueville's call for "a new science of politics." I want to suggest that although Tocqueville may have borrowed this phrase from *The Federalist,* the actual substance of the "new science" was less indebted to that source than to Montesquieu. The crucial element here is that Montesquieu held to a conception of science different from that of most Enlightenment thinkers, including *The Federalist.*

Most readers have associated Montesquieu with a Newtonian conception of science that was most clearly embodied in Montesquieu's view of constitutionalism as set out in book 11, chapter 6 of *De l'esprit des lois* and its classic discussion of the separation of powers. Although there is an undeniably Newtonian flavor to some of the passages in that chapter and to a few elsewhere in the work as a whole,[25] the theoretical outlook of *De l'esprit* was diametrically opposed to the constitutional gadgeteering inspired by Newtonian physics and to its implicit ideal of a constitution as a unified theory of power, as a founded entity conceived and instituted as God had conceived and instituted the universe.

Montesquieu believed political societies to be historical accretions, the artifact of no single founder, strongly shaped by physical conditions (climate and geography), and consisting of complex accommodations over time between religion, morality, customs, economy, and civil and political laws. The main target of *De l'esprit* was despotism. Together with *The Persian Letters* it constitutes the most sustained meditation on despotism to be found anywhere in modern political theory. He was convinced that despotism was the dominant tendency in the monarchical state system of his day, and he sought to counter it with a theoretical construction that was deeply influenced by the practices of feudalism and by the vestigial remnants of that system preserved in the so-called intermediary bodies (*les puissances intermé-*

diaires).[26] These consisted of provincial estates or assemblies, municipal governments, and the judicial institutions of *les parlements*.[27] It was not an urge to restore feudalism that had led Montesquieu to emphasize the value of some of its practices, but rather the imagery that it inspired of a decentered political system in which power was dispersed among many centers and thereby limited by the natural rivalries among them.

The feudal element in Montesquieu's theory was decisive to Tocqueville's "new science" and to its antimodern thrust. Its presence in Tocqueville's theory resolves the logical paradox of how it is possible to find a "new" language of theory for a "New World," which, for Europeans, was only now emerging. A truly New World would be one without precedent and hence without a language appropriate to it. For Tocqueville what was ultimately most new about the New World was its capacity for reproducing sameness. This capacity could be variously described as uniformity, conformity, leveling, egalitarianism, or democracy. It all came back, however, to the same point. Never before in human history had there been a society in which so many people thought alike, dressed alike, lived alike, or occupied the same middling social station. To appreciate the radical novelty of New World newness required the startling effect produced by observing it from the vantage point of the Old World, that is, from the vantage point of an idealized oldness that cherished variety, gradation of social rank, difference, and rareness with a passion equal to that felt by democratic man for equality. These were the feudal elements in Tocqueville's conception of the Old World. They were not only associated with the old but were essentially archaic in the new context being shaped by the forces making for egalitarianism. They were, Tocqueville knew, dead in the literal sense that the institutions that embodied them, such as a privileged aristocracy, could not be restored. They could be treated as a principle, however, and in that form they might be useful in an entirely different political and theoretical context. They could help to clarify the theoretical meaning of the new and at the same time serve as the center of an antimodern practice or pragmatics. They are what Tocqueville meant by a new science.

More than a quarter century ago, the late Louis Hartz attempted to retrieve and restate Tocqueville's fundamental interpretive principle. In *The Liberal Tradition in America* Hartz maintained that to understand America was to appreciate the fact that it had no feudal past.[28] Using this insight as a departure point, I might expand it by saying that to have no feudal past means to have a politics without history. In my interpretation feudalism, the system in which inheritance, with its implicit historicity, is the master notion, serves as a metaphor for historicized politics. By a historicized politics I mean a politics that over time inevitably produces inherited privileges and unequal powers. The result is a social space crowded with prior claims to unequal ownership and status and the transformation of a manifold of injustices (unlawful conquest and forcible seizures) from the dim past into vested rights of the present. Historicized politics is postlapsarian.

The New World of America, in contrast, appears as a fresh land, seemingly without limits or boundaries and innocent of past inequities. Land was easily available, and opportunities for wealth and higher status seemed limitless. Accordingly, America's politics was natural rather than historical. America's political practices developed as though written on a *tabula rasa* much as the contract theorists of the seventeenth century had imagined men imposing a civil association upon a state of nature.[29] Inscribing politics upon nature rather than history was the essence of what was modern about America. "The case and circumstances of America," Tom Paine wrote, "present themselves as in the beginning of the world. . . . We are brought at once to the point of seeing government begin, as if we had lived in the beginning of time."[30] From the standpoint of natural politics, "history" does not signify a narrative of events but obstacles such as are represented by vested interests, traditional networks of influence, and settled expectations—in short, everything that has to be taken into account by political actors. To have no history is to face only natural obstacles and one's own limitations. Natural politics presents a vista of unimpeded action, and it aroused Tocqueville's deepest apprehensions. It seemed made to order for despotism or for centralized bureaucracy. A lack of traditions and customary institutions allows the will to extend itself almost without limit. America was spared that fate, at least for the moment, because central power remained underdeveloped.

When Tocqueville remarks that America became democratic and egalitarian without having to pass through a destructive revolution, he is recalling that in the great revolution of 1789 the French had tried to establish democracy by overthrowing feudalism. France, in other words, had tried to accomplish by force what Americans had inherited by accident, the elimination of history and the founding of natural politics. The lesson that the new science wants to impart is that although both societies spawned by revolution are antifeudal, each should strive to preserve archaic elements that derive from a feudal past, as in the case of France, or are the functional equivalents of feudal institutions, as in America. Unrelieved newness is the stuff of despotism.

One of Tocqueville's favorite examples of archaism in America was

the judiciary and the legal profession.[31] They represented the presence
of an aristocratic principle in a political system that otherwise embodied newer principles of majoritarianism and a plebiscitary president.
Observing America during the Jacksonian presidency, Tocqueville
concluded that the principle of an independent judiciary, coupled with
the high social esteem enjoyed by the bench and bar, operated to check
the majority and to secure the property rights, and hence the loyalty,
of the bourgeoisie. The principle was elitist and ran contrary to the
democratic ethos, which Tocqueville had encountered everywhere. Its
archaic character was suggested by analogy with the *noblesse de robe*
and the *parlements*. These institutions perpetuated a feudal element in
the Old Regime, and both came to be renowned for their resistance to
the centralizing efforts of the monarchy. The *parlements* were law
courts that belonged to the privileges of a particular stratum of the
French nobility. Among their powers was the authority to grant or
withhold registration of royal decrees, thus denying them full legal
authority. The power could be invoked to block, at least temporarily,
the efforts of monarchs to extend their powers. Not infrequently the
parlements were accused of being more interested in defending narrow
class privileges than in controlling the excesses of the monarchy.[32] Parenthetically, historians of our day have viewed a substantial part of
royal activity during the decades before the Revolution as modernizing
and reformist. In that light, the actions of the *parlements* appear as ob-
structionist and antiprogressive.[33]

The point of Tocqueville's comparison between New and Old
World institutions was not to restore the *parlements* in France or the
system of class privilege. It was to teach democracy the importance of
providing a counterprinciple at the center of its system. The advice
was less obvious than it seemed. Americans had extolled the values of
the law and the independence of the judiciary long before the writing
of *Democracy in America,* but typically this perspective on the legal system had been accompanied by self-distrust. Law and the judiciary
were viewed as valuable counterweights to the "excesses" of popular
rule. But this was to think in terms of checks and balances rather than
to think archaically. It was, in other words, to think within the categories of the political culture rather than outside it. That culture, as the
second volume of *Democracy* would emphasize, weighed heavily on
American society and compelled its members to view the political
world in a way that suppressed differences. In order to grasp the implications of democracy, therefore, one had to get outside the new and,
"nicely balanced between the past and future," view it from a vantage
point that enabled one to look at the new with an eye toward the old.
A theoretical eye sensitive to the possibilities of archaism can exploit

them in order to reinsert historicity into societies whose "natural" bent is to extirpate it.

ARCHAISM TAKES ON a special urgency when the new nation that was once thought to have no past now has one and when it once had no feudal past but now has one. Putting the matter this way might seem to be straining the Tocqueville-Hartz thesis beyond recognition. The slightest familiarity with American history is sufficient to demonstrate that America has always had a past in which differentiated societies and complex cultures flourished before the colonists arrived early in the seventeenth century. At best one is only entitled to claim that before 1607 America did not have a European past. Tocqueville himself attached great importance to the colonial heritage of English practices and political ideas and of biblical examples.[34] Yet these qualifications do not take away Tocqueville's basic point, that America's newness, its vast spaces and natural resources, the egalitarianism promoted by the availability of land, and the opportunities for social mobility had conspired to make America a society perpetually in movement and continually changing. Americans were always changing laws, jobs, locations, tastes, beliefs, and status, not once but several times. To live the new was to accept instability and dislocation as normal features of existence. "The woof of time is every instant broken, and the track of generations effaced."[35]

Conceptions of change are also susceptible to change, and Tocqueville's understanding of it reflects a bygone era. For him change was the result of the uncoordinated strivings of largely autonomous, and mostly isolated, individuals acting out their hopes across a huge and often empty social space. That conception of spontaneous change seems remote from the conception of change fostered by the culture that contemporary science and technology have built under the bidding of corporate capitalism. For an "advanced society" struggling amidst the rigors of the international economy, change is necessary for survival. It must, therefore, be produced as a matter of deliberate policy. The organization of scientific research and its subsidization by public and private funds signify that change has been institutionalized.

The resulting intensification and rationalization of change, the continuous reproduction of the new and the simultaneous subversion of the old, justify calling such a society postmodern, for there is no longer any old world to be transformed, only the changing of change. Instead of being a special case, fashion, with its seasonal character and inexhaustible ingenuity, may be the general emblem of advanced societies. A postmodern society produces its own archaeological strata at an almost daily rate as its members change cars, clothes, genders, bodily organs, heroes, wives, sexual preferences, and intellectual truths. For their part, politicians complain of "volatile electorates" and seek ways of insulating party organizations from supporters who seem highly susceptible to brief enthusiasms and whimsies. To seek continuity between generations one must turn to computers, which, we are reliably informed, are into their fourth and fifth "generations." "And they shall eat sour software . . ."

One of the most striking recent changes stands Tocqueville on his head. It is the steady de-democratization of American society, both as a "social condition" and as a political "civilization," to use Tocqueville's vocabulary. Social inequalities have widened and deepened; bureaucratic centralization of governmental power continues to grow; the American electorate remains the most lethargic of any major democracy; and real power is remote from public control, although not from control over the public. Today it is difficult to imagine that any political scientist or political sociologist in good repute would write a book about the irresistible tide of democracy or its incarnation in America, except either as parody or, what amounts to the same thing, as an antithesis to the Soviet Union.

Tocqueville feared the overdemocratization of society. He warned that the dynamic of democracy, in the form of the "tyranny of the majority," would level all distinctions of status, wealth, and merit and impose uniformity of opinions. During the past half-century, however, democratizing forces have been engaged in periodic struggles, not to extend a system of total ideology or uniform practices, but to establish certain democratic principles of equality and fairness that ran against the grain of a now-dominant ideology of merit. Ironically, the person who has often had to sacrifice has not been the affluent or upwardly mobile but the worker who is asked to accept "reverse discrimination." There have been democratic gains during the past half-century, but these have been mainly initiated, not by the state, but by an increasingly politicized civil society. Thus, the various movements represented by civil rights workers, students, women's groups, churches, and gay rights advocates have done much to equalize freedoms in the society. Each of these movements was importantly a protest against the antidemocratic practices being enforced by political and legal authorities. The same can be said, I would argue, about the ecological movement. Although it originated largely as a romantic protest against the destruction of natural resources and the pollution of environments, and displayed an elitist mentality that seemed more intent upon preserving the pleasures of nature for the few, the movement has evolved in a direction that can fairly be called democratic.

This has been the result of the antinuclear protests and the rising resentment over the handling of toxic wastes. Both developments have had the effect of broadening the base of protest and of deepening the reaction against the state.

Although these groups appear to be the inheritors of Tocqueville's "civil associations," there is a crucial difference in the situation. Tocqueville's associations took advantage, so to speak, of a political vacuum; they were not disputing ground that had been preempted by the state but undertaking activities that no existing agency was performing. Today, however, the groups in question are contesting existing practices and policies, the vast majority of which are legitimated by the state.

The assortment of programs associated with "welfare" is one area in which the role of the state is predominant, but it also represents an area about which a democrat might well have equivocal feelings. The condition of the poor and of the working classes generally has been improved, whatever may have been the waste, inefficiencies, and corruption. At the same time, however, it seems clear that widespread dependencies have been created, and a large population has become marginalized and their marginality institutionalized. Whatever benefits may have been bestowed by the welfare state—and they are considerable—it is becoming plainer that the welfare state is not a synonym for the democratic state, not a complement to democracy but a threat.

Although the development of a more politicized civil society suggests that democracy is on the defensive rather than being the universal and irresistible tide prophesied by Tocqueville, the concept of "tyranny of the majority" is still invoked to explain so-called populist invasions of freedom, such as mandating prayers in public schools, censorship of public libraries and of the books read by students in school, antibusing legislation, and the campaign to replace evolutionist theory with "creationism." Although there are many ways of interpreting these phenomena, they do seem to have in common a protest against change. As such they raise the question of whether a more critical attitude toward change is not necessary if democracy is to be preserved in any except a rhetorical form.

The attitudes underlying the urge to censor, introduce prayer, or eliminate sex education, especially when they emanate from fundamentalist religious groups, are archaic in the sense discussed earlier. Historically, however, their roots are also closely intertwined with democratic traditions. Religious fundamentalism, "moralism," and racial, religious, and ethnic prejudices belong to the same historical culture as traditions of local self-government, decentralized politics, participatory democracy, and sentiments of egalitarianism. These traditions may be said, therefore, to constitute American feudalism. Like feudalism they favor decentralized power, local cultures, and local distinctions of rank, achievement, and value. They are suspicious of distant authorities, centralized power, and new moral fashions. Their prejudices appear as anachronisms. But then, so does democracy itself.

This reversal in the status of democracy, from being modern to being archaic, is connected with another feature of America that astonished Tocqueville almost as much as the phenomenon of widespread social equality. America seemed to him to lack the one political institution all European societies accepted as fundamental: it had not created a state. One looked in vain for an administrative apparatus, a large professional army, a horde of officials, mountains of records, and a society whose members were conditioned to look toward the center. America was a land where there was little evidence of the state's existence.[36]

The relative absence of the state meant that in a fundamental respect America was, politically speaking, premodern. Virtually every historian, including Tocqueville himself in *The Old Regime,* had underscored the central role played by the state in promoting the transition to modernity. Yet America, the archetype of modern society in so many respects, appeared to have become modern without the crucial agent of modernization. It was not only a society without a feudal past but a society without an antifeudal past.

It is true, of course, that Tocqueville understated the actual role of that state during the first half of the nineteenth century, especially in terms of its assistance to native capital. Nevertheless, it is roughly true that the concept of the state did not figure significantly in American political thought until the slavery debates began in earnest. The great stimulus to state power and to state consciousness was the Civil War just as that terrible event destroyed the last serious defense of feudal politics. It is easy to forget that the Civil War was the bloody culmination of a long series of opposition movements against the centralized state. The antifederalists emerged to oppose the founding of the American state and initiated a persistent antistatist line that extended to the Virginia-Kentucky resolutions (1798–99), the Hartford Convention, the nullification controversy, and the Civil War.

Since the Civil War the state has grown steadily, aided by the centralizing impulses encouraged by periodic economic depressions and the total mobilization of society during two world wars, until in our own time it stands as the seemingly unchallenged definer of the terms of political and social life. The triumph of the state, although late in coming to America, has repeated the European experience. It has come to its present power and dominance at the expense of America's version of feudalism.

One of the most striking claims of Tocqueville's *The Old Regime and the French Revolution* concerns the participatory character of local and provincial politics under the Old Regime. Village and municipal councils and provincial estates were merely the most obvious examples of a rich political culture that was destroyed by the modernizing thrust of the centralizing monarchy. The American state was no less destructive of local participatory practices, or regional cultures, and the pluralism and diversity nourished by these forms. State action was, of course, responding primarily to the needs of an evolving corporate economy. National markets, predictable consumers, and a minimally educated work force were objectives that made local differences appear to be antimodern or antiprogressive. The rationalization of markets, culture, and education has proceeded in tandem with the rapid rationalization of the state and the reduction of politics to management, trends that were self-consciously formulated in the *President's Report on Administrative Management of 1937* and authored by what would become a familiar team of technocrats, corporate executives, and academicians.

The pervasive presence of the state, the rise of technocratic elitism, the closely knit structure of state and corporate bureaucracies, and the decline of the ideology of egalitarianism in favor of meritocracy are the signs of a postmodern politics in which democracy serves primarily a rhetorical function with little or no correlative in official institutions or practices. Surprisingly, despite the attenuation of democracy at the level of national politics, there still exists a highly flourishing archaic political culture that is democratic, participatory, localist, and, overall, more egalitarian than elitist in ideology. As a factor in national politics, it is negligible. Yet every day it absorbs the energies, skills, and commitments of thousands of Americans. Sometimes it involves the founding of new political associations (e.g., to protest actions of public utilities or rates commissions); other times it means politicizing certain services that were traditionally set aside as the preserves of experts (medical clinics, schools, waste disposal, nuclear energy). Like Tocqueville's feudal element these, too, are antistatist, antibureaucratic, and anomalous. Like Tocqueville's aristocracy, they do not always appear in an attractive light. They can be bigoted, provincial, myopic, and anti-intellectual. Yet their archaism represents the main, perhaps the only, democratic counterthrust to statism. Thus, unlike its hegemonic status in Tocqueville's *Democracy in America,* democracy is now the feudal element, the counterprinciple to a new, postmodern regime.

Five / Tending and Intending
a Constitution:
Bicentennial Misgivings

"Tending" and "intending" refer broadly to two persistent modes of thinking about and practicing politics which first confronted each other during the ratification of the Constitution. Ratification might be thought of as a contest in which the intending conception triumphed, while the tending conception was so deeply wounded by the encounter that its viability remained in doubt for most of the two centuries that followed. The bicentennial observances of 1987 commemorated the ratification of the Constitution, but they also celebrated the triumph of one version of a constitution without commemorating the defeat of the other. This is because a bicentennial is a ritual of remembrnce that contributes to the continuing formation and reformation of a public memory and collective identity. Such rituals, like memory itself, are selective and profoundly political. They are an element in a continuous process of interpretation, a public hermeneutics, by which various authorities shape collective understandings, which, in turn, produce reliable social behavior in support of the regime and its leaders.

We might, therefore, want to step back and ask, What is it "we" are doing when we celebrate the ratification of the Constitution? Are "we" reenacting a collective role that "they," the Founding Fathers, first defined in the primal text that begins, "We, the People, in order to form a more perfect Union . . ."? Was that "we" as much an artificial construct as the Constitution itself and hence not the creator of the Constitution, as the Preamble alleges, but its creature? And who is the "they" that, as it were, is momentarily being resuscitated by and for the bicentennial occasion? Are "we" and "they" both artifacts constituted to serve a constitution of which neither "we" nor "they" are or were fully aware? Is that constitution The Constitution?

If a bicentennial celebration is a civic ritual as well as a political act, of what kind is it and for what ends? If we were to follow the lead of the cultural anthropologist, we might want to say that as ritual it strives to promote collective self-renewal, to reconfirm loyalties to an idealized version of the political system.

A ritual of reconsecration is not, however, instinctively credible in an age of advertising and media politics; and solemnity is an uncongenial mood for citizens whose response mechanisms are attuned to electronic images rather than grounded in a religious sensibility—assuming that that distinction still matters. A bicentennial is necessarily a manufactured, managed reproduction of certain selected public values, institutions, and processes. Concretely, it is ritual evolving in response to the needs of state power which finds itself beset by rapid technological change and intense international economic competition.

The bicentennial is also a political act, not solely because power and resources have been mustered to promote and enforce a desired conception of "we" and "they," but also because a civic ritual of this kind makes a political point by what it selects for remembrance and what for forgetting. Civic celebration serves in this instance to expurgate the pain and costliness of past choices so that they appear as unmitigated blessings, inevitable culminations. Fourth of July celebrants do not commemorate the confiscation of Loyalist estates; America's victory in World War II is remembered but not the Japanese relocation camps.

Civic forgetfulness is, however, the tribute that the political unconscious pays to the power of the forgotten. A civic celebration organizes forgetfulness so as to ward off the return of the repressed, which, though overcome or rejected, is still perceived as threatening. Lost causes are incorporated into civic rites precisely because they are, indeed, lost, harmless. The repressed, in contrast, poses a threat: not from the possibility that it may inspire a movement for the restoration of some archaic institution or practice but that it may be used to legitimate contemporary social forces that conceive themselves to be excluded, forgotten, passed by, archaic.

Bicentennialism represses the memory of deep-seated controversy over fundamental choices not primarily to redescribe the past but to inscribe the present. The choice can be understood in terms of my two ideal types, the "politics of intending" and the "politics of tending." The choice can also be described as one between a constitution of government on the one hand and a political culture on the other. The politics of intending has dominated the American political mentality and political practices since 1787. It did not, however, eliminate its rival nor completely overcome its own internal incoherencies. In fact, the incoherencies internal to the ideology of intending required that its rival, the politics of tending, be preserved in attenuated form and periodically exhumed to create a national nostalgia and sentimentalism that serves to blur the realities of public power in America.

The Philadelphia Convention produced a spare document that identified and assigned the powers belonging to the various branches of the proposed national government. The document was not accompanied by an interpreter's apparatus that could help to decode its lean language. As though to ensure that their "real" intentions might not become a part of the intense debate over ratification, which they expected, the framers swore not even to divulge the proceedings.

A text had been produced but not a constitution. The first step in the establishment of the Constitution required not only legitimation of the structure of political authority proposed in the text but, most importantly, a coherent conception of power that would both reflect and promote the master idea behind the work of the convention, "the consolidation of our Union." What was lacking was a constitutional theory that would set out the ends or purposes of the arrangements and show how the arrangements were supposed to work. In short, what was lacking was a theoretical conception of the Constitution and a theory of constitutional practice.

The achievement of legitimacy and the first formulation of a theory and practice were the result of the ratification controversy. The debate that followed the convention allowed those who had been influential in shaping the document to defend it publicly; and the only way they could defend it was to expound and interpret it.[1] By virtually all accounts, the most influential and certainly the most enduring of interpretations was that produced by the authors of *The Federalist Papers*. That work was the nation's first significant public hermeneutic; it may be said to have constituted that genre.[2]

Hamilton, Madison, and Jay invented a political theory of the Constitution, and they did much to establish an authoritative conceptual language for interpreting its provisions. The center of the theory was defined by Hamilton: "Government is only another word for POLITICAL POWER AND SUPREMACY."[3] *The Federalist* set out the nature of power under the new system, explained how it was to be exercised and why it had to be limited in some matters but enlarged in others, how power was to be generated, the qualities and qualifications of those who would be expected to govern, and what sort of citizenry was required by a system that had been designed to allow them only a limited influence while extracting from them the raw materials of power in the form of taxes, military skills, enthusiasm, and opinion.

Over the two centuries since ratification, the influence of *The Federalist* has, if anything, increased. Its conception of politics and national power has become so ingrained in the American political consciousness that few realize the extent to which they have absorbed a particular theory of the Constitution.

A theory is not, however, a constitution. It becomes one only when it is put into practice. Practices consist, first, in offices that designate the location of authority and, second, procedures or formalities that legitimate the exercise of power. There is, however, more to "high offices." They are publicly visible, and those who hold them not only are said to discharge an office's responsibilities but also to perform the office. High political office is a symbolic per(form)ance. Those who hold them are expected to display public virtues and to preserve public formalities. The authority of office is, therefore, both a right to power and a rite of power.

Rites are cultural rather than legal artifacts. Their value lies in the responses that they evoke, and these depend upon the store of beliefs, memories, customs, and values in the society—all that makes up the political culture. A political culture sets standards of performance not only for its authorities and rulers but for its members. Modern constitutionalism has neglected the importance of member skills, preferring to emphasize instead the concept of citizenship in terms of formal rights and duties. Not surprisingly, modern constitutionalism, from Hobbes and Locke to Rawls and Nozick, has developed its notions of citizenship almost exclusively through the language of contract.[4] Although that tradition of political argument puts great stock in the notion of "performance," what it means by performance is the virtual opposite of its political-cultural meaning.

To perform a contract is to complete it, to fulfill certain specified obligations in what is essentially a relationship of exchange, as when the Hobbesian citizen exchanges obedience for protection. It is not a question of special skills but of knowing what a promise is and then of discharging it. In this connection it is worth noting that the official letter, signed by George Washington as president of the Philadelphia Convention and affixed to the proposed constitution when it was transmitted to the Congress, incorporated the language and assumptions of contract. "Individuals entering society," it noted, "must give up a share of liberty to preserve the rest."[5]

Although the contractual idea is widely identified with the protection of freedom, its classical version stipulated a basic transaction in which power was surrendered in order to gain protection. The surrender of power was often masked by language that referred to (natural) rights, which, it alleged, had to be given up in return for civil rights, as defined by public authorities. What was being masked by the transaction was the redefinition of rights, which would enable those same authorities to gain lawful access to the resources of the individual, to tax his property and to conscript or make other use of his body. In this context Washington's letter contains a most revealing formulation of the exchange, for it is compelled to deal with the question of political culture, something that classical contract theory never faced until Rousseau. "It is [the letter states] at all times difficult to draw with precision the line between those rights which must be surrendered, and those which must be reserved; and on the present occasion this difficulty was encreased by a difference among the several States as to their situation, extent, habits, and particular interests."[6]

The "difference" to which the letter alluded was nothing less than the political cultures of the thirteen states, "their situation, extent, habits, and particular interests." The existence of diverse cultures was depicted as a barrier to, even inconsistent with, "the consolidation of our Union." But the most important barrier represented by the political cultures of the states was barely mentioned: the fact that for well over a century Americans had been learning political skills and acquiring the arts of participation in their local and state institutions. Ratification could not mean, therefore, that they would be entering civil society from a state of nature, as in the classical conceptions of contract and as implied in Washington's letter; nor could it mean that they would be surrendering natural for civil rights. As citizens of their respective states, they were already in possession of civil or legal rights. Ratification meant instead a paradox: there was an important sense in which the new constitution signified that insofar as Americans would surrender or modify the rights that they held in their state polities they would, in part, be leaving civil society for a state of nature.

That paradox, while overdrawn, points up an important fact about the ratification controversy and some of its neglected implications. Americans did not adopt a constitution in anything but the most formal sense of a paper document. Instead they chose, on the one hand, between a sophisticated theory of a constitution, as represented most brilliantly by *The Federalist Papers,* but a theory with only a minimally developed practice or a supporting culture of its own; and, on the other hand, a variety of constitutions supported by flourishing political cultures and practices, as represented by the colonial and revolutionary history of the several states, but constitutions without a coherent or compact theory.

Accordingly, the Philadelphia constitution can be seen as the product of a radical, even revolutionary strategy to establish a central government, a system of nation-state institutions where virtually none had theretofore existed. It deserves to be called "revolutionary" in the precise sense that it broke with the established direction of political development and available political experience. It had, therefore, to propose a constitution without a political culture distinctive to it. At the same time, it was revolting from and against an existing political constitution and its political culture.

The radical nature of the drive for ratification has been obscured by the popularity of the metaphors of birth, creation, and founding, which have been in use for almost as long as the Constitution itself. Each of these metaphors represents a distinct type of narrative. Each implies a story of an entity, in this case the Constitution, which came into existence by unusual effort but without seeming to dislodge a prior arrangement, as though it were merely occupying empty space. Each suppresses the memory of a rival; for there was in fact an existing political constitution of which the Articles of Confederation was simply the symbolic expression, not the exclusive representation. Supporting the confederation, and often obstructing it, was the political structure of American life: state governments, various institutions of local government, jury systems, and a vast array of spontaneous ad hoc life forms that arose and disappeared according to their usefulness. These were the institutions by which Americans tended to the common concerns of daily life. Thus, when the Philadelphia Convention proposed a constitution and *The Federalist* furnished an exegesis of it, these were not solutions to a political vacuum but the superimposition of a new form of politics, national politics, on top of political life forms that, at the time, did not represent local politics because there was virtually no national politics to which they could be compared. Ratification of the new constitution necessarily signified the subjugation of other forms of politics. The myth of The Founding belongs not to the archetype of Athena springing full-blown from the brow of Zeus but is instead a muted version of the fratricidal story of Romulus.

THE TWO VISIONS of politics which I have been sketching are conventionally described as "federalist" and "antifederalist." Certainly it is possible to ascribe important differences to the two positions, some of which were sharply drawn, while others were more nuanced. Although exceptions would have to be noted, the antifederalists can be described as leaning more against inequality and toward citizen participation, strongly opposed to the enlargement of the powers of the new central government, deeply concerned over the lack of a bill of rights in the original constitution, and suspicious that the proposed system was a disguise for the introduction of aristocratic government.

The antifederalist vision might be summed up by saying it was not one single vision or a master narrative in which past political history had been a preparation for the "miracle at Philadelphia"; it was, instead, the expression of diverse local narratives. The vision was partially conveyed in a speech by George Mason at the convention when he set out his conception of the House of Representatives: "It ought to know & sympathise with every part of the community; and ought therefore to be taken not only from the different parts of the republic, but also from different districts of the larger members of it, which had . . . different interests and views arising from difference of produce, habits, etc. . . . We ought to attend to the rights of every class of the people."[7]

The labels of "federalist" and "antifederalist" are, however, inadequate. The first fails to convey the radical nature of the position represented, a radicalism unlike any of the visions associated with socialism or communism. It is now the dominant vision, and so it appears conservative because it remains the outlook of the governing elites, which, historically, have controlled the natural, human, political, economic, cultural, and scientific resources of our society. Because it is not static it cannot be described as a conservatism of the status quo. Rather, it is a conservatism *in statu ascensi*. It is not about justice but about directing the unique forms of power made available by modern science and modern organizational theory and entrepreneurial practice for the exploitation of a uniquely rich land and of the innocent energies represented by hopeful immigrants seeking a fresh start.

The other vision wants to conserve, but it is driven to radicalism because there is no way for its conception of life forms to be maintained without opposing a system of power in which change has become routinized. The two visions of politics are represented by the notions of "intending" and "tending." Tending inclines toward a democratic conception of political life, intending toward an authoritarian conception as the nineteenth century understood that term: one who loves the principle of authority, that is, the right to command and enforce obedience.

I BEGIN WITH a simple dictionary definition of tending: to apply oneself to looking after another, as when we tend a garden or tend to the sick. It implies active care of things close at hand, not mere solicitude. Active care is not, however, a synonym for expert knowledge. Expert knowledge is typically predicated upon attitudes of detachment, upon disavowing personal involvement and disregarding historical associations. Perhaps skill would be a better prerequisite, but the crucial point is that tendance is tempered by the feeling of concern for objects whose nature requires that they be treated as historical and biographical beings. The beings are such as to need regular attention from someone who is concerned about their well-being and is sensitive to historical needs. Going one step farther, we might say that proper tendance requires attentiveness to differences between beings within the same general class, whether students, patients, plants, or animals. Tendance implies respect that is discriminating but not discriminatory.

But how is the idea of tending concretely expressed? What does it mean practically? The idea of tending is one that centers politics around practices, that is, around the habits of competence or skill that are routinely required if things are to be taken care of. Ritual practice emphasizes formalities, and while these are an important element of the tending mentality, they are not the whole of it. What, it might be asked, makes practices possible? That question was posed squarely in one of the classic theoretical works on American politics, Tocqueville's *Democracy in America.*

When Tocqueville tried to account for the success of the American political system, he listed two closely related reasons. One he called "mores" (*moeurs*), or "habits of the heart,"[8] the other he described as "a real, active political life" centered around a "local community."[9] *Moeurs* referred to the moral and religious beliefs of ordinary Americans which he thought necessary "to support political institutions." The second was the product of the intimate political experience which Americans acquired in their everyday existence. "Interests, passions, duties, and rights took shape around each individual locality and were firmly attached thereto."[10]

Tocqueville was, in effect, describing a political culture, a complex of shared beliefs, values, habits, practices, and experience that define the particularity of a place and envelop its politics. In this setting politics is not so much practiced as cultivated in ways analogous to tending fields or flocks. Tocqueville summed it up in a famous chapter on political associations in which he described these associations as "the great free schools" of democracy:[11] "It is through political associations that Americans of every station, outlook, and age day by day acquire a general taste for association and get familiar with the way to use the same. Through them large numbers see, speak, listen, and stimulate each other to carry out all sorts of undertakings in common. Then they carry these conceptions with them into the affairs of civil life and put them to a thousand uses."[12]

TURNING NOW TO the conception of "intending a constitution," I want to take note, first, of the richness of meaning associated with the word "intend." The usual understanding is that "to intend" means to seek deliberately to bring about some desired effect or purpose (e.g., "I intend to arise at 6:00 A.M. tomorrow."). There are, however, additional suggestive meanings starting with the etymological root, *intendere*, "to stretch forth." From this basic meaning have come the following: "to stretch, strain, make tense, intensify, to direct (the mind) toward some objective."

These meanings might be summarized by saying that they suggest a straining toward the future, an effort that requires power, and hence the agent intensifies, focuses, his or her powers. There is an expansionist ideology implicit in the idea of intending that is evident in a letter of 1803 by Gouverneur Morris, one of the important members of the Philadelphia Convention: "I knew as well then as I do now that all North America must at length be annexed to us. Happy, indeed, if the lust of dominion stops there."[13]

In contrast, to tend is to be concerned about something that exists, something that requires being taken care of, if it is to perdure. It represents, one might say, a concern for the historicity of things, for the preservation of pastness because the past is an important element in the narrative structure of identity attributed to the object of tendance and shared by the one who is tending. Accordingly, power is regarded as subordinate to identity and in its service. The Articles of Confederation reflected these attitudes when it limited membership in Congress to no more than three years in any six. In a similar vein, many of the state constitutions introduced shortly after the Revolution sharply reduced the power and tenure of many state governors, and there were widespread demands for annual elections and rotation in office.[14]

Intending, however, is less concerned with taking care of things than with acting effectively, not in the future, but toward it. At the Philadelphia Convention, James Wilson was one of several speakers who expressed this outlook: "We should consider that we are providing a Constitution for future generations, and not merely for the peculiar circumstances of the moment."[15] The intending mode emphasizes efficacy and seeks the elimination of what appears to stand in the way of fulfilled intentions. Unlike the tending mode, intending will subordinate collective identity to the needs of power.

One way this is expressed is in an indifference toward historicity and in a two-dimensional conception of time in which present and future alone figure. Accordingly, the intending mentality thinks in terms of obsolescence, of an order of things being threatened by time, becoming outdated in the specific sense that certain things are hampering the exercise of power and so prevent the realization of objectives. We see it in Madison's attack on the Articles of Confederation as based "on principles which are fallacious. . . . We must consequently change this first foundation and with it the superstructure resting on it." [16] Achieving objectives is understood as a problem of establishing conditions that will facilitate or smooth the exercise of power. Conditions have to be "rationalized," as Max Weber would have said; that is, shaped so as to reduce the costs of power and thereby make it more efficient: efficiency and efficacy are consanguineous members of the same family of intendance.

The intending mode of power is not peculiar to late twentieth-century revisionists who want to reform the present constitution. It has an old genealogy, in fact one of the oldest. Too often it is assumed that because the Founding Fathers favored the rights of property and a system governed by a political elite they were, therefore, conservatives. This is to misunderstand not only the Founders but also the dominant form of American conservatism.

THE FOUNDING FATHERS were revolutionaries twice over: in 1776 they led an armed rebellion against the British Crown and in 1787 a political rebellion against the constitution under which the colonists had fought the revolution. A common theme of the leaders of both revolutions was to protest excessive interference in internal affairs, first at the hands of British authorities, later from populist-oriented state legislatures. A complex, entrepreneurial mentality, political as well as economic and social, public-spirited as well as competitive, began to take shape and to perceive the future in terms of new opportunities for wealth, power, and intellect. At the Philadelphia Convention, the discussion of whether the chief executive should be eligible for reelection was importantly framed by those considerations. "Shut the Civil road to Glory," Gouverneur Morris warned, and ambition may take "a dangerous turn." [17] Conversely, Hamilton wrote disparagingly that "the regulation of the mere domestic police of a State [government] appears to me to hold out slender allurements to ambition." [18]

The seizing of the future was conceived in terms supplied by a new mode of discourse which was partially hidden in the language of constitutionalism. It might be called the discourse of organizationism. It was expressed by Hamilton when he defended the idea of a national navy: "Every institution will grow and flourish in proportion to the quantity and extent of the means concentered towards its formation and support." [19] The organizationist ideology of the Founders was best captured by a remark in a pamphlet written by an antifederalist critic: "The late revolution having effaced in a great measure all former habits, and the present institutions are so recent, that there exists not that great reluctance to innovation, so remarkable in old communities, and which accords with reason." [20]

Like the constitutional revisionists of today, the Founders spoke the language of intendment: the problem of the Articles, they argued, was that it had created a weak government unable to preserve domestic order, protect the society from foreign threats, launch military actions, or ensure the conditions for economic prosperity. Intendment's mode was established by Hamilton in the very first sentence of the first *Federalist,* where he asserts that "after an unequivocal experience of the inefficacy of the subsisting Foederal Government . . ."[21] That Hamilton's opening note should be "inefficacy" signified a strikingly different notion of legitimation from that used by the colonists when they had attacked the authority of the British Crown. Then they had argued that they were justified in throwing off British authority because of the unjust and illegal acts of the Crown. Now, however, they were rebelling, as it were, not against arbitrary power but against weakness.

The decentralized structure of power sanctioned by the Articles represented obstructions that prevented the concentration of power necessary for the realization of the Founders' vision of a single, unified society governed by a strong state. That vision was captured in a passionate lecture by Gouverneur Morris at the convention. After warning his colleagues against worrying about protecting individuals and the state governments instead of "the aggregate interest of the whole," he urged them to support "the dignity and splendor of the American Empire. It has been our great misfortune," he concluded, "that the great objects of the nation had been sacrificed constantly to local views, in like manner as the general interests of States had been sacrificed to counties." [22]

Weakness was thus associated with difference—the different governments of the separate states, different policies on commerce, taxation, money, militias, and debtors. Difference presented a problem because it did not comport with the Founders' conception of power.

Difference signified exception, anomaly, local peculiarities, and a thousand other departures from the uniformity that a certain kind of power prefers. Difference rejects the notion of a single narrative history and a unifying single purpose. It favors a pluralistic conception of history, or histories rather than history. Difference is not about a unified collective self but about the biography of a place in which different beings are trying to live together. As one of the antifederalists put it, "The idea of an uncompounded republick, on an average one thousand miles in length and eight hundred in breadth and containing six millions of white inhabitants, all reduced to the same standard of morals, or habits, and of laws, is in itself an absurdity, and contrary to the whole experience of mankind."[23]

The Founders, however, looked upon the new society with a vision in which local differences seemed divisive, even destructive, while the conditions of uniformity seemed to form a natural basis for a truly national power. This conception of power was expressed by John Jay in a way that reveals how uniformity had become such a crucial assumption in the Founders' notions of power that they ignored the numerous differences that existed even among the population of the eighteenth century in favor of an idealized version of the society as proponents of power would have liked it to be: "Providence has been pleased to give this one connected country, to one united people, a people descended from the same ancestors, speaking the same language, professing the same religion, attached to the same principles of government, very similar in their manners and customs."[24]

THE THEME OF weakness and difference was given its authoritative expression in *The Federalist Papers,* and thanks to the influence that those commentaries were to have over later interpretations of the Constitution and the political understanding of educated Americans, it was to play a powerful role in elevating the politics of intendment over the politics of tendance. For the *Federalist* argument was not about political weakness generally but about the weakness inherent in democratic states. "The instability, injustice and confusion introduced into the public councils, have in truth," Madison declared, "been the mortal diseases under which popular governments have every where perished."[25] This indictment was broadly cast to prove that throughout history popular governments were incapable of providing effective governance: "It is impossible to read the history of the petty Republics of Greece and Italy [Hamilton declared], without feeling sensations of horror and disgust at the distractions with which they were continually agitated, and at the rapid succession of revolutions, by which they were kept in a state of perpetual vibration, between the extremes of tyranny and anarchy."[26]

As we shall see shortly, the argument from historical experience was intended to suggest that democracy, instead of representing a modern type of politics, was something of an anachronism because it was unsuited to the size and scale of New World politics. New World politics would have to deal with an "enlarged orbit" of government, and hence it could not practice a politics of tendance proper to a small-scale democracy. An enlarged scale for politics was a momentous decision, as momentous certainly as the Revolution itself. It was symbolized by a radical switch in discourse, from a localist and decentered discourse or political theory to a centered one. It required a different vocabulary from the one employed to justify rebellion against the Crown. The older vocabulary was used to mount a protest of the periphery against the center, of the colonies united not so much among themselves as against the sovereign center, of local liberties and institutions against the remote and hence abstract imperial authority. It was a protest cast in the language of tending and directed against a huge power that defined itself in the language of superintending.

There were two precise moments in *The Federalist Papers* where we can see the new discourse of intendment emerging. The first is where Hamilton confronts the charge that, judged by Montesquieu's claim, a large-scale republic is a contradiction in terms and that, therefore, the proposed constitution is a monstrosity and the existing system of a number of small-scale republics loosely confederated seems the natural one for America. The second moment is when Madison argues that democracy is a practical impossibility as well as undesirable and that an "extensive Republic" is to be preferred.

The idea of an extensive republic had to find its appropriate discourse because the language of tendance was inadequate for the vision of centralized and expanding power, or "the majesty of the national authority."[27] A basic principle of the new theoretical discourse was to insist upon the importance of power but to wrap it in nonthreatening, apolitical language. Hamilton praised the proponents of the new constitution for defending the principle of "the firmness and efficiency of government."[28] Terms such as "systematical," "efficient," "well-administered," and "energy" appear with studied frequency in *The Federalist* and are meant both as a recommendation for the new system and as a criticism of the Articles.[29] "I believe," Hamilton declared, "it may be laid down as a general rule, that [the people's] confidence in and obedience to a government will commonly be proportioned to the goodness or badness of its administration."[30] These principles culminate in an intendment vision of a powerful state defined, not by its ground in the aspirations and needs of the people, but in reference to abstract principles of organization: "The safety of the whole is the interest of the whole . . . .[It depends on] one good Government. . . . One Government can collect and avail itself of the talents and experience of the ablest men. . . . It can move on uniform principles of policy—It can harmonize, assimilate, and protect the several parts and members, and extend the benefit of its foresight and precautions to each. . . . It can apply the resources of the whole to the defence of any particular part. . . . It can place the militia under one plan of discipline by putting their officers in a proper line of subordination to the Chief Magistrate, will as it were consolidate them into corps and thereby render them more efficient." [31]

THE NEW DISCOURSE of intendment developed by *The Federalist* brought a new language of legitimation that linked the several notions of "system," "efficiency," "energy," "power," and "administration." The new language was summed up in Hamilton's phrase "the new science of politics." [32] The old language of legitimation by the popular will was ritualistically observed by the Founding Fathers in the Preamble to the Constitution. It begins, "We the People . . ." and ends by having the people "ordain and establish" the new constitution.

The notion of a "science of politics" was introduced to lend an aura of authority otherwise lacking in the *Federalist* case. The authors acknowledged that there were serious questions about the legitimacy of the proceedings at Philadelphia. [33] The convention had been summoned ostensibly to revise the Articles of Confederation, yet it had produced a document that called for the abolition of that system. *The Federalist* recognized that the political form that they were promoting was a radical departure, an "experiment of an extended republic," in Madison's phrase, and required its own justification. [34]

The new justification had a distinctly positivist quality. As I have already suggested, the new language of "system," "administration," and "efficiency" conveyed an objectivist character to the case being made on behalf of the new constitution. At the same time, *The Federalist* also made repeated appeals to the facts of "history" and "experience," not to "prove" the validity of the new system, for it had not yet been tried, but to discredit the Articles of Confederation, the populist tendencies in state politics, and an incipient, though inchoate, democratic ideology. Specifically, the appeal to science was raised in order to counteract the widespread claim that republics could not survive if, like the Roman republic of antiquity, their participatory institutions were stretched to fit a great expanse of space. The stakes in the argument were, at bottom, about democracy, for the parties to the debate all agreed that a small republic was virtually a synonym for a participatory democracy in which all citizens managed the common affairs. Or stated differently, the larger the republic, the less democratic.

The basic text in this controversy was the ninth *Federalist*. Hamilton began with a vivid description of the history of small republics as "continually agitated" and marred by "the rapid succession of revolutions." He then confessed, disingenuously to be sure, that if "models of a more perfect structure" of republicanism could not be "devised," then republicans would have to concede that republicanism had failed. Enter the new "science of politics." "Like most other sciences," Hamilton noted, it "has received great improvement. The efficacy of various principles is now understood, which were either not known at all, or imperfectly known to the ancients." The specific principles that are scientifically warranted are the system of checks and balances, an independent judiciary, and the institution of representative government, all of which, in Hamilton's significant characterization, "tend to the amelioration of popular [i.e., democratic] systems of civil government." Hamilton then announced that he wanted "to add one more," admittedly "novel," scientific principle. The novel principle marked a crucial step toward a politics of intendment and away from a politics of tendance. The principle was "the enlargement of the orbit" within which the several state governments were to "revolve," that is, a new scale of politics that reduced the states to satellites revolving around a new center of power. Thus, size and concentrated power, the two natural enemies of democracy, were invented by science to show how republics could control the excesses of democracy while enjoying "the advantages of monarchy," effective administration by "one Government watching over the general and common interests." [35]

Hamilton and Madison both expatiated at length on how the scientific basis of the new order would generate an unprecedented amount of power. Government by representation was the secret of power because it allowed a virtually unlimited territory to be incorporated under one system. This meant that the system could avail itself of the greater resources potentially present in the larger area. Madison presented the proposition in abstract, quasi-scientific language that was a perfect specimen of the discourse of intendment: "If Europe has the merit of discovering this great mechanical power in government [made possible by 'the great principle of representation'], by the simple agency of which, the will of the largest political body may be concentered and its force directed to any object, which the public good requires; America can claim the merit of making the discovery the basis of unmixed and extensive republics." [36]

THE DISCOURSE OF intendment framed in the vocabulary of science was used to place a particular interpretation on the Constitution and to assimilate the Constitution to that discourse. The key text here was Hamilton's *Federalist* Number 31. There he returned to the theme of a science of politics and proceeded to list certain "primary truths," such as "the whole is greater than the parts," and "all right angles are equal to each other." Then he declared that there are "other maxims in ethics and politics," which, "if they cannot pretend to rank in the class of axioms are yet such indirect inferences from them, and so obvious in themselves, and so agreeable to the natural and unsophisticated dictates of common sense, that they challenge the assent of a sound and unbiassed mind, with a degree of force and conviction almost equally irresistible." [37] These maxims turn out to be exclusively about power, and they promote a grandiose conception of it which foreshadows virtually all of Hamilton's later arguments about "the necessary and proper clause" and the constitutionality of a national bank, as well as Chief Justice Marshall's expansive conception of national power: "A government ought to contain in itself every power requisite to the full accomplishment of the objects to its care . . . free from every other control but a regard to the public good and to the sense of the people. . . . As the duties of superintending the national defence and of securing the public peace against foreign or domestic violence, involve a provision for casualties and dangers, to which no possible limits can be assigned, the power of making that provision ought to know no other bounds than the exigencies of the nation and the resources of the community. . . . the federal government must of necessity be invested with an unqualified power of taxation in the ordinary modes." [38]

The appeal to science was, in effect, a means of elevating *Federalist* notions about central powers—over taxation, commerce, and war—to an objective plane where *The Federalist*'s teaching about them could appear as axiomatic rather than contestable. The scientific conception of power and the whole intendment ideology had to face, however, the question with which Tocqueville would be concerned and which was crucial to the politics of tendance. If the scientific system was to be superimposed upon the politics of localism, where were the *"moeurs,"* the political culture, to come from that would support the new system? As Hamilton acknowledged, "A man is more attached to his family than to his neighborhood, to his neighborhood than to the community at large. . . . A government continually at a distance and out of sight, can hardly be expected to interest the sensations of the people." [39] The question was provoked because the new system preceded its practice. There was virtually no conception of national political habits or traditions, no conception of national civic virtue, hence no sustaining political culture.

The Federalist had to invent a new and abstract conception of the citizen, a citizen who would be national in character, an unmediated subject designed for a politics of intendment. As Madison later described it, the very essence of a "national government was to operate within the extent of its powers directly and coercively on individuals." [40] But such a citizen had first to be extricated from the political culture of intendment and to be the direct object of the new form of power emanating from the center. This is what lay behind the famous *Federalist* argument that, unlike the mode of governance under the Articles, the new system would "carry its agency to the persons of the citizens." [41] The new power would regulate him, tax him, and legislate for him without passing through the intermediary authority of the states; and it would institute its own agencies, courts, and officials for that purpose. [42] At the same time, the political nature of the new citizen would be diminished. His political nature would be confined to periodic elections once every two, four, or six years.

But what would then be the appeal of the new system? How would citizens be attracted into the nonpolitical culture of the intendment system when they "feel a stronger byass towards their local governments than towards the government of the Union?" [43] Hamilton's answer revealed a vision of power in which participatory terms had become irrelevant: The national government could "destroy" the natural attraction of local governments "by a much better administration." [44]

Administration seems the natural form by which a scientific approach deals with the threat presented by politics. For, as we see in Hamilton's discussion of the executive branch, administration stands above the partisan, interest-dominated conflicts of politics. It embodies rational energy or, in Hamilton's words, "decision, activity, secrecy, and dispatch. . . . and the power of directing and employing the common strength." [45]

ALTHOUGH THE BICENTENNIAL celebrates the triumph of the politics of intending, that triumph was not assured until after the Civil War. In the twentieth century, two world wars and a major economic depression have established intending as normal politics. Its forms are the cult of leadership and personality; managerial modes of governance; a mass electorate, which is encouraged to be politically passive until aroused by media stimuli at election time; and a steady increase in mass control and surveillance. Its political culture can be accurately described as shallow: at one end, an elite culture in which education exists primarily to produce technocrats and, at the other, a mass culture founded on changing fashions in which impotence masquerades as impudence. The politics of tendance experienced something of a renascence during the 1960s, when a protest culture emerged and participatory politics became a shibboleth. It has persisted with surprising tenacity and has developed a wide variety of political forms: ecological politics, feminism, sexual and civil rights, antinuclear protests, and much more. Despite the attempts on the part of the politics of intendment to co-opt it, either by sublimating it into a rhetoric of nostalgia and of religious and moral fundamentalism or by sanitizing it by appeals for "voluntary" efforts, the politics of tendance persists stubbornly.

Six / Montesquieu and Publius: The Crisis of Reason and The Federalist Papers

In a famous letter of 1790, Thomas Jefferson sketched out a critical bibliography of sorts for the study of politics. After recommending Adam Smith's *Wealth of Nations*, he praised Locke's "little book on government" as "perfect as far as it goes." When he came to Montesquieu's *Spirit of the Laws*, however, he entered a qualified judgment, saying that while it "is generally recommended," a reader should be careful because of "the mixture of truth and error found in this book." Jefferson then concluded with an observation about the genre to which *The Federalist Papers* belonged that would be reechoed countless times during the next two centuries. "Descending from theory to practice, there is," Jefferson declared, "no better book than the Federalist." [1]

Tocqueville may possibly have had *The Federalist* in mind when he characterized American political culture as pragmatic rather than theoretical; and in our own century a long succession of scholars beginning with Charles Beard has unanimously agreed that practicality was the hallmark of this first classic of American political thought. *The Federalist*, it was said many times, should be read as a work of "political science," even of "constitutional technology." The essays by "Publius," the pseudonym under which Jay, Hamilton, and Madison wrote, were prompted by the practical political objective of promoting ratification of the Philadelphia constitution, and so their task was the mundane one of explaining and justifying each provision of the Constitution and the workings of its institutions.[2]

In this interpretation, *The Federalist* appeared as the harbinger of the distinctively American, perhaps even Anglo-American, approach to constitutionalism as a combination of law and practical politics leavened by distrust of theory—so distrustful, indeed, that American political scientists from Woodrow Wilson to Carl Friedrich preferred the prosaic term "constitutional government" to "constitutionalism." Daniel Boorstin summed up a half-century of scholarly fashion when he declared that "the genius of American politics" consisted of a politics without theory. Jefferson's judgment might then have been revised to read: *The Federalist* marked an ascent from theory to practice.

The view of *The Federalist* as atheoretical has been sharply challenged in recent years, beginning with Douglas Adair's investigations into the influence of Hume's political essays upon Madison's classic, *Federalist* Number 10. Lately it has become commonplace to refer to the "political theory" or even the "philosophy" of *The Federalist*.[3] These changes advance the interpretative claim that a richer and truer understanding of *The Federalist* can be reached by means of the categories of theory or philosophy. Thus, to grasp what *The Federalist* meant by a "science of politics," we need to consult what Hume wrote on that subject; or if we would understand what was involved when its pseudonymous author, Publius, appealed to "reason" or to "experience," we should turn first to Locke.

These efforts are to be welcomed, but only with certain reservations. For the most part, they adopt a method in which a theoretical text is taken to be a structure of connected arguments of greater or lesser complexity. The challenge is to get the arguments "right" and thereby reduce the text to being unproblematic. The method proceeds like this: Hume's views on "science" or "matters of fact" are isolated, identified, and then presented as exercises in philosophical definition or as argument. The next step is to compare Hamilton's or Madison's usage and to interpret it in the context established by the abstracted ideas of Hume. The result is to purge discourse of its political stratagems. Thus, "science" is discussed without any awareness that there are important political stakes in how science is conceived. Consider, for example, the authoritarian ambience created when a writer describes science, as Hobbes did, in terms that stress the infallibility of scientific method, the rigid character of its reasoning, and the authoritativeness of its findings.

Contrast that with a view that stresses the probability of certain forms of scientific reasoning, the corrigibility principle built into it, and the important role of consensus in a scientific community. Political elements have not been incidental or external to the understanding of science but internal to conceptions of its methods and modes of thought. This is not surprising if we remember that the three writers who did most to missionize the cause of early modern science, Bacon, Descartes, and Hobbes, extolled the potential of science for expanding the power of society. Accordingly, science has not been a discourse in which power and affiliated notions are absent.

FOR MANY YEARS, historians of American political thought have noted that Montesquieu's *Spirit of the Laws* was widely cited during the debates over the ratification of the Constitution. By and large, they have discussed his political theory in terms of influence or arguments. My concerns are rather different: I want to explore the turn toward modern constitutionalism embodied in the constitution drafted at Philadelphia and given its authoritative exegesis soon thereafter by the authors of *The Federalist Papers*. That turn can be called a modern one because it represented a self-conscious attempt to design a constitution according to the principles of reason and to justify it by appealing to the authority of science.

Montesquieu's constitutional thinking followed a different route in that it resisted eighteenth-century attempts to found a science of politics based upon scientific and mathematical modes of analysis. Stated sharply, Montesquieu dissociated constitutionalism from a science of politics and, at bottom, saw them as deeply antagonistic to each other.[4] Publius, however, saw the two as fruitfully connected and even claimed that a science of politics would save modern constitutionalism by curing republicanism of its democratic maladies. The tensions and antagonisms that Montesquieu perceived between science and constitutionalism were present, I shall claim, in the version of constitutionalism offered by Publius and not resolved by him. And the consequences are still with us.

Montesquieu offered an opposing vision that is fascinating precisely because it did not issue from antiscientific or antirational attitudes. Indeed, for the most part it employed the same science-inspired vocabulary as his critics. He, too, would refer to "laws" and their "necessity." He accepted unquestioningly that the responsibility of mind was to render man and the world as intelligible as possible. But he departed from his contemporaries and from the next generation of philosophes on the crucial question of what constituted intelligibility.

To many of his contemporaries and to most of the philosophes who came after him, intelligibility was equivalent to transparency. For something to be understood it had to be made clear, stripped of myth, superstition, and religious fable so that its operations and their effects were visible. That was the function of reason. This conception of reason can be called Cartesian. It displays Descartes' conviction that truth and clarity were inseparable; that the model of truth is best exemplified in mathematical modes of reasoning; and that custom and tradition are, at best, makeshift solutions, which, ideally, should be replaced by rational principles.

The paradox of Cartesian reason was that it served as both a principle of liberation and a justification of subjection. In the name of freedom, equality, and progress, reason was enlisted to criticize accepted beliefs, established authorities, and traditional hierarchies. Its targets were the historically derived identities—ruler and subject, priest and believer, noble and bourgeois—which it exposed as discordant, contingent, and without coherence or logical structure except for the certainty that their irrationality served the power of those who inherited or succeeded to positions of rank and eminence. To critical reason differences appeared as differentials, as unequal and unjust advantages or disadvantages.

But reason could also be coercive. The liberatory and the repressive tendencies of rationalism can be seen coexisting in a mind like Condorcet's, which believed that political and mathematical truths shared the same structure. Where Montesquieu would note approvingly that "it would be a remarkable coincidence if the laws of one people were to agree with those of another,"[5] Condorcet insisted that "truth and justice are the same in all countries and for all men. What is good in one province cannot be bad in another. Uniformity in all objects of public order is an additional bond among men; every difference is a seed of discord."[6]

Eighteenth-century conceptions of scientific laws drew heavily on mathematical notions of "necessary" truths, of truths that had the "force" to "compel" the understanding or which, like Newton's laws of gravity, were "irresistible." A necessary truth stood for an unarguable truth or, better, a truth that could be argued only according to prescribed terms of what constituted an argument. Such truths placed the human mind in the same relation to the "laws" of logic or reasoning as an operative law of nature placed certain select natural phenomena. Both were "under" law, that is, under its prescriptive power: the mind "obeys" a syllogism, the planet "follows" a prescribed course. Power in both cases is transmuted into law, and law exercises absolute control. In the one case it "demonstrates," and in the other it "operates."

That today we are a certain type of persuadable being is a tribute to the critical work of reason. Historically reason served as the great ground-clearer whose labors make it possible for the individual to be free to obey a policy that appears rational. By discrediting the claims of rival authorities, reason deposits a self abstracted from social context, liberated from the rival powers that have constituted it and facing the uncontested power of reason. Reason appears "irresistible" and "self-evident" because the self has nothing to resist with. Selves, so to speak, have been severed from their "evidence," which has been left behind in the context from which they have been abstracted. Freedom has now become interchangeable with necessity. To be free is to obey necessary truths, truths that, like a mathematical proof, demand as a condition of their truthfulness that they be independent of social or historical context.

Montesquieu's quarrel with that mentality issued from a deep distrust of monological conceptions of man, society, and world that insisted upon a single conception of what constituted rational discourse and demanded that the world be understood in terms which enabled that discourse alone to seem reasonable when, in fact it was rigid and repressive. "If things are seen ever so little from a certain perspective, the sallies of imagination vanish; for these are usually inspired because the mind launches itself from one direction and abandons all of the others."[7]

That distrust was not so much a product of philosophical skepticism as of a profoundly political outlook.[8] The fundamental problem, which recurs in many of his numerous writings, is about despotism and its relationship to reason, science, and hence to modernity generally. The political question for Montesquieu, therefore, was not, in the first instance, about constitutions, actual or ideal as such, but about the constitution of beings and things (*la nature des choses*).

There is, Montesquieu would claim, a lawlike structure to all things and beings, but it cannot be described by means of universal laws valid for all phenomena, for all time, and for all circumstance. Universality is equivalent to a vision of universal monarchy—benevolent, all-encompassing, uniform. Montesquieu's countervision began from multiplicity: "Laws in their most extended meaning are the necessary relations which derive from the nature of things; and in this sense all beings have their laws, Divinity has its laws; the material world has its laws; minds superior to man have their laws; man has his laws."[9] Thus, law becomes a subversive notion rather than the sign of a unitary scheme of things. Montesquieu insinuates that when we employ the word "law" in our talk about nature or society, and when we habitually introduce such phrases as "governed by law" or "kept to their appointed places by law" to describe, say, the movements of the planets, we are not just indulging our need for metaphorical language. We may be, instead, expressing a political wish that not only the planets but all things, including human relationships, were similarly controlled in the interests of total harmony.

The various laws were, according to Montesquieu, "fixed" and "invariable" because they prescribed the conditions that enable things and beings to persist. The laws governing matter and motion as well as the existence of sensible beings were traceable to *"une raison primitive,"* to God "the Creator and Preserver" of the universe. Yet laws are not to be understood as commands but as reciprocal relationships expressive of the natures of those to whom the laws apply.

Man as a "physical being" is, like the rest of Creation, "governed by invariable laws," yet he is also endowed with a nature that is "free" and "intelligent." His nature leads him to "violate endlessly the laws that God has established and to change those he has established himself." It is, Montesquieu declares, a "necessary" law of man's nature that he "must find his own way." Necessity was thus transformed from a repressive term implying closure to one suggesting openness. Among several of his contemporaries, necessity was connected with a univocal, unambiguous conception of truth. It was that connection, between truth, necessity, suppressiveness, and univocality that Montesquieu sought to dissolve.

The necessary law that says man is free means among other things not simply that he is free to make mistakes but that in fact he does. As Montesquieu put it, man is a being of limited understanding, prone to err and subject to "a thousand passions." It is his nature "to forget"— to forget his Creator, to forget his duties to others, even to forget himself in blind obedience. Neglectful man is, therefore, in need of counsel. To help man God has given him religious laws, philosophers have instructed him in the moral laws, and lawmakers have inscribed his duties in political and civil laws.[10]

Transgressive, changeable, and forgetful man is heteronomous man, the subject of a variety of laws. He is, by nature, not the malleable object of a single and sovereign lawmaker or law-declarer. Instead, he is the object of multiple claims and the subject of multiple constitutions: the laws of nature, divine laws, international laws, "the general political laws whose object is the human wisdom which has founded all societies," the particular political laws of each country, the law of conquest, civil law, and domestic law. The conclusion to be drawn is that reason should not constitute itself into an instrument for discovering some universal principle applicable to all social phenomena.

When reason aspires to have its laws universally acknowledged, it is tempted into a certain politics that entails discrimination, exclusion, and simplification. Particulars will have been stripped of some of the accommodations and multiple relations that define their natures and legitimate their various claims. Thus, in pursuit of its ideal, reason practices a version of "reason of state," sacrificing particulars to the higher good of the universally true statement or proposition.

The alternative that Montesquieu proposes is a reason that, while it will not eschew generalization altogether, will particularize and contextualize: "There are then different orders of law, and the sublimity of human reason consists in knowing precisely to which of these orders the matters that should be acted upon are principally related." [11]

We might call Montesquieu's conception of reason "politic judgment." It is concerned with rendering intelligible a social whole, which has not been assembled by theoretical reason but deposited by historical actions and inactions and is apt, therefore, to be marked by ignorance, foolishness, and immorality. The closest Montesquieu came to defining what I have called politic judgment was in a passage written in response to critics: "Good sense consists in large measure of knowing the nuances of things." [12]

Although a social whole is likely to display incongruities and surprising conjunctures, these are not necessarily the signs of irrationality. They are the results of accommodations worked out by unequal powers for concrete circumstances and amidst competing "laws." Their rationality is in the rendition of complexity, not in the achievement of the "best" solution: "Even the strongest commitment to reason is not always desirable; mankind is nearly always better accommodated in means than extremes." [13]

When the mind is engaged, not in acting but in theorizing about reality and about the actions incorporated in it, it should accept the variety of forms and relationships in which rationality is outfitted. Rationality is bound to assume varied forms because when theoretical reason attempts to analyze the "laws" in which certain types of relationships are being realized, for example, the relationships between governors and governed, it will have to take account of the influences of climate, geography, religion, morals, manners, and political understandings. "The truest and holiest dogmas can have the very worst consequences when they are not connected with the principles of society; and, on the contrary, the falsest dogmas can have admirable results when they are brought into relationship with those principles." [14] For Montesquieu, irrationality does not take the form of inconsistency, lack of rigor, or absence of method. It is, instead, disregard of the several structures of relations, the "laws," which constitute beings.

FOR MONTESQUIEU, CONSTITUTIONALISM involved more than the limitations upon power and its discretionary exercise. It stood for the domestication of power by an unplotted conspiracy of difference, that is, the modification of power by the several modes of accommodation which the complex being called mankind had resorted (or submitted) to over the centuries. These included physical conditions (climate, soil, etc.), laws, religion, moral codes, customary norms and practices, economic modes of activity, such as commerce and agriculture, and, above all, manners (*moeurs*), or what might be called "habits of accommodation." What men call "society" is composed of sets of relationships and interrelationships which are the result of historical adaptations and accommodations, of thousands of actions which time and custom have smoothed into 'a working arrangement. Unlike many of his contemporaries among whom the concept of society as a "system" of rationally arranged and interconnected institutions was much in vogue, Montesquieu employed the image of a "labyrinth" to convey the tortuous character of society, its undesigned, unpremeditated qualities, its opaqueness to linear and univocal reasoning.[15]

Montesquieu called his ideal form of constitutionalism "moderate government" or, more literally, "moderated government." His ideal might be restated as power moderated by the complexities of political culture or, more briefly, acculturated power. His description makes it clear that the complexities are so great that it is virtually impossible to set out to create such a system: "To form a moderated government it is essential to combine powers, to regulate them, temper them, and cause them to act, to give, as it were, a ballast to one to enable it to resist another. It is a masterpiece of legislation that chance rarely creates and that prudence rarely attains."[16]

A moderated government was not a distinct form but a principle that could be applied either to a republic or to a monarchy. As the above quotation suggests, Montesquieu seemed to be expressing a common eighteenth-century conception of a constitution as a Newtonian balance of forces, but while that element was certainly present in his thinking it tends to subvert that conception rather than follow it consistently. Each constitution has, Montesquieu emphasized, its own "principle." For a republic, whether it be aristocratic or democratic, the principle is a public-spiritedness that places the common good above private interest. Monarchy depends upon honor, which was

Montesquieu's way of insisting that only a monarchy that respected as "fundamental laws" the claims of "intermediate, subordinate, and dependent powers," such as the aristocracy, could avoid becoming arbitrary and absolute.[17] But honor, as Montesquieu carefully explained, was a substitute for "political virtue," and strictly speaking it was a "false honor" in the form of "ambition" that gives life to monarchy. Hence, the full description of monarchy was a kind of ironical combination of Mandeville's principle that private vices can unintentionally produce public benefits and of a mechanical Newtonianism in which ambition checks ambition: "[Monarchy] is as with the system of the universe, where there is a force which constantly repels all bodies from the center, and a power of gravitation that calls them back. Honor sets in motion all parts of the body politic; it connects them by its very action; and the result is that each advances toward the common good while believing that he is going toward his particular interests."[18]

The worst form of government was despotism. It was the simplest in structure, and it appealed to the commonest passions. Despotism means, first, power operating with a minimum of cultural constraints, unmediated power. The "emblem" of despotism, as Montesquieu put it, was the savage who, in order to secure the fruit from a tree, cuts down the tree.[19] Despotism means, second, power exercised without cultural support. That was why Montesquieu identified fear as the basic principle of despotism. Fear sapped human bonds, which were the basis of social groupings. Despotism appears as power at its most efficient because, following the laws of physics, it is force without resistance or friction, pure power.

DESPOTISM IS USUALLY accompanied by predicates such as "arbitrary," "willful," or "capricious" and appears, therefore, antithetical to the measured, deliberate, even relentless images evoked by mathematical conceptions of reasoning. Montesquieu accepted this received view as his starting point: a despotic government is rule by a single man "without law and rule, directing everything by his will and caprices."[20] But these notions do not reveal the true nature of despotism, because resorting to categories of willfulness and capriciousness presupposes the existence of established norms which enable us to recognize the presence of arbitrariness.

The distinctive mark of Montesquieu's despotism is that it operates in a setting in which these norms have been destroyed. Montesquieu established that context by describing other political constitutions, such as aristocracy and monarchy. Each of these, he notes, "diminishes simplicity and establishes a thousand exceptions." A monarch, for example, may rule his several provinces either by "establishing diverse laws or permitting different customs." But a despot will, by nature, be indifferent to difference. "Nothing is heard but the voice of fear, which has only one language, instead of nature which expresses itself so diversely and appears in so many different forms." [21]

The indifference to diversity is what Montesquieu had in mind when he described the despot as one who "knows nothing and takes care of nothing"; hence, for him things appear simply as "a general appearance," and so "he governs by a rigid will which is everywhere the same; everything is smoothed beneath his feet." By eliminating class differences, diverse bodies of law, regional variations, and all other significant exceptions to uniformity, despotism simplifies space and time: space is unoccupied by anything other than his will, time is simply his present whim. "Despotism is sufficient unto itself; around it there is only emptiness." [22] While emptiness permits unlimited caprice, it also has the effect of converting commands into uniform laws, which, like the laws of nature, are indifferent to differences: "A despotic government is, so to speak, self-evident; it is uniform throughout: since only passion is needed to establish it, everybody is capable of it." [23] Thus, contrary to the received understanding, which depicted despotic rule as law-breaking, Montesquieu suggests that once despotism succeeds in reconstituting a context in which difference has been obliterated, "will," as the saying goes, "becomes law."

IN THE ABOVE formulation, despotism signifies an ideal-typical temptation of thought and practice that is peculiarly modern. It was inspired not as premodern notions of despotism were, by images of conquerors or theologies depicting willful deities, but rather by notions of an impersonal order governed by rational laws. Science represents knowledge of the laws that govern natural phenomena; a science of politics represents knowledge of the laws that prescribe how power must be constituted in the political domain.

The important consequence of rendering politics into a scientific discourse is that description comes to be represented as a necessity that demands a certain prescription. In the process political choices are turned into extensions of necessity, into dependents who have surrendered their autonomy, "bowed to necessity."

Although necessity comes garbed in the language of science, its persuasiveness is parasitic off a deeper layer of myth. The biblical account of creation taught that order had been originally constituted by God and subsequently sustained solely by His power. If God were to withdraw his power, order would collapse and chaos would follow. In

The Federalist, biblical myth is recast into the language of modern science to warn Americans of their fate if they were to fail to constitute power sufficient to secure order. Just as chaos prevails in the universe if the laws of nature cease to "rule," so the "dismemberment of the Union" and "the violent death of the confederation" would surely happen unless a new and stronger power were established and men would obey it.

Thus, the secularization of the cosmos that accompanied the eighteenth-century Enlightenment did not dislodge the biblical belief that order was a function of power. It merely transferred the function from the deity to the laws of nature. The laws of nature acquired the moral force of "God's decrees" to accompany their "physical" laws. As a result, norms acquired the quasi-physical force of necessity, while necessity was invested with quasi-moral authority.

The moral force of natural necessity was illustrated in *The Federalist* by Publius's attempt to justify the provision of the proposed constitution (Article 7) declaring that only nine states need approve the document to put it into operation. The provision clearly circumvented the principle of unanimity stipulated in the Articles of Confederation. Publius dealt with this admittedly "delicate" problem in a less than delicate way by appealing to the overriding force of necessity, or, in his words, "by recurring to the absolute necessity of the case; to the great principle of self-preservation; to the transcendent law of nature and of nature's God, which declares that the safety and happiness of society are objects at which all political institutions aim, and to which all such institutions must be sacrificed." [24]

The force of necessity was invoked by Publius to defend two of the most contentious and important clauses in the new document, the "necessary and proper clause" (Article 1.8.18) and the "supremacy clause" (Article 6.2). [25] Critics charged that these provisions would open the door to a huge expansion of national power. Publius responded that the enlarged powers of the proposed government had to be acknowledged once the decision to have a government was accepted: "They [the two clauses] are only declaratory of a truth which would have resulted by necessary and unavoidable implication from the very act of constituting a Federal Government and vesting it with certain specified powers." [26]

This mode of reasoning came to supplant the famous starting point of the very first *Federalist* paper, in which Publius presented the debate over ratification as posing the most fundamental of political questions, "whether societies of men are really capable or not, of establishing good government from reflection and choice" or were to remain dependent on "accident and force." [27] What began as an invitation to deliberation eventually became so hemmed in by the rhetoric of necessity that by the time Publius had reached the very last of his essays the problem had been reduced to a starkness beyond deliberation: "a Nation without a National Government is . . . an awful spectacle."[28]

The constitution drafted at Philadelphia was the first modern constitution to be presented to the citizenry for its approval and, thanks to *The Federalist,* the first to be recommended and defended by appealing to the science of politics.

The first reference to the science of politics occurs in the ninth *Federalist.* The opening sentence of that essay contains the crucial theme concerning the constitution of order and the suppression of chaos. "A Firm Union will be of the utmost moment to the peace and liberty of the States as a barrier against domestic faction and insurrection." Publius then proceeds to paint the history of previous republics in the dark colors of chaos: "continually agitated . . . rapid succession of revolutions . . . a state of perpetual vibration . . . the extremes of tyranny and anarchy."[29] The science of politics is then introduced as the knowledge that will redeem republicanism from its wretched history. In part this involves appealing to certain "principles," which Publius attributes to recent "great improvements" in the science of politics such as separation of powers, checks and balances, an independent judiciary, and representation.[30] But the appeal to a science of politics also involves a subtler appeal than the one to specific achievements. It relates to a kind of politics submerged in the abstractions of eighteenth-century conceptions of scientific discourse.

One such conception was "space." Mathematics and physics had presented a way of thinking about space which reduced it to a dehistoricized abstraction, as having, in Hobbes's words, "no other accident [i.e., attribute] but only that it appears [outside] of us."[31] Such a conception might be contrasted with the notion of "place," of specific location that has become inscribed by those who have occupied it. We might now turn to the great debate over space and place that took place in *The Federalist.* I suggest that the proponents of the new constitution relied on conceptions of space, while their opponents were defending a politics of place. Appropriately, the debate specifically centered around Montesquieu.

"The experiment of an extended republic," as Madison called it,[32] would demonstrate that it was possible to establish and maintain a republican constitution of power while attempting to rule an expanse of space so large that only monarchies and despotisms had ever tried. But to persuade Americans that the experiment was feasible, Publius had to refute the great authority on the question. Montesquieu had warned that in attempting to constitute power to govern a huge area, the temptation of reason would be to expunge the differences attaching to concrete places so that place turns into space, empty and abstract, thereby affording reason the freedom to define power according to laws that would expand it commensurately rather than confuse it. Abstract space invited a Cartesian rather than a Montesquieuean reason. Antifederalist critics of the proposed constitution were quick to invoke Montesquieu and to charge that only a despotism could rule the vast territory represented by America.[33] The response of Publius was to seize upon the sheer size of America and to use it as an argument for an enlarged conception of power: "The extent of the country is the strongest argument in favor of an energetic government; for any other can certainly never preserve the Union of so large an empire."[34]

Certainly the vastness of the new country posed the most direct challenge to established notions of what constituted proper political space. To many observers at the time, the state governments resembled nothing so much as the ancient Greek polities: they had the same tendencies toward autonomy, even autarchy; the same instability and sharpness of class conflict; and the same rough-and-tumble politics with comparatively widespread political participation. To the Framers the states appeared as so many competing centers of power, loyalty, and ambition, so many barriers to the founding and exercise of an effective state power.

How, then, was reason to constitute power amidst such Montesquieuean diversities? Did "the novelty of the undertaking," as Madison said of the proposed system, require that critical reason first sweep away "the existing Confederation" by demonstrating that it was "founded on principles which are fallacious" and then proceed to "change this first foundation, and with it, the superstructure resting upon it"?[35]

Posed in that form, *The Federalist* would seem to have come down on the side of Cartesian rather than Montesquieuean reason. The politics of a Cartesian reason dictated a strategy that depicted the current national condition as akin to a state of nature, "an infinity of little jealous, clashing, tumultuous commonwealths, the wretched nurseries of unceasing discord."[36] Thus, the distinct polities and cultures represented by the thirteen states appeared as the irrational elements—inherited and regressive, the traditional forms of politics—which, in the eyes of *The Federalist,* had all too successfully prevented the establishment of effective national power and authority. Reason could then intervene, declaring that "a Nation without a National Government is an awful spectacle"[37] and proceed to fill the empty national space by introducing rational foundations where none existed. The irrational politics of particularism would then be replaced by a rational administra-

tion concerned with "an unbiassed regard to the public weal." Instead
of a politics based upon "immediate interests . . . done . . . without
that knowledge of national circumstances and reasons of state, which
is essential to a right judgment, and with that strong predilection in
favour of local objects which can hardly fail to mislead the decision," [38]
there would be "one good Government . . . [that] can move on uniform principles of policy." [39]

Throughout *The Federalist,* reason is enlisted to promote the idea of
(national) state power. In this project, reason is aided by frequent appeals to "the science of politics." [40] Together reason and science are
used to delineate a distinct discourse of power. Its vocabulary includes
such notions as "proper and efficient management," "energetic government," and that "the true test of a good government is its aptitude
and tendency to produce a good administration." [41] It was also a vocabulary that displayed some of the despotic tendencies associated with
Cartesian reason. There were claims to "absolute demonstration" and
to "rare instances in which a political truth can be brought to the test
of mathematical demonstration." [42] There were justifications that referred to "the uniform course of events" and to the "solid conclusions
drawn from the natural and necessary progress of human affairs,"
which seemed to assume the existence of social laws. [43]

The intimate connection that Publius wanted to establish among
science, reason, and power was best illustrated in *Federalist* Number
31, written by Hamilton. It begins with a perfect illustration of how a
conception of power relationships can inform a linguistic structure:
"In disquisitions of every kind there are certain primary truths upon
which all subsequent reasonings must depend." [44] These truths, Publius continues, "command the assent of the mind"; and if they do not,
it can only be the result of an imperfection of the mind or of some
"strong interest or passion." Some "maxims of geometry" are then
adduced, but the crucial passage occurs when Publius turns to "maxims in ethics and politics." He lists four: no effect without a cause; "the
means ought to be proportioned to the end"; "every power ought to
be commensurate with its object"; and "there ought to be no limitation of a power destined to effect a purpose, which is itself incapable of
limitation." [45] The last three maxims were to play a major justificatory
role in Publius's defense of a broad reading of the "necessary and
proper" clause, the war powers, and the taxing power. He acknowledges that these primary "truths" of politics are less exact than those
of science or mathematics, yet he insists that interest and prejudice
alone explain why critics of the proposed constitution fail to find his
reasons compelling. "A sound and unbiassed mind" would find, he
argues, the following maxim "irresistible": "A government ought to

contain in itself every power requisite to the full accomplishment of the objects committed to its care, and to the complete execution of the trusts for which it is responsible; free from every other control, but a regard to the public good and to the sense of the people." [46]

To the criticism that he had provided a justification for virtually limitless power, Publius argued that the science of politics supplied its own antidote in "the internal structure of the proposed government." Various devices had been developed in modern times which allowed a government "to be modelled in such a manner as to admit of its being safely vested with the requisite powers." [47] These included the separation of powers, checks and balances, representative government, and the newest advance of all, "enlargement of the orbit" so that the sheer diversity and number of interests could be expected to produce endless squabbles that would cancel their power to do mischief.

Thus, Publius argued that limitations on power should be sought in the structure of government, not in the definition of its powers. But what if the structure is designed to check power rather than to exercise it? Would reason then produce stalemate? Would a Montesquieu-type reason be at odds with a Cartesian reason? By posing these questions, a startling disagreement is exposed at the very center of *The Federalist,* and Publius suddenly drops his mask to reveal a divided *persona.* The dispute is between Hamilton and Madison. It concerns the possibilities of a science of politics and the conditions necessary for a rational system of power to operate. That disagreement also sheds light on the question of how reason responds when constitutional constraints seem to frustrate reason from dealing with what it conceives to be political necessities.

Broadly speaking, Hamilton consistently appealed to reason and to a science of politics to defend a strong interpretation of national power. He saw a science of politics as sufficiently well founded to justify vesting a new state with magnitudes of power previously thought to be dangerous. As I have noted earlier, Hamilton argued that the huge scale of America made a powerful state imperative. Madison, in contrast, displayed far less confidence in the ability of a new science to demonstrate that men can safely exercise large and concentrated forms of power. Indeed, his reservations are reminiscent of Montesquieu.

The crucial text was *Federalist* Number 37. Madison begins by reminding his readers of the necessarily fallible nature of those who drafted the proposed constitution and of "the difficulties inherent in the very nature of the undertaking." The "most" that can be expected, he cautions, is to avoid past errors and to leave the door open to future changes. [48] The main difficulty is that contradictory principles have to be accommodated, such as the need for "stability and energy in Government" on the one hand and, on the other, certain republican principles that require power to be dependent on the people and entrusted for "a short duration." Or there is the difficult task of "marking the proper line of partition between the authority of the general and that of the State Governments."[49] These difficulties in drawing precise lines are ascribed by Madison to a more general difficulty that men have in making distinctions in complicated matters. Despite many efforts, philosophers have failed to establish precise distinctions between "sense, perception, judgment, desire, volition, memory, [or] imagination" or marked clearly the "boundaries between the great kingdoms of nature."

In turning to "the institutions of man," we need to qualify "our expectations and hopes" even further. "Experience has instructed us that no skill in the science of Government has yet been able to discriminate and define with sufficient certainty" the three great branches of government or "the precise extent" of various legal codes. Madison goes on in this Montesquieuean vein to argue that it was not just "the obscurity arising from the complexity of objects" that defeats efforts at precision, but the inadequacy of language itself for communicating complex notions.[50] He concludes with a peroration that subverts Hamiltonian science and even temporarily abandons the authority of reason for that of religion. "Would it be wonderful if under the pressure of all these difficulties, the [Philadelphia] convention should have been forced into some deviations from that artificial structure and regular symmetry, which an abstract view of the subject might lead an ingenious theorist to bestow on a Constitution planned in his closet or in his imagination? . . . It is impossible for the man of pious reflection not to perceive in it a finger of that Almighty hand which has been so frequently and signally extended to our relief in the critical stages of the revolution."[51]

Madison did not abandon the claims of the science of politics. But instead of using that science to advance the cause of power, as Hamilton had, he used it mainly to restrain or negate it. This would be consistent with Madison's basic concern, which was not to establish a strong state but to protect liberty and property from state legislatures. Thus, where Hamilton seized on the huge scale of America to argue for a strong state, Madison argued that the science of politics has shown how a huge territory, with all of its diverse factions and interests, serves to discourage the formation of "an unjust and interested majority."[52] Madison also attributed to science the discovery of the modern principle of representation, one of whose virtues is that it reduces the power of democracy by filtering the views of the people.[53] In the same vein, he attributed the system of checks and balances to a new science, and it, too, was in Madison's eyes a crucial device for preventing accumulations of power. It was also, incidentally, the occasion for Madison's explicitly invoking Montesquieu in support of "this invaluable precept in the science of politics." [54]

THE DIFFICULTY OF Madison's constitutionalism was that it was so intent on checking power that it could not give a satisfactory account of how government could generate power for positive goals. "The principal task of modern Legislation," he writes in *Federalist* Number 10, is "the regulation" of "various and interfering interests. . . . Justice ought to hold the balance" between the demands of the numerous interests and factions that infest society. The problem is that "the spirit of party and faction" have become involved in "the necessary and ordinary operations of Government." [55]

Despite all of the scholarly attention that has been lavished on this classic of American political thought, few seem to have noticed that Madison never resolves the problem of how justice is to be served. Instead, he shows how a large-scale republic, based on representative institutions, will frustrate factions and majorities and prevent then from dominating governmental policy. He shows, in other words, how injustice will be prevented, not how justice will be promoted. In his concern that society should "be broken into so many parts that the rights of individuals or of the minority will be in little danger from interested combinations of the majority," his argument seems to point toward a deadlock where the only solution is to establish some institution whose relative isolation will enable it to play the role of reason in a society torn by "human passions," "mutual animosities," and factional conflicts.

Again, in *Federalist* Number 51, while explaining how the separation of powers will cause "ambition to counteract ambition" so that the danger of tyranny, especially from the legislature, will be averted, Madison once more confronts the problem of government and justice; he manages little more, however, than an argument that perhaps explains how government acquired the power to protect and control the governed, but not how it could develop and promote policies. "Justice," he declares, "is the end of government" and "civil society." It "ever will be pursued, until it is obtained, or until liberty be lost in the pursuit." His solution to the problem of justice turns out to be an echo of Montesquieu's notion of a constitutional monarchy where self-interest keeps the system balanced and makes civic virtue superfluous—only it is an echo without Montesquieu's irony. Justice will be obtained, Madison claims, when the "more powerful factions or parties" come to realize that they will be secure only if they establish a government that will "protect all parties."[56]

One of the unnoticed features of Madison's celebrated analysis of factions is that it causes the state governments virtually to disappear as significant foci of political life and along with them the rich and complicated political cultures represented by thirteen distinct polities. Politics is reduced to the self-interested activities of economic interests, ideological sects, and demagogic politicians. The possibility of an American version of Montesquieu's constitutionalism of diverse laws, "intermediary groups," and intricate accommodations went unexplored. The consequences were considerable.

Madison's constitutionalism with its distrust of politics and its preoccupation with checks and restraints has the paradoxical result of forcing the rationale for state power to an extra-constitutional plane where state rationality, and hence state power, can operate relatively unhampered. On one of the few occasions in *The Federalist* when Madison attempted to confront questions about the specific powers of the national government, he adopted a position close to Hamilton's, defending a broad interpretation of the "necessary and proper clause" and of the principle that "wherever a general power to do a thing is given, every particular power necessary for doing it is included." This reading, as Madison recognized, rendered a specific enumeration of powers superfluous.[57]

Madison's tergiversations, if such they be, could also be matched by passages from Hamilton in *The Federalist* where he endorsed most of the constitutional restraints favored by Madison. The important difference was, however, that Hamilton believed that a constitution must provide a rational basis for the exercise of unlimited national power. It was not only the demands of war and diplomacy or the dangers of domestic insurrection that made unlimited power necessary, but the contingent and unpredictable nature of politics itself. Thus, "the care of the common defence" required powers "without limitation because it is impossible to foresee or define the extent and variety of national exigencies. . . . The circumstances that endanger the safety of nations are infinite."[58] This doctrine of "reasons of state" or "necessities of the State" thus finds reason seeking release from the constitutional trammels that reason itself had erected in order to contain power.[59]

The specific form constitutional reason of state takes is the executive, both in its bureaucratic or administrative side and in its presidential or leadership role. Hamilton's great *Federalist* papers on the nature and power of the executive envisage a mode of power that is as insulated as possible from the "irrationality" of legislatures, able to act decisively, and in possession of knowledge and information denied the parochially-minded Congress.[60] The executive becomes the embodiment of disinterested rationality that finds expression in the notion of administration as the vital center of the state: "The true test of a good government is its aptitude and tendency to produce a good administration."[61]

An insulated executive, presiding over an administrative state that would develop rational policies, yet enabled by his aloofness to deal energetically with crisis and contingency, was Hamilton's vision of constitutional rationality. It is a vision of power with no inherent limits because it is power that has been dissociated from politics and absorbed into reason. What makes that vision so remarkable is that, in the guise of Publius, both Hamilton and Madison repeatedly warned their readers about the dangerous lust for power that afflicts all men and the passions that corrupt judgment and make all political schemes that appeal to virtue appear utopian.

Once put into that form, the passion for reason and the search for a science of politics appear as the yearning for a pure politics conducted according to impersonal laws and objective knowledge. The stronger the revulsion to politics, coupled with a passionate involvement in it, the greater the longing for a plane of purity. That longing may express itself in the elevation of "national security" to a sacrosanct plane above partisan bickering; or it may be the drive to convert political questions into administrative solutions; or it may be the attempt to justify contentious social policies by appealing to some quasi-scientific formula, such as "cost-benefit analysis" or "rational choice theory"; or, as in the hearings on the nomination of Robert Bork to the Supreme Court, it may take the form of a profoundly ideological and politicized quest for jurists whose alleged commitment to judicial self-restraint and non-political, rational deliberation makes them the perfect contrast to the process by which they have been selected, thereby expiating the sinful passions of those who engineer the selection.

Two tendencies seem to be at work. Each carries the mark of that reductionist rationality which Montesquieu had worried about, and each, as it were, feeds off the other. One is rationality that takes the form of rationalization of activities, the reduction of diverse practices to a more systematic form that is justified on grounds of efficiency, rational allocation of resources, and expertise. It promotes the bureaucratization of both public and private sectors. The other is a higher rationality reserved to the state alone. In the name of national security, or "defense" against terrorism, or the "war" against drugs, or the "fight" against AIDS, or the "struggle" against foreign economic competitors, there is a constant pressure to relax legal and constitutional restraints, especially those relating to the executive branch.

Critical reason is enlisted to discredit the politics of parties, the role of legislatures, and popular participation—while exhorting judges to self-restraint—and thereby to clear a space for rational action by the executive.

The difficulty in getting a purchase on these problems is that criticism appears as an attack upon rationality inspired by an atavistic urge to return to a simpler age. Perhaps, however, the solution to the crisis of reason, as Montesquieu suggested, is not in simplification but in complexity. But how does complexity itself avoid appearing as a simple solution? Perhaps it has to do with treating complexity as signifying diverse claims and life forms so that the marks of a solution are not simplicity or elegance or reduction, as we have been taught, but the creation of conditions which encourage complexities that live by different laws and defy Cartesian solutions. Montesquieu would, I suspect, have approved.

Seven / E Pluribus Unum:
The Representation of Difference and the Reconstitution of Collectivity

The title of this chapter is familiar as the motto that appears on our national coinage. The sentiments expressed by this emblem seem unproblematical, and never more so than in the afterglow of the Great Year of the bicentennial of the American Constitution. *Unum* connotes national unity. Unity is, one would judge, a widely accepted value in America. It is toasted in beer commercials and celebrated by automobile manufacturers; it pervades the staging of sporting events such as the Olympics; and it is invoked by politicians to demonstrate resolve in the face of demands from foreign terrorists.

But as one reflects on the motto, its self-evident quality soon clouds over; and the longer one reflects, the more problematical, and richer, its contents. One discovers that in puzzling over an emblem, one has chanced upon a mode of discourse whose origins are intertwined with those of the Republic itself.

The motto engraved on the coinage is meant as a statement of collective self-understanding, but of what kind? One difficulty is that the grammar of the motto, the tense it wants to convey, is enigmatic. Since the motto lacks a verb, it is not easy to say whether it means to express a hopeful project or a complacent assumption, whether the condition of unity signified by *unum* is an aspiration to be fulfilled in the future, or a description of an accomplished fact in the present. Is *unum*, in other words, the expression of a teleology, and where does this leave *pluris?* Although we may be in doubt whether the motto refers to the present or the future, we tend to be certain that it could not have been intended to refer to the past. We "know" this because we read the motto as members of a political culture who have been taught that "in the beginning" we were many, not one, divided rather than unified, *pluris* rather than *unum. Pluris* is thus the antithesis to *unum*, the negativity of an abandoned past, as a Hegelian might put it.

We know, moreover, that less than one centennial after The Beginning a bloody civil war was fought over the proper meaning of *unum* and *pluris*. The appropriate national motto nearly became *"e uno pluris,"* from one to many. Although the war for Southern independence failed, the narrow margin of failure sets one to wondering whether *unum* can be realized only at the expense of plurality. We may even be led to reflect that despite celebrating the bicentennial of *unum*, a substantial part of current national political debates is taken up once more with *pluris:* with controversies over immigration policies, migrant workers, sanctuary for political refugees, and the influx of hundreds of thousands of immigrants representing a bewildering variety of cultures and political values. In the current context in which old-fashioned immigration seems mixed up with the ironies of recolonization, the choice of the Latin *pluris*, indeed the choice of a dead language to represent a national ideal, seems less a tribute to classical republicanism than an intriguing obscurantism.

Pluris, or "many," is a bland word. How was the choice of it supposed to affect the meaning of *unum?* Was it to mean an aggregate of similars or one of differences? Was it simply a head count or a reference, say, to varieties of regions, cultures, economic interests, and religions? Is *pluris* a refractory stuff such that *unum* cannot replace it but only displace it? Can *unum* issue from *pluris* or only be superimposed upon it?

Perhaps, however, the resistant qualities of *pluris* can be overcome if *pluris* is not treated as a sign of differences but as a neutered expression of the ideal conditions needed to make *unum* possible. The phrase *e pluribus unum* may have been suggested by Cicero's *unus de multis*, since *pluris* is the comparative form of *multus*. In Latin, *pluris* simply means "several, many," and it lacks the corporate, solidaristic connotations of, for example, *populus*, or people, that are implied by the Preamble when it invokes "We, the People" and attributes sufficient unity to that entity such that it is capable of willing "a more perfect Union." Parenthetically we may want to take note of an objection to the Preamble made by some Pennsylvania antifederalists who were quick to detect the political strategy behind the "populist" rhetoric about "We, the People." According to these dissenters, in elevating the people to sovereignty the federalists were really intent upon diminishing the status of the several states. The men of Philadelphia had affected "the style of a compact between individuals entering into a state of society, and not that of a confederacy of states."[1] To restate it, we might say that the antifederalists had exposed the language of *unum,* its emphasis upon abstract homogeneity—a compact, individuals, and people—and its suppression of real political differences represented by the several states.

When translated as "many," *pluris* asserts the presence of homogeneity rather than heterogeneity, of a lack of differentiation among the components which makes possible their easy amalgamation into a *unum.* Put aphoristically, as *unum* loosens, power weakens, *pluris* reasserts itself. Not surprisingly, homogeneity has often been recommended as a condition favorable to power. *Cuius regio eius religio.* Oneness of religion, race, ideology, language, nationality, and culture has been attractive to rulers, policy makers, and generals because it implies massed support and minimal discord. Since there is no need to placate, suppress, or even pay attention to dissidence, homogeneity promises a more perfectly focused use of power's resources and more predictable consequences for policy choices.

Undifferentiation was implied in Locke's magisterial formulation concerning the relationship between power and the nature of political community: "and it being necessary to that which is one body to move one way; it is necessary the Body should move that way whither the greater force carries it, which is the consent of the majority; or else it is impossible it should act or continue one Body, one Community."[2]

Oneness, then, is a metaphor for power. This seems implicit in a remark by Madison in *The Federalist* concerning "the great principle of representation": "If Europe has the merit of discovering this great mechanical power in government, by the simple agency of which, the will of the largest political body may be concentred, and its force directed to any object, which the public good requires; America can claim the merit of making the discovery the basis of unmixed and extensive republics."[3]

Typically, discourse about *unum* will avoid setting up heterogeneity as *unum*'s antithesis. Instead, "anarchy" is the usual candidate—as in Hobbes's "state of nature"—and it implies disordered and possibly violent differences verging on chaos. If, however, a society is peacefully heterogeneous, the choice of *pluris* works to conceal significant differences in order to enable *unum* to act in a unified manner. A significant difference would be one with sufficient organization and resources to pose a difficulty for public order or an obstruction to public policy. When the differences are real, *unum* performs as a useful fiction designed both to conceal differences and to legitimate power, thereby representing power as having to be exercised on behalf of a society too divided to act collectively. For in Hobbes's equally magisterial formulation in the chapter entitled "Of Persons, Authors, and things personated": "A multitude of men . . . naturally is not One . . . [They] are made One Person, when they are by one man, or one Person, Represented."[4]

If, then, *unum* is a fiction, on whose behalf is it a fiction? The answer is, I think, reason's fiction. Reason wants to generalize, to universalize. That aim is obstructed by differences. The political consequences of what reason needs if it is to operate with maximum efficiency, or what is needed by the social groups who adopt reason as their distinguishing principle, are serious. Following a Hobbesian reading, *unum* would signify that in "ordaining" a constitution, *pluris* has simultaneously legitimated a new arrangement of power and alienated its own powers.[5] Or, stated slightly differently, alienation of power by *pluris* is the necessary condition of the peculiar constitution of power for which *unum* stands. This is possible only if *pluris* comes to acknowledge the dangers inherent in its own diversities, to recognize that alienation is rational.

The dualism of the one and the many is, of course, one of the oldest in the history of Western thought.[6] For our purpose, however, genealogical evolutions are less significant than the fact that each of the terms, *unum* and *pluris*—mythemes, as I shall call them, after Lévi-Strauss—came to be connected in eighteenth-century America to a whole network of subthemes which not only provided the distinctive pattern of meaning associated with the mytheme but itemized it, so to speak. Thus, *unum*'s pattern is woven of such primary elements as national unity, patriotism, centralization, and state. Its subthemes are power, majesty, and control. Its tempo is progressivist and oriented toward the future. In what follows I suggest that the overall pattern of *unum*'s mytheme is profoundly mimetic of an older mytheme, that of Old Testament monotheism.

One of the earliest and grandest expressions of *unum*'s mythematics is to be found in the second *Federalist,* by John Jay: "Providence has been pleased to give this one connected country, to one united people, a people descended from the same ancestors, speaking the same language, professing the same religion, attached to the same principles of government, very similar in their manners and customs."[7]

Jay's invocation of Providence presages what can fairly be described as a Hebraic or Old Testament conception of society in which lineage, cultural homogeneity, religious uniformity, and political institutions are represented as a seamless web. The historical genealogy goes further to suggest an analogy in which the founding of *unum,* which is symbolized by the new constitution being recommended by Jay, is interpreted as belonging to the same ontology as the Creation myth set out in the Old Testament book of Genesis.[8] In the Genesis account, world creation is a monument not only to power but to the triumph of order over chaos. But order is not conceived by the Old Testament as monolithic. Rather, it is a structure of discriminations between night and day, between earth, sea, and sky, and between god and man. That structure is reproduced in the ordering of life when Adam is given full sovereignty over all living creatures. Each creature is carefully named, that is, differentiated, so that its integrity is not obliterated when man's dominion is instituted. Thus, in the Old Testament mytheme, the constitution of monotheistic power does not require the deconstitution of difference. *Unum non tollit naturam sed perficit,* if I may modify Aquinas.

In Jay's account, however, with its emphasis upon oneness of language, ethnicity, religion, and political ideology, difference drops out; there is, instead, a striking reassertion of the heresy of the Tower of Babel. In that story it is precisely because the men of Shinar have one language and a highly unified social organization and thus have suppressed their differences that they are able to mobilize the power necessary to erect a tower whose rising pinnacle signifies a challenge to the heavens. Yahweh dissolves the threat by the simple device of introducing a multiplicity of languages. Disunion and scattered power result.[9] *E pluribus infirmitas.*

Jay's version reverses the biblical narrative. The Constitution promises to overcome the dispersion of power produced by difference. For in the paragraph that follows directly upon the one just quoted, Jay contrasts, on the one hand, "the design of Providence" for "a band of brothers, united to each other by the strongest ties," with, on the other, the present condition under the Articles of Confederation where the states are "split into a number of unsocial, jealous and alien sovereignties." Disunity, even dismemberment, weakness, and division, all seem to be the consequence of a nonsystem without a center, a decentered and polytheistic condition of "jealous and alien sovereignties" whose "unsocial" character was meant as a grim reminder of a primal condition, a state of nature. *Unum* signifies political exodus from a condition of political polytheism to one of political monotheism, an overcoming of local worshipers and their deities. Thus, the biblical themes merge with revolutionary and postrevolutionary themes. Weakness is associated with the pluralism, the polytheism of the Articles of Confederation; the diverse political cultures of the separate states appear as polytheism, local shrines identified with particular places, values that cannot be separated from the physical places where they have been experienced.

The new constitution is, of course, not explicated by appealing to theological notions. Instead, *The Federalist* invokes the "science of politics," the Enlightenment's functional equivalent. Yet the conception of power by which the Constitution's provisions were interpreted was not derived from any science but was, instead, an exact imitation of theological discussions concerning the vast powers needed by a deity who was responsible for the workings of an entire universe.[10] In Hamilton's secular version of providential power, "A government ought to contain in itself every power requisite to the full accomplishment of the objects committed to its care, and to the complete execution of the trusts for which it is responsible; free from every other control, but a regard to the public good and to the sense of the people."[11]

The discourse of power is schematically represented by Hamilton in *Federalist* Number 23, where he outlines the central questions that have to be posed if there is to be an "energetic constitution: "the objects" to be pursued by the government, "the quantity of power necessary to the accomplishment of those objects," and "the persons upon whom that power ought to operate."[12] For Hamilton and many of the other Founders, the "objects" or purposes of the new system were to define the "quantity" of power. Those objects were, first and foremost, defense against "internal convulsions" and "external attacks."[13] It is impossible to overestimate the influence, especially upon Hamilton's thinking, of the military weakness of the Confederation and of the frustrating experience of the Revolution concerning raising supplies, recruiting troops, and acquiring revenues to fight the war. The profound effect of that experience, the negative experience of a system rooted in the autonomous power of the individual state governments, was registered in Hamilton's sweeping interpretation of the war powers contained in the new constitution. "These powers," he wrote, "ought to exist without limitation." The reason for unlimited power proved to be an argument that presupposed as its model of power an omnipotent god whose omniscience gave him perfect foresight. For Hamilton the lack of omniscience becomes the reason for enlarging the power of the state: "It is impossible to foresee or define the extent and variety of national exigencies, or the corresponding extent and variety of the means which may be necessary to satisfy them."[14]

Omniscience is not, however, abandoned as an ideal. Rather, it begins to assume the modern form of "information." The collection of information, and the advantages it gives, are crucial to the centering of power. The central government assumes the form of a surveillant father-deity, "the guardianship of the public safety" in Hamilton's phrase, distanced from the welter of local interests/deities and able to judge dispassionately: "As the center of information [it] will best understand the extent and urgency of the dangers that threaten—as the representative of the WHOLE [it] will feel itself most deeply interested in the preservation of every part." [15]

How, then, would difference be represented so that the case for *unum* and political monotheism appears compelling? The "mischiefs of faction," which the Tenth *Federalist* made a permanent part of the American political consciousness, provides a clue as to how difference would be represented in the ideology/theology of *unum*. In Madison's view, factions originated in difference: "a zeal for different opinions concerning religion, concerning Government and many other points, as well of speculation as of practice; an attachment to different leaders . . . [different] parties . . . distinct interests [which] . . . grow up of necessity in civilized nations, and divide them into different classes, actuated by different sentiments and views." [16] In his classic essay Madison was not praising "interest group politics" or admiring the varied political life forms spontaneously emerging; rather, he was expressing the fear of being overwhelmed by differences.

The deepest nightmare was that diversity might manage to combine to form a majority, perhaps a majority of the unpropertied allied with some of the numerous forms of propertied interests. The nightmare was expressed by Madison in the form of a dilemma which was the expression of a fundamental ambivalence that found *unum* unable to live with *pluris,* yet unable to live without it. Madison formulated the problem of "curing" the mischiefs of faction by reducing it to a stark choice between destroying liberty, which allows faction to flourish, or "giving to every citizen the same opinions, the same passions, and the same interests." [17] Since the one course was undesirable and the other impracticable, the solution lay in devising methods of controlling the effects of faction.

For the moment we need not be concerned with Madison's solution, which, in imitation of Yahweh's strategy against the men of Shinar, relied upon the great geographical expanse of America to dilute the intensity of organized faction and scatter its power. The important move was Madison's transformation of difference so that certain forms of it became privileged.

"The diversity in the faculties of men from which the rights of property originate," Madison argued, militates against "a uniformity of interests." Thus, property is founded in difference, "different degrees and kinds of property" and "different and unequal faculties of acquiring [it]." "The protection of these faculties is," Madison concluded, "the first object of Government."[18] The great threat to difference is democracy: it wants men to "be perfectly equalized and assimilated in their possessions, their opinions and their passions."[19] Thus, difference becomes praiseworthy when it is associated with inequality of ability and acquisition. *Unum*'s relation to *pluris* now appears equivocal: it needs to prevent the coalescence of certain differences while protecting those differences of ability which produce inequalities. It would be but a small step from Madison's concept of unequal faculties to a full-blown conception of meritocracy in which a just society is one where social goods are distributed in accordance with one's deserts and the only significant differences will be earned and hence deserved.

WHEN WE COME to consider *pluris*, there does not seem to be intuitively a coherent mytheme, only a rhetorical antithesis to *unum*. The vagueness that surrounds *pluris* is a tacit tribute to the influence of the political culture which has collected around and supported the myth of *unum* for two centuries.

The hegemony of *unum* has encouraged a kind of collective amnesia that has forgotten what *pluris* meant, what historical allusions it carried. Did *pluris* once possess a richer range of reference, a political culture, a theory and a set of practices? In trying to identify the mytheme of *pluris*, I want to begin by juxtaposing two famous remarks by Tocqueville. "Americans have this great advantage, that they attained democracy without having to suffer democratic revolutions and that they were born equal instead of having to become so."[20] The second remark is briefer: "America has no feudal past."[21]

In these remarks, as well as throughout his classic study of American politics and political culture, Tocqueville proceeded by means of a contrast between democracy and aristocracy. In France, he argued, democracy required a great revolutionary upheaval because it could not be established without first destroying a "feudal system." In Tocqueville's eyes, much of what distinguished America was attributable to what America had not experienced, namely, an Old Regime politics of monarchical absolutism and centralization and a feudal society of largely inherited inequalities and corresponding privileges.

In our own day, Tocqueville's thesis was revived by the late Louis Hartz. Although Hartz explicitly adopted Tocqueville's thesis that connected the uniqueness of America to a lack of feudal experience, he extended it by claiming that this historical vacuum allowed Lockean liberalism to become America's traditional ideology, its ideology of order, and thus to play the role that conservative ideologies typically performed in European politics. In Hartz's terse formula, "the absence of feudalism and the presence of the liberal idea" were the main clues to the American political tradition.[22]

In what follows I want to reconsider the Tocqueville-Hartz thesis insofar as it applies to American political thinking during the Revolution and the dispute over ratification of the Constitution. My claim will be that, contrary to that thesis, America had a feudal tradition; that the American Revolution, unlike the French Revolution, was in its political theories importantly a revolution for, not against, feudalism; that the Revolution of 1776 was, in a Weberian sense, a counter-revolution against the slowly evolving pressures toward "rationalization" on the part especially of British administrators; and that the revolution that actually overthrew the premise of feudalism, or suppressed it, occurred when the Constitution was ratified in 1787. A truer version of our motto might be *e feudalibus unum,* a very free rendering of which might be, unity must suppress feudalism because feudalism signifies primal chaos and political polytheism.

E pluribus unum, then, is the appropriate emblem for the revolution of 1787, and the *unum* is the mytheme for the transformation of several states, with their diverse and conflicting interests and loyalties, their thirteen sovereignties, into something new, a "consolidation of power," as the Founders described it, a unified people whose oneness would for the immediate future be represented by the state, a state that, as Jay had argued in the second *Federalist,* could find support in a preexisting national culture but a state that, as everyone recognized, did not have a corresponding practice.[23] The abstract character of *unum* was praised by Hamilton in a remarkable passage in which it was strongly suggested that one of the positive qualities which recommended the new constitution was that its "benefits" would be more appreciated by those of a theoretical bent, "speculative men," rather than by "the mass of citizens." The Constitution would be concerned with "general interests" whose very generality was not likely to "inspire" either "a habitual sense of obligation" or "an active sentiment of attachment" on the part of ordinary citizens.[24]

Thus, *unum* represents a different political plane, abstract rather than immediate, intellective rather than sentimental, administrative or executive in its outlook rather than participatory or suffrage-oriented, and drawn to a general, one might say, monotheistical overview rather than to "minute interests." It will, as Hamilton made clear, attract a different type of political man. The "strong propensity of the human heart" is to be attached first to family, then to neighborhood, then to community and local government.[25] These "affections" will not attract the *unum* type of political man because these are the petty concerns of local politics, "the mere domestic police [policy] of a state," and consequently they "hold out slender allurements to ambition." Even to discuss their details would be "too tedious and uninteresting to compensate for the instruction it might afford."[26]

Unum politics, in contrast, is for ambitious men with a larger than normal appetite for power. For "minds governed by that passion," the "charms" that lure them have to do with grander stakes of "commerce, finance, negociation, and war."[27] These were, of course, the main domains carved out by the Constitution for the new state. The Revolution of 1776 had a very different attitude toward power, one that cannot be captured by setting up a simple contrast between the "democratic" impulses in the Revolution and the "elitist" impulses at work in the counterrevolution of Philadelphia. That contrast matters, but as numerous historians have pointed out, there were too many ambiguous ideas among those who opposed ratification to describe them as "democratic." Nor can that attitude be delineated by following the well-worn path of argument in the pamphlet literature that preceded the break with Britain, from arguments about charters and the rights of Englishmen through further arguments about the differences between internal and external regulation or between taxation and legislation, to the ultimate argument from natural rights.

Some of these difficulties can be resolved, I would suggest, if we think of the opposition to British rule as a unique compound of democratic and feudal elements which later reappeared in the antifederalist opposition to the Philadelphia constitution. The Revolution of 1776 was importantly a feudal revolt because it was a revolution against centralized power, rule from a distance, and uniform principle. It was expressed in one widely circulated pamphlet this way: "The colonies are at so great a distance from England" that Parliament "can generally have but little knowledge of their business, connections and interests."[28]

As is well known, a self-conscious effort was begun in 1763 by British administrators seeking to tighten up control over the colonies generally and over their representative assemblies in particular. Although British spokesmen and defenders of British policy appealed to the authority of the Crown, the sovereignty of Parliament, and the nature of the British Constitution, there was also a very strong sense in which they were appealing to a rather different order of considerations having to do with the "objective" needs of administration. In Thomas [later Governor] Pownall's influential work, *Principles of Policy* (1757), an attempt was made to offer a new meaning for the term "empire." That attempt was significant not only for the reason Koebner has pointed out, that Pownall's new term, "civil empire," was used to mean "the efficient functioning of administration," but because the meaning of administration was being drawn from industrial analogies that were profoundly antifeudal. Good government, Pownall maintained, depended on property owners who must act together, not on the model of landed proprietors but "like some engine and machine, the silk-mills for instance, where one common great first movement is communicated and distributed thro' the whole." And "empire," he went on to say, must likewise be directed as "one whole," so people must be "modelled into various orders and subordination of orders."[29]

The indifference to local circumstance implicit in Pownall's notion of empire was given practical expression in the famous claim of the Declaratory Act of 1765 that Parliament "had, hath, and of right ought to have, full power and authority to make laws and statutes of sufficient force and validity to bind the colonies and people of America . . . in all cases whatsoever."

A very different mentality was being expressed in the protests of the colonists. In a well-known pamphlet of 1764, the concept of empire reflected an outlook that was polytheistic rather than monotheistic; decentered rather than centered; oriented toward representative assemblies, not toward regulatory boards. "An imperial state," according to Stephen Hopkins, "consists of many governments, each of which hath peculiar privileges."[30] The emphasis upon difference, pluralism, and the dispersion of power among several centers forms a striking contrast with the imperial emphasis upon unity and centered administration. It reappears in numerous colonial pamphlets and is the basis for my hypothesis that the colonies and their evolution into state governments during the course of the Revolution represented the expression of an American feudalism that made it a feudal revolution; and insofar as it represented a reaction to administrative rationality, it had a reactionary element. If this is correct, then the formation of the American political tradition is not to be explained by the absence of a feudal experience but by its later suppression.

Feudalism is associated historically, first, with a system of land tenure which correlated specified rights and duties between the landowner and those who worked the land or held it from him; second, feudalism was a regime of inherited privilege and social status, personal dependence, and inequalities of power, influence, status, and rights.[31] If these features are taken as essential marks of feudalism, then clearly feudalism had at best only marginal significance in America. There are, however, sound historical reasons for not insisting exclusively on medieval and early modern versions of feudalism.[32]

During the seventeenth and eighteenth centuries, particularly among French political theorists, feudalism began to be conceptualized rather than simply chronicled. The major figure, for my purposes, was Montesquieu, who, as is often noted, was frequently cited by Americans, especially at the Philadelphia convention and during the subsequent debates over ratification. The concept of feudalism played a major role in Montesquieu's celebrated *De l'esprit des lois*. But he was only one of several writers who dealt with what was a very lively topic in France during the first few decades of the eighteenth century. Feudalism was at the center of an intense controversy over the so-called ancient constitution.

The ancient constitution was a construct developed to protest and, if possible, even halt, the consolidation of royal absolutism and the centralization of state power associated with the rule of Louis XIV. The opponents of royal power appealed to a loose assemblage of ancient statutes and customs which, they claimed, established certain rights, immunities, and institutions of the aristocracy, as well as of local and provincial bodies. These rights and practices were said to form a constitution, which placed limits upon royal power and its bureaucracy. The *thèse nobiliaire,* as it has been called by later historians, maintained that the ancient constitution was the true constitution; that the growth of royal claims was a usurpation; and that the old arrangement should be restored and power shared between king and aristocracy.[33]

At the hands of Montesquieu the class bias in the *thèse* was toned down, and the *thèse* became the basis for a broad defense of decentralized power and a critique of royal absolutism and the centralized state. Montesquieu adopted the idea that inherited rights and aristocratic institutions formed a natural barrier to absolutism, but he expanded it to include a complex array of local institutions and local bodies of law and custom. These elements formed what he called "intermediary bodies" whose function was not simply to defend or mediate between state and civil society but to complicate power. At his hands feudalism became a term to designate an alternative to the centralized state. It stood for the periphery against the center, for the diversity of local institutions and practices against the uniformizing tendencies of administrative rule, in short, for political polytheism against political monotheism. The incorporation of feudalism produced a conception of political society in which anachronism was used to challenge the modern conception of the sovereign, centralized state. Because it was a conception that depicted and explained political society as a concatenation of differences—of moral beliefs, religious customs, local practices, class structures, economic systems, and geography—it could be said to pit political culture against political rationality, the centrifugal tendencies of the one against the centripetal impulses of the other.[34]

Feudalism thus becomes much more than a system of land tenure or aristocratic privilege, or even a defense of local home rule. It introduces a distinctive discourse, one that proposes a conception of power that challenges the modern conception of the state first set out by Hobbes and later reinterpreted by Weber.

In eighteenth-century America, as we have seen, there were elements of the feudal outlook in the prerevolutionary protests against British commercial policies, protests that can be fairly characterized as imparting a pronounced antimercantilist and antistatist cast to colonial political thinking. That outlook did not jell into a coherent theory, primarily because there was no available theoretical language to give adequate expression to a distinctive blend of ideas that seemed at once progressive in the Enlightenment sense of emphasizing individual rights, responsible government, rule of law, and a certain formal equality, and, at the same time, regressive in the sense of emphasizing the values of place, local interests, and local arrangements while defending the status of local notables.

The uncertainties to which this unstable amalgam could give rise were evident in the familiar arguments used by the colonists in attacking British policies. The appeal to the rights of Englishmen had the curious quality of attempting to defend the differences in the situation of the colonists, as embodied, for example, in the diverse charters of the individual colonies, while claiming the same rights as Englishmen. The effect was to universalize English rights, that is, to dissociate them from place (England) while at the same time trying to confine British power to a mainly local suzerainty over the British isles and to an external regulation of colonial trade but not of the internal life of the colonies.

The same problem reappeared when the colonists began to appeal to theories of natural law and natural rights: they were becoming increasingly self-conscious about the separateness of their interests and identity, but they attempted to defend what was concrete and local by appeals to what was universal and transcendent, that is, to what was "true" regardless of time and circumstance. These competing considerations were all brought together in the "Declaration and Resolves" of the first Continental Congress of 1774, which appealed to difference, "their several local and other circumstances," and to principles that overrode them: "That the inhabitants of the English colonies in North America, by the immutable laws of nature, the principles of the English constitution, and the several charters or compacts, have the following Rights . . ."[35]

The principle of difference was preserved in the closing paragraph of the Declaration of Independence where it was asserted that "these

United Colonies are, and of Right ought to be Free and Independent States" that "have the Power to levy War, conclude Peace, contract Alliances, establish Commerce, and to do all the other Acts and Things which Independent States may of right do." It was a discourse that its opponents quickly charged with being archaic, anachronistic, democratic, and feudal.

The push for the new constitution was self-consciously a critique of the political constitution of the Revolution. The American Revolution, it should be noted, was distinguished from modern revolutions in that the usual course has been to establish a constitution or settle a new form of government once the revolution has succeeded. But in the American Revolution constitution-making occurred during the Revolution and mostly in the earlier years when the former colonies adopted new constitutions in place of royal charters. The Articles of Confederation was not adopted until 1781, and that system, as is well known, expressed rather than replaced the so-called sovereignty of the state governments. The *Federalist* attack upon the revolutionary-constitutional system emphasized weakness and anarchy. Although many historians have noted that the *Federalist* argument included several numbers devoted to reciting the history of confederations and to drawing lessons about how such systems inevitably disintegrated, few have given much, if any, thought to the fact that *The Federalist* also tried to affix the stigma of feudalism to the Articles of Confederation by arguing that while "the ancient feudal systems were not strictly speaking confederacies, yet they partook of the nature of that species of association. . . . The separate governments in a confederacy may aptly be compared with the feudal baronies."[36] The common characteristics of confederacies and feudalism, other than a proclivity toward anarchy, were incessant internecine rivalries for power and "the concentration of large portions of the strength of the community into particular depositories."[37]

At a deeper level, the analogy between feudalism and the current system of state sovereignty exposed the fundamental worry of *The Federalist* and its cause concerning the positive strength of "feudalism" in America. The feudal factor was implied whenever *The Federalist* referred to the "corporate" character of the states and to their role as "intermediary" powers between their citizens and a central authority.[38] Thus, "feudalism" signified the presence of distinct political cultures, not just paper constitutions—as the new federal constitution was. These polities, as the supporters of the new constitution never failed to point out, even had their local barons, or local elites, who jealously opposed the Constitution as a threat to their entrenched power.[39] Above all, American "feudalism" possessed one unique feature that

distinguished it from ancient feudalism and presented the gravest difficulties to the proponents of the new system: the state governments
were firmly rooted in the affections of their citizens, a condition that,
as *The Federalist* repeatedly acknowledged, ancient feudalism had
failed to achieve.[40]

The authors of *The Federalist* acknowledged on several occasions
that the new government would be unable to compete with the state
governments for the affections of the citizens. Thus, the new government resembled an alien authority and alienated power: it was remote,
abstract, concerned with matters that did not directly affect the daily
concerns of citizens, and unable to count on that "confidence and good
will of the people" which was natural to the state governments.[41] As
one antifederalist argued, "The idea of an uncompounded republick,
on an average of one thousand miles in length and eight hundred in
breadth containing six millions of white inhabitants, all reduced to the
same standard of morals, of habits, and of laws, is in itself an absurdity, and contrary to the whole experience of mankind."[42]

The difficulty was embodied in what *The Federalist* argued was the
real innovation and absolutely fundamental principle of the proposed
constitution: it could exert power directly upon the individual citizen
and thereby avoid having to solicit the consent of the several states, the
major hindrance to effective action under the Articles. This meant, in
effect, circumventing the political culture of the states by abstracting
the citizen from his local culture and reconstituting him as a new kind
of being, one who would be the object of national administration
rather than an active subject in local self-government.[43]

The conflict between *unum* and *pluris* took the form of rationality
versus difference, between national power based upon what *The Federalist* called "the new science of politics" and the "imbecility" of the
constitutional system embodied in decentralized systems.[44] The conflict was presaged in the course of Hamilton's critique of feudalism
where he alludes to the case of Scotland as a warning of how "ties
equivalent to those of kindred" could generate powerful resistance to
central government which only rational governance could overcome.
Only "the incorporation with England subdued [Scotland's] fierce and
ungovernable spirit, and reduced it within those rules of subordination, which a more rational and a more energetic system of civil polity" had previously established in Britain.[45]

The conflict in its American version was set out in the *Federalist*
argument for a different national taxing power than that provided in
the Articles of Confederation. Under that system, taxation required
that each state consent to an exaction that would be the same for each.

Hamilton seized upon the principle of difference to demonstrate that the provision was bound to be virtually inoperable. The differences in "circumstances," "and many much too complex, minute, or adventitious, to admit of a particular specification," made impossible any "common measure of national wealth" or any "general stationary rule" for judging the ability of the individual states to pay. But, Hamilton pointed out, since the new constitution provided for the authority of the national government to coerce individuals, then the standard could be a simple one of taxes on consumption.[46] Thus, individuals are, as it were, extricated from their context of state citizenship and identified as objects of power far more simplified than if the objects of power were the several and diverse states. Difference is not so much suppressed as circumvented.

The association of rationality with *unum* and its state and of nonrationality with *pluris* was apparent when Hamilton warned against the dangers of obstructionism in *Federalist* Number 22: "When the concurrence of a large number is required by the constitution to the doing of any national act we are apt to rest satisfied that all is safe, because nothing improper will be likely to be done; but we forget how much good may be prevented, and how much ill may be produced, by the power of hindering the doing what may be necessary, and of keeping affairs in the same unfavourable posture in which they may happen to stand at particular periods."[47]

IT HAS BEEN noted many times that the case for *pluris* never managed to find a theoretical voice comparable to that of *The Federalist*. I have tried to suggest that one reason was the ability of *The Federalist* to combine two powerful mythemes, one drawn from Old Testament conceptions of monotheistic power, the other from eighteenth-century conceptions of a rational science of politics, especially as these latter fitted into *The Federalist's* vision of the administrative power of the executive branch. The suppression of polytheism or difference made possible a unified or single national narrative, *e pluribus unum*.

On the other hand, *pluris* never managed to achieve a theory, and the fact that it did not may suggest something about our basic preconceptions of theory. Stated briefly, we experience the same difficulties in grasping the antifederalists' arguments as they experienced in making them. We and they are both confronted by a notion of theory which favors the reduction of difference to enable us to advance generalizations. We classify and categorize, we simplify, and we quantify; we regularize phenomena so that we can subsume them under general

statements or hypotheses. In this we duplicate the administrative outlook, which seeks to fit individual cases under general rules and abhors
exceptions as the scientist does anomalies.

Precisely because the case for *pluris* is a case for diversity, those who
would theorize it are put in the paradoxical position of seeking to generalize about difference, of trying to make a theory about exceptions,
local idiosyncrasies, regional differences. Politically that position appears vulnerable to charges of defending the archaic against the modern, of obstructing progress. And this was precisely what *The Federalist* was arguing when it attacked the political system of the Articles
of Confederation as feudal and democratic. In the *Federalist* critique,
democracy is represented as a premodern political system, invented by
the Greeks and foolishly perpetuated in the Italian city-states of their
own day, but hopelessly unsuited to the large territory of the modern
nation-state.[48] Yet, as I suggested at the outset, American history, especially the history of the present, is a story of differences. It is a history that suggests that the true archaism is *unum* with its myth of a
single people and a single narrative. And perhaps the supreme archaism is *unum*'s proudest achievement, the state.

Eight / Contract and Birthright

> Once when Jacob was boiling pottage,
> Esau came in from the field, and he was
> famished. And Esau said to Jacob, "Let me
> eat some of that red pottage, for I am fam-
> ished!" . . . Jacob said, "First sell me your
> birthright." Esau said, "I am about to die;
> of what use is a birthright to me?" Jacob
> said, "Swear to me first." So he swore to
> him, and sold his birthright to Jacob. . . .
> Thus Esau despised his birthright.
> —GEN. 25:29–34

The story of Esau recounts how a man sold his birthright. In ancient times, a birthright usually fell to the eldest son. He succeeded his father and received the major portion of his father's legacy. A birthright was thus an inherited identity and implicitly an inherited obligation to use it, take care of it, pass it on, and, hopefully, improve it. An inherited identity is, by definition, unique: Esau was the inheritor of his father, Isaac, and hence a descendant of Abraham, the founder of Israel. Esau was also the inheritor of the profound experiences of his father, whom Abraham had been prepared to sacrifice for his God; and Esau was also the inheritor of his father's father, and so on, according to the genealogies so beloved in the Old Testament, back in time to Adam and Eve. Esau's was thus a collective identity, bound up with a people and extending over time.

This unique identity Esau had bartered to fill a need that could be satisfied by any number of different foods. He had bartered what was unique and irreplaceable for a material good for which there was a number of available substitutes.

Although Esau is depicted as a crude man, the Old Testament leaves no doubt that his decision was free and uncoerced, even though there had clearly been an element of cunning on Jacob's part. The power of the biblical narrative depends upon the juxtaposition between the free nature of the choice and the unfree nature of a birthright. One does not choose to be the eldest son of a particular father: that is a matter of one's special history. Contrary to what Jean-Paul Sartre would claim, the idea of a birthright denies that we are "thrown into the world." It asserts, instead, that we come into the world preceded by an inheritance. This is why if Esau is to disencumber himself of his inheritance he has to enter into a mode of discourse contrary to the mode of discourse surrounding a birthright. Accordingly, the biblical narrator says that Esau "swore" and "sold," that is, Esau entered into a contract of exchange. But the contractual mode presumes precisely what the birthright mode rejects, that the exchanged objects are equal in value. It is not that it is impossible to reduce a birthright and a bowl of pottage to a common measure of value but rather that the nature of one is more deeply violated than the other by that operation. In other words, there is an intuitive sense that protests that a birthright is not the kind of thing that should be the object of a contract—in much the same way, perhaps, that we feel that Faust committed an act of self-violation when he contracted with Mephistopheles to make over his soul in exchange for power.

The idea of a contract is familiar to us not only as a legal instrument by which most business transactions are negotiated but also as one of the archetypal metaphors of political theory. It is associated with such masters of political thought as Hobbes, Locke, Rousseau, Paine, and Kant. It has represented a distinctive vision of society, and nowhere has it been more influential, both in theory and in practice, than in the United States. It is a core notion in two of the most widely discussed political theories of recent years, those of John Rawls and Robert Nozick.

Briefly put, contract theory conceives of political society as the creation of individuals who freely consent to accept the authority and rules of political society on the basis of certain stipulated conditions, such as each shall be free to do as he or she pleases as long as his or her actions do not interfere with the rights of others; or that an individual shall not be deprived of property except by laws that have been passed by duly elected representatives; and so on. The contractual element is needed, according to the theory, because all persons being free and equal by nature and society being by nature in need of coercive power to protect rights, preserve peace, and defend against external invasion, the freedom of individuals will have to be limited and regulated. Individuals will contract, therefore, to surrender some part of their rights in exchange for the protection of the law and the defense of society from foreign or domestic enemies.

For more than three centuries the contract way of understanding political life has been criticized for being unhistorical, but the criticism has usually taken the form of arguing that contractualism gives a false account of how societies have actually come into existence. To which the contract theorist has quite properly replied that he has not been engaged in historical description but in prescribing the principles of a rights-oriented society. Yet that reply does expose an assumption, namely, that it is possible to talk intelligibly about the most fundamental principles of a political society as though neither the society nor the individuals in it had a history. It stands, therefore, in sharp contrast to the conception of a birthright, which, while not strictly historical in the approach to collective identity, might be said to have a quality of historicality.

I want to suggest that the conception of a birthright provides a more powerful way of understanding our present political condition than does contract theory, and that contract theory is less a solution to the political problem of our times than an exacerbation of it. I began with the story of Esau because it bears on the birthright that each of us has. Like Esau's, our birthright is an inheritance. Like Esau's, it is inherited from our fathers. Like Esau's, it is a birthright that concerns a unique collective identity. Like Esau, our birthright is not being extracted from us by force; it is being negotiated or contracted away. Finally, like Esau, we have made it possible to contract away our birthright by forgetting its true nature and thereby preparing the way for its being reduced to a negotiable commodity with the result that its disappearance is not experienced as loss but as relief.

The birthright that we have made over to our Jacobs is our politicalness. By politicalness I mean our capacity for developing into beings who know and value what it means to participate in and be responsible for the care and improvement of our common and collective life. To be political is not identical with being a part of government or being associated with a political party. These are structured roles, and typically they are highly bureaucratized. For these reasons, they are opposed to the authentically political.

A political inheritance or birthright is not something we acquire like a sum of money or our father's house; nor is it something we grow into naturally without effort or forethought, like reaching the age of eighteen and automatically being entitled to vote. It is something to which we are entitled, as Esau had been, but we have to make it consciously our own, mix it with our mental and physical labor, undertake risks on its behalf, and even make sacrifices. What the "it" is was suggested more than twenty-five hundred years ago, when Heraclitus implored his fellow citizens to "cling to the common," that is, to search out the concerns that represent what our collective identity is about and seek to use them, take care of them, improve and pass them on.

Politicalness comes to us as a birthright, as an inheritance, and hence it has a historical quality without being merely historical. A birthright is defined by the historical moments when collective identity is collectively established or reconstituted. For Americans, these moments include the seventeenth-century beginnings in New England; the revolutionary founding and the redefinition of it signified by the ratification of the Constitution; the Civil War, with its vision of a nationalized society and its inconclusive attempt to radicalize republicanism; and two world wars that have annexed collective identity to the dream of world hegemony and have reconstituted the moments represented by the New Deal and the civil rights movement of the sixties so as to make them functional elements in a more broadly grounded system of state power.

Historical things "are"; they have spatial and temporal attributes that can be described. But, as elements of a birthright, they have to be interpreted. Interpretation is not historical description but a theoretical activity concerned with reflection upon the meaning of past experience and of possible experiences. Because birthrights need interpretation, they are contestable; and because contestable, there is no absolute finality to the interpretation. Birthrights are transmitted, and because of that their meaning will have to be reconsidered amidst different circumstances. We inherit from our fathers, but we are not our fathers. Thus, the Constitution is part of our inheritance. Its formation and contents can be described historically, but the interpretation of its origins and its contents have been highly contestable subjects and remain so. No interpretation enjoys undisputed hegemony.

Now, one reason for the contestability of historical things, whether located in the more remote past or the more immediate present, is their ambiguousness. Human actors intervene to enact a law or promote a policy, but they are never able to circumscribe its consequences, many of which prove to be unwanted. Or the intervention itself embodies contradictory motives, such as when a law reflects the aims of those who hope to prevent the law from achieving the ends of its proponents and so attach a rider to it. Most, if not all, defining historical moments are full of ambiguities. Our Constitution, for example, proclaims liberties and inhibits democracy. Every war since the Mexican War has its ambiguities, although this is not to say that some wars are not less ambiguous than others: World War II, for example, was less ambiguous than World War I—and World War III may be totally unambiguous.

Our birthright is composed of these ambiguous historical moments, and so its political meaning is rarely obvious. If we are to deal with the ambiguities of our birthright, we need an interpretative mode of understanding that is able to reconnect past and present experience, and we need to think in different terms about what it means to be political. We can, however, share in the symbols that embody the experience of the past. This calls for a citizen who can become an interpreting being, one who can interpret the present experience of the collectivity, reconnect it to past symbols, and carry it forward.

This conception of the citizen differs from the conception made familiar by contemporary liberal and conservative thinkers and their neovariants. The latter conception tends to be two-dimensional. The individual is usually pictured as responding to the world as if in a situation of choice in which he or she will decide according to whether a choice will advance or reduce, protect or threaten the interests of the chooser. The temporal dimensions of choice are typically reduced to two, the present and the future. In this context, recall President Reagan's famous query to the voters, "Ask yourself, are you better off now than four years ago?" Thus, the citizen was asked to think about the past as a thin slice of time, four years, to reduce its political meaning to economic terms, and then to assess it in personal rather than communal or collective terms. It was not a request for an interpretation of the meaning of four years of the Reagan regime, but for a calculation of personal gains. It was a question that tacitly rejected as nonsensical the possibility that "I" could be better off, but that "we" were not.

The reason that the president could successfully address this appeal to the voters is that social contract thinking has become so ingrained as to seem to be a natural part of the social world. There are two crucial assumptions made by social contract theory which present a particularly sharp contrast to the notion of a birthright. One is that the contracting individuals are equal because they have no prior history, the other that the contract represents a beginning in which society starts afresh like the beginning of a new footrace.

Each of these assumptions is deeply antihistorical. Individuals could be considered equal, that is, uniform in some important respects, only if they had no autobiographies with different backgrounds and experiences; that is, if they had no personal histories. Obvious as this may seem, the contract theorist has to deny it, at least for the moment prior to the act of consent, otherwise no one would agree even to equal terms if they knew that others would be carrying forward previous advantages and hence could perpetuate or even increase their advantages. Thus, the contract theorist has to posit a memoryless person, without a birthright, and so equal to all others.

In the seventeenth and eighteenth centuries, the memoryless person was said to exist in a state of nature where no social, political, or economic distinctions existed. In our own day, the notion has been perpetuated most ingeniously by John Rawls in his conception of a "veil of ignorance." Rawls asks us to imagine an apolitical condition in which individuals who know nothing specific about their personal identities choose certain conditions that they would accept precisely because they do not know who they are or what advantages or disadvantages they enjoy. They are forced by the logic of this situation to choose conditions that will be fairest to all. The same lack of historicality surrounds the society that results from the Rawlsian contract. It begins with no past, no legacy of deeds or misdeeds, nothing to remember. The contract depends upon collective amnesia.

In suggesting this, I do not mean to devalue the idea of equality but to claim that its present chimerical status, where it seems impossible to achieve yet impossible to abandon, is due in no small measure to the spell cast by contract thinking. We tend to assume that equality represents a condition we are trying to recapture, that once we were equal, as in the moment before the contract, and so the task is to eliminate barriers, such as segregation or sex discrimination. When this is done, equality is restored because equality has come to be identified with equal opportunity. But equal opportunity merely restarts the cycle of competition in the race, and races are designed to produce a single winner. Then it becomes obvious that social competition cannot be compared to a footrace between trained athletes; that the race for education, jobs, income, and status is rarely between equals, but between those with greater advantages and those with greater disadvantages. The end result is that the quest for equality becomes an exercise in guilt which is typified in Rawls's solution. Rawls argues that inequalities can be advantageous if they spur economic activity that improves everyone's situation, which, by definition, would include that of "the least advantaged." But this is an argument for improving the lot of those who are unequal. It does not follow that in doing so inequality is reduced, much less eliminated.

In reality, the issue may be a different one: what kind of collectivity is it that approaches its central value of justice by making the lot of the disadvantaged the test? The answer is that necessarily such a society will have to commit itself mainly to developing the economy because only in that way will the lot of the disadvantaged be improved. As a consequence, the elites will be formed in response to that need, and the structure of society will be shaped toward economic ends. The answer presupposes a polity that is, in reality, a political economy rather than a democracy. I shall return to this point.

I want now to set over against the social contract's conceptions of membership and collectivity the notion of inheritance as suggested by the Esau story. One reason why Esau may have bargained away his history or inheritance was because in addition to the material benefits—his father's flocks and land—a birthright brought with it some accumulated burdens. He would inherit his father's "name," that is, a family history that would likely have included its share of debts and obligations, responsibilities, quarrels, feuds, and so on. To live in the world for any length of time is to know shame, guilt, dishonor, and compromise.

It is not irrelevant to the notion of inheritance as a burden that the Old Testament described Esau as a hunter, which signified someone who prefers to travel unencumbered and who is disinclined to settle down. His brother Jacob, in contrast, was characterized as "a quiet man, dwelling in his tents" (25:27). The Old Testament clearly aimed to depict opposing types. It noted that before their birth, "the children struggled together within" their mother's womb (25:22). Their mother, Rebekah, was told:

Two nations in your womb,
and two peoples, born of you
shall be divided;
the one shall be stronger than
the other,
the elder shall serve the younger. (25:23)

Even when they were being born, Jacob was said to have grabbed hold of Esau's heel (25:26). In their encounters, it was Jacob who always won by virtue of some stratagem. Thus, as their father, Isaac, lay dying, Jacob and his mother, Rebekah, conspired to deceive Isaac into believing that Jacob was Esau. As a result, the dying father gave his precious blessing to the wrong son.

Our natural response is to say, "Foolish father!" But the truth is that all fathers are foolish and all birthrights are a mixture of good and evil, justice and injustice. When Esau learns that Jacob has also tricked him of his blessing, he demands that Isaac give him another. Isaac complies but, under the rules, he cannot retract the first and superior blessing given to Jacob. So he gives Esau another but inferior blessing, with the predictable result that Esau is resentful and threatens to kill Jacob, who then flees. Thus, the birthright sows seeds of conflict, and the effort to mitigate the effects creates further conflicts.

An inheritance, then, is a mixed blessing from foolish fathers. And, lest we forget the scheming Rebekah, from foolish mothers as well. The same is true of our birthright. The Founding Fathers left us a mixed blessing, a Constitution that showed how power might be organized without leading to arbitrary authority, but also a document that was silent about women and accepted the institution of slavery. What is true of the Constitution is also true of the legacy of later centuries of American history. There is unparalleled economic opportunity and social mobility, but there are numerous blots and stains: the treatment of the Indians, the aggression against Mexico, the cruel war between the states, and, beginning in 1898, the imperialist expansion of American power abroad, and, not least, the use of the atomic bomb.

When set over against this ambiguous legacy, the function of social contract thinking becomes clear: to relieve individuals and society of the burden of the past by erasing the ambiguities. This function assumes practical importance because contractualism is not solely an academic philosophy. It is part of American political mythology, of the collective beliefs that define our identity and help shape our political attitudes and opinions.

Parenthetically, while myth is a feature of so-called advanced societies—which might for the present purposes be defined as societies in which science and rationality become identified and their promotion becomes an object of public policies—there is a difference between the status of myth in such societies and its status in premodern and primitive societies. In an advanced society, the study of history is highly sophisticated, and as a consequence myth and historical consciousness coexist uneasily; while in premodern societies, especially primitive ones, the historical consciousness is less evident.[1]

This point has a practical bearing. President Reagan was rightly described as a president who appealed to "traditional values" and to the "nation's past." However, if those appeals are governed by the dehistoricizing tendencies of contract theory, as I believe they are, his appeals were not to history even when they appeared to make reference to it. Rather, history returned as myth because the critical relation between myth and history dropped out.

Returning now to the main theme, anthropologists tell us that myth is kept alive by rituals. Accordingly, we should expect our political rituals to perpetuate the myth of contractualism.

One of our firmest rituals is the inauguration of a president. In his second inaugural address, President Reagan gave expression to the myth and so preserved it: "Four years ago I spoke to you of a new beginning, and we have accomplished that. But in another sense, our new beginning is a continuation of that created two centuries ago, when, for the first time in history, government, the people said, was not our master. It is our servant; its only power that which we, the people allow it to have."

Reagan's formulation repeated the mythic formula of contract that there is not only a political beginning but, in principle, there can be any number of new beginnings. The basic myth that ties the beginnings together is that "the people" was the dominant actor in the mythic drama: like an Old Testament god, the people spoke and said, "Let government be servant and its powers limited." Note, however, that the myth was also utilized to delegitimate as well as legitimate. The president also spoke disparagingly of recent efforts to employ governmental power to correct perceived social ills and wrongs: "That system [presumably the original Constitution] has never failed us. But for a time we failed the system. We asked things of government that government was not equipped to give. We yielded authority to the national government that properly belonged to states or to local governments or to the people themselves."

Thus, a new beginning can, like a form of magic, absolve us of past wrongs and put us in a saving relationship to "the system," which, like some patient father-god, will welcome back the prodigals. By restoring the original contract we are washed clean and made innocent once more. Moreover, we are all, potentially, made equal again: blacks, Chicanos, Puerto Ricans, Jews, northern WASPs, and Southern gentlefolk can each and all accept the sacrament: "Let us resolve that we, the people, will build an American opportunity society in which all of us—white and black, rich and poor, young and old—will go forward together, arm in arm."

The sacrament of innocence is absolution from the foolishness of our fathers and mothers. It soothes us with the knowledge that we were not there when blacks were treated as a species of property; when Indians were massacred and deprived of their ancestral lands; when suffragists were attacked and humiliated; when the early strikes of workers were broken by the combined force of government and business corporations; when the liberal government of FDR refused to admit refugees from Hitler's Germany; or when the Bomb was dropped, not once but twice. As Reagan remarked in the inaugural address, "We, the present-day Americans, are not given to looking backwards. In this blessed land, there is always a better tomorrow."

Against this conception we might set the words of Richard Hooker, an English theologian of four centuries ago: "Wherefore as any man's deed past is good as long as he himself continueth; so the act of a public society of men done five hundred years sithence standeth as theirs who presently are of the same societies, because corporations are immortal; we were then alive in our predecessors, they in their successors do live still." [2]

Clearly, by Hooker's understanding, and that of the birthright idea, we can never renounce our past without rendering the idea of a political community incoherent. The reason why we cannot has to do with the power that is aggregated by a political community. A political community exercises power in the world and against it. When we accept our birthright, we accept what has been done in our name.

Interestingly, President Reagan also alluded to the idea of a birthright: "We will not rest until every American enjoys the fullness of freedom, dignity and opportunity as our birthright. It is our birthright as citizens of this great republic." At the center of the president's conception of birthright was the fundamental notion of contract theory, the idea of freedom: "By 1980 we knew it was time to renew our faith, to strive with all our strength toward the ultimate in individual freedom consistent with an orderly society. We believed then and now there are no limits to growth and human progress when men and women are free to follow their dreams. . . . The heart of our efforts is one idea vindicated by 25 straight months of economic growth: freedom and incentives unleash the drive and entrepreneurial genius that are the core of human progress."

Freedom was thus conceived in essentially economic and material terms: it was not Esau's birthright that was at stake for the president but Esau's contract with Jacob for disposal of his birthright. For Reagan nowhere in his speech suggested that our birthright includes our right to participate, our right to be free from political surveillance, our concern to protect urban habitats and natural environments—in short, what was omitted was our birthright as political beings. Perhaps the most striking example of the reduction of our birthright to a bowl of pottage occurred in the use that President Reagan made of Lincoln's Emancipation Proclamation for freeing the slaves: "The time has come for a new American Emancipation, a great national drive to tear down economic barriers and liberate the spirit in the most depressed areas of the country."

Reagan's image of "the opportunity society" symbolizes a profound transformation in collective identity that has been accelerated during the years since World War II. We have virtually ceased to think of ourselves as a political people. Our politicalness is interjected only as a convenient contrast with the Soviet Union. Then, suddenly, we are a "democracy." Democracy is not invoked when the discussion is about enforcing desegregation statutes, intruding religion into the schools, or preventing discrimination excepting reverse discrimination. On most occasions, the Reagan administration identified democracy with a threat to orderly and efficient decision-making or to rational cost-benefit analysis. There is no evidence that the Bush administration will follow a different understanding.

The silence about politicalness and the cynicism about democracy are related. Politicalness is at odds with the conditions required by the form of polity which has come into being, but that form lacks legitimation, and so the democratic principle of "we the people" is shamelessly exploited to provide it. The new polity can be christened "the political economy." The name stands for an order in which the limits of politics are set by the needs of a corporate-dominated economy and of a state organization that works in intimate collaboration with corporate leadership.

In the theory of the political economy, society is absorbed into "the economy"; and instead of economic relationships being viewed as embedded in a complex of social and political relationships, they are treated as though they constituted a distinct system that is at once autonomous, or nearly so, as well as constitutive or defining of all other types of relationships. The primacy of economic relationships does not operate solely as an explanatory device but as a first principle of a comprehensive scheme of social hermeneutics. Economic relationships constitute an interpretative category of virtually universal applicability. It is used to understand personal life and public life, to make judgments about them, and to define the nature of their problems. It supplies the categories of analysis and decision by which public policies are formulated, and it is applied to cultural domains such as education, the arts, and scientific research. It is, we might say, a conception striving for totalization.

To the political economy a genuinely democratic politics appears as destabilizing. This is because those who govern fear that democratic institutions, such as elections, a free press, popular culture, and public education can become the means to mobilize the poor, the less well-educated, the working classes, and aggrieved ethnic groups and to use them to bring demands for a revision of social priorities and a redistribution of values. This would kindle inflationary pressures and divert social resources to nonproductive uses, such as health care, low-cost housing, and toxic waste disposal. Accordingly, the ruling elites have to discourage the mobilization of poorer groups by asserting that a rational investment policy requires different priorities. So, for example, during the Reagan years Pentagon officials mostly opposed congressional attempts to trim the defense budget, insisting upon the priority of defense over so-called social spending.

The depoliticalization of the poor and the working classes was most clearly demonstrated in the anti-inflation strategy adopted by the state. Virtually every commentator agrees that the rate of inflation was successfully lowered at the expense of employment, which is to say, at the expense primarily, although not solely, of the working classes and minorities. The significance of this choice goes beyond the important matters of jobs and standards of living to the vital question of whether an unemployed person has not been deprived in some crucial sense of membership. For if the economy is the crucial sector of a political economy, it means that employment is, so to speak, a mark of citizenship in the important sense of being involved in productive activity. Such activity is widely believed to be the most important function in society and, ultimately, the foundation of American power and security. Economic production, we might say, is to the political economy as political citizenship was to Aristotle, namely the mark of whether one was inside or outside the polity.

It is clear that in today's high-tech society there is a substantial number of persons, mostly minorities, who are superfluous: they are unemployed and have practically no foreseeable prospect of becoming employed, except perhaps temporarily, and many are trapped in a cycle of unemployment that comprehends two and sometimes three generations. In a rapidly changing economy that replaces the skills of human operatives with machines in accordance with the relentless pace of technological innovation, superfluous members are constantly being created. If by chance some are returned to the work force in a period of economic upturn, this does little to reduce their anxieties about the future. Everyone knows that business cycles return. The consequence is to produce noncitizens who will be most reluctant to take political risks of the kind required by politicalness.

Similarly, when in the name of "the economy" public spending on social programs is cut, this means more than the loss of substantial economic benefits. It reduces the power of individuals. Health care, education, aid for dependent children, job training—each of these holds out hope to an individual that she/he can increase their power to cope with the world. When social programs are reduced, then restored somewhat, only to be reduced again, tremendous power is lodged in the hands of the state, or of those who operate it. The economy becomes a means of denying power to some and denaturalizing them, as it were, rendering them wary of political involvements.

Underlying these programs, which combine pacification with demoralization and depoliticalization of the lower classes, is a fear of Esau. We should recall the "blessing" that Isaac finally gave to the frustrated and enraged Esau, who had been doubly cheated:

By your sword you shall live,
and you shall serve your brother;
but when you break loose
you shall break his yoke from
your neck. (Gen. 27:40)

The advent of the political economy does not signal the disappearance of the state, despite the frequent and well-subsidized rhetoric extolling the free market and attacking government regulation. Under the regime of political economy, the state is actually strengthened. Lest we forget, the military has for over three thousand years been a key element in political power and a crucial one in the apparatus of the modern state. The astronomical rise in defense budgets and the revival of an interventionist foreign policy signify an increase in the power of the state. The same can be said of the increasing control over information being exercised by the state.

The basic reason why the Reagan administration was concerned to mystify the presence of the state and to denigrate its value is obvious: they wanted to discredit the state as an instrument of popular needs without substantially weakening it. It should never be forgotten that the state is not necessarily weakened by reducing social welfare programs, but that it is often strengthened under the guise of introducing more efficient management practices.

For those who care about creating a democratic political life, a strong state must be rejected because the idea of a democratic state is a contradiction in terms. By its very nature the state must proceed mainly by bureaucratic means; it must concentrate power at the center; it must promote elitism or government by the few; it must elevate the esoteric knowledge of experts over the experience of ordinary citizens; and it must prefer order and stability to experiment and spontaneity. The result of state-centeredness is a politics in which at one extreme are the experts struggling to be scientific and rational while at the other is a politics of mass irrationality, of manipulated images, controlled information, single-issue fanaticism, and pervasive fear.

A democratic vision means a genuine alternative. It means the development of a politics that cannot be co-opted, which is precisely what has happened to the original democratic dream of basing democracy upon voting, elections, and popular political parties. These forms, as we know from the experience of this century, can be taken over by corporate money and manipulated by the mass media. Democracy needs a non–cooptable politics, that is, a politics that renders useless the forms of power developed by the modern state and business corporation. This means different actors, different scales of power, and different criteria of success.

First, democracy means participation, but participation is not primarily about "taking part," as in elections or officeholding. It means originating or initiating cooperative action with others. This form of action is taking place throughout the society in response to felt needs, from health care to schools, from utility rates to housing for the poor, from nuclear energy to nuclear weapons, from toxic waste disposal to homesteading in urban areas. One of the most important aspects of these developments is that political experience is being made accessible, experience that compels individuals to deal with the complexity of interests and the conflicting claims that have hitherto been reserved to politicians and bureaucrats. In this way the political can become incorporated in the everyday lives of countless people.

Nine / Democracy and the Welfare State: The Political and Theoretical Connections between Staatsräson and Wohlfahrtsstaatsräson

In this chapter I sketch a theory of state power. I try to show how the power of the state has drawn from two sources, each of which claims a democratic genealogy. One is Reason of State (*Staatsräson*), the other is "welfare." Although I make several references to the history of European states and to recent socialist debates about the welfare state, the chapter is directed mainly at the American context.

Misreadings

Although it is doubtless true, if uninteresting, to say that there are many different ways of understanding the problems that the welfare state presents to democracy, it is also true, and more interesting, to suggest that there are also some ways of misunderstanding it. One such misreading interprets the welfare state as the teleological completion of liberalism. By administering programs that provide for the basic needs of individuals and families, the state allegedly helps to establish the material foundations for the exercise of citizenship, which liberalism, in its zeal for procedural and political rights, has historically neglected.

Another, more misleading reading treats the welfare activities of the state independently of other state interests. Thus, much of the contemporary controversy about the welfare state, particularly in the United States, proceeds as though the intense preoccupation with military power, which has dominated American politics and claimed a substantial percentage of social resources for more than two decades, is not related to the same state that administers social services. As Thucydides reminds us, the imperial state and its needs for legitimation raise questions about an "elective" affinity between democracy and empire that were raised by the first democracy to found an empire and, at the same time, to support its citizens by a comparatively elaborate system of public allowances and subsidies. In our own century, Max Weber insisted that social welfare did not represent a special category of state functions but was shaped by the fundamental purpose of promoting state power: "In the final analysis, in spite of all 'social welfare policies,' the whole course of the state's inner political functions of justice and administration is repeatedly and unavoidably regulated by the objective pragmatism of reasons of state. The state's absolute end is to safeguard (or to change) the external and internal distribution of power."[1] In the matter of the relationship between state power and welfare, Ronald Reagan's secretary of defense, Caspar Weinberger, was being a better guide than many of his critics when he remarked that "strong defense is the best social welfare program."

Finally, there is the misunderstanding produced by modern socialist theories. There is no question, of course, about the sincerity of the democratic convictions of most Western socialists. The difficulty is, in part, that many socialists have come to identify socialism with the welfare state, thus incorporating socialism into the problem posed for democracy by the welfare state. The development that saw socialism evolve toward a statist mentality was facilitated by the theoretical failure of socialist theorists to decide whether socialism is, so to speak, a subcategory of democracy or democracy a subcategory of socialism. The difference would be crucial, for it would involve either the conditioning of socialism so as to realize the possibilities of democracy or the reverse: democracy would be subordinated to the requirements of socialism, specifically those of a socialist economy.

But there is another part to the difficulty. It has to do with the historical inadequacy both of the socialist understanding of the political and of the socialist political imagination. Historically, socialist theory arose as a critical response to capitalism understood primarily as a system of economic power rather than as an economic formation that evolved into a system of power that penetrated and conditioned the political institutions emerging from the English civil wars of the seventeenth century and the American and French revolutions of the eighteenth century. The political transformation of capitalism was captured in Marx's notation that "civil society is political economy." Unfortunately, as is well known, Marx sketched but never developed a systematic theory of the state, and hence the idea of a political economy remained overdetermined economically and underdescribed politically. Accordingly, the socialist critique remained importantly mired in a historical moment in the first half of the twentieth century when the systemic character of capitalism qua economy was first becoming apparent and when it seemed as though the basic wrong of capitalism was an incapacity to distribute fairly from the cornucopia it was developing.

Twentieth-century socialist theorists then compounded the difficulty created by Marx. In setting about to supply socialism with a theory of the state, they assumed that the state was the equivalent of the political; if the role of the state in assuring the conditions for the reproduction of capitalism were correctly described, then the meaning of the political, for all practical purposes, was exhausted. With a theory of the capitalist state as the essence of their political theory, yet reluctant to face the implications of the increasingly antidemocratic character of the capitalist state and of the political practices that legitimated it, socialists of the post–World War II years nonetheless assumed it to be axiomatic that socialism was the natural twentieth-century heir of democracy. In their view, there was no democracy other than "social democracy" or "democratic socialism." However, after four decades of socialist theorizing and socialist governments it is not easy to identify what is uniquely socialist in the socialist idea of *social* democracy or what is democratic in its idea of democratic socialism. One can say that socialism has helped to affix welfare policies as a strong feature of the capitalist state, and that when socialists have served as the parties of government in West Germany, France, Italy, and Spain, among their main achievements have been the modernization and increased efficiency of their respective state apparatuses.[2] With its economic and statist vision, socialism has established itself as a variant rather than an alternative to the political formation, to be described shortly, created by twentieth-century capitalism. Unfortunately, by identifying itself as the residuary legatee of democracy, socialism helps to postpone a confrontation between democracy and the welfare state.

The claim that welfare should be considered in the context of state power forms the premise of my inquiry. My contention is that a principal task of democratic theory in America today is to establish a democratic critique of the welfare state. For that purpose I shall have to be content to postulate an abbreviated conception of democracy. Democracy involves more than participation in political processes: it is a way of constituting power. Democracy is committed to the claim that experience with, and access to, power is essential to the development of the capacities of ordinary persons because power is crucial to human dignity and realization. Power is not merely something to be shared, but something to be used collaboratively in order to initiate, to invent, to bring about. A democratic critique of the welfare state is a critique of a political arrangement that denies this conception of democracy as political action in the most fundamental sense of using power to constitute a collaborative world. A democratic critique means thinking about welfare in essentially political terms. It asks, what are the political implications of humanitarianism, of classifying citizens as needy and of making them needful objects of state power? A political analysis of welfare requires that we revise our conception of the state to take account of certain historical developments of capitalism of which welfare policies are the expression.

What is the appropriate name for this formation? The name should not be chosen because it serves some system of typologies such as the ancients were fond of. The ancient classifications of political constitutions, Aristotle excepted, resembled a Procrustean bed that tolerated little evolution or change in the archetypal forms of kingship, aristocracy, and democracy, save for a radical transformation of each into its alleged opposites of tyranny, oligarchy, and ochlocracy or anarchy. Postmodern polities have their theoretical origins in Hobbes, who demolished the theoretical basis of the ancient typology while formulating the motor principle of postmodern politics, "a perpetual and restless desire of Power after power that ceaseth only in Death." Postmodern polities are continuously changing so that a name can only hope to capture temporarily certain predominant features and to intimate a general political direction.

New Name, New Polity

Following Marx, we might call the new formation "the political economy of capitalism," a formulation that asserts the primacy of a specific type of economic organization and strongly implies that the "political" comprehends the public institutions and legal system whose function is to promote and protect the interests of the social groups that own and control the means of production. A formulation of this sort immediately encounters the criticism, both of revisionist Marxists and of anti-Marxists, that it gives insufficient emphasis to the positive role of the state. I want to suggest, however, that in naming the new power formation it is important to retain Marx's emphasis upon the primacy of economic organization and its class character, but at the same time to recognize that "the economy" represents the ontological principle of modernizing ideologies, not a neutral construct for describing the organization of production and distribution of material goods. The ideology of "the economy" and the positive role of the state in advanced capitalist societies share a common tendency toward the depoliticalization of society; or, stated more sharply, both are not only opposed to the redemocratization of society, they are committed to reshaping the attenuated remains of democratic practices to accord with the needs of a corporate vision of politics.

The name "Economic Polity" best captures the ontological and ideological assumption of an underlying reality to which ideally the life of society should be attuned and of a conception of power that is shared by two sectors, the public and the private, which ideally ought to coexist in a nonadversarial relationship. The Economic Polity, unlike the ideal polities of Plato and Aristotle, is positively committed to a conception of an unlimited expansion of power. It is the creature of late modern forms of power made available by the practical application of scientific knowledge. Late modern power is unique. In principle it is endlessly reproducible and is increasingly independent of civic virtue. Given a few oil wells, a few investors, a few technicians, it is possible to construct a nuclear device or finance revolution. The ideology of the Economic Polity, like its sources of power, envisions endless expansion but its imperialism tends to be nonterritorial, degrounded, projecting its influence throughout the world, while militarizing the emptiness of space.

The ideology of the Economic Polity was expounded by Ronald Reagan in a statement of 14 March 1986, in which he set out the American commitment to "a global foreign policy." According to the president, the aim of the policy was to create "a free, open, and expanding market-oriented global economy." Democracy, which ordinarily is an object of derision among the Economic Politicians because of its association with a politics of modest scale, was also to be promoted, although it, too, would be ex/distended to fit the imperial design of a "global foreign policy" and a "global economy." The world, the president alleged, was in the throes of a "democratic revolution," and American resources should be sent to the democratic forces struggling in Afghanistan, Cambodia, El Salvador, and Nicaragua. The ultimate enemy was "Soviet adventurism," which seeks "to destabilize and overthrow vulnerable governments on nearly every continent." The president summarized the essence of the Economic Polity when he declared that the United States had two main tools in its struggles against the USSR, "military strength and the vitality of our economy."

There was also a depoliticalizing message in the president's vision. American support for "resistant forces fighting against Communist tyranny" could succeed only if accompanied by a suspension of democratic politics in the United States. "American interests," he explained, "will be served best if we can keep the details of our help—in particular, how it is provided—out of view." As president he needed to be able to grant support "without publicity." "To hobble ourselves" by ordinary procedures "makes it harder to shape events while problems are still manageable." Presumably the reference to "manageable" meant a situation where the actual fighting could still be left to indigenous forces. For, as the president warned, if clandestine politics were not permitted at home, "it means we are certain to face starker choices down the road." Thus, the global policy and the global market seem to mean exporting democratic revolution abroad and importing counterrevolution at home.

The president's appeal to forgo the normal public scrutiny of executive actions belongs squarely in the time-honored, if constitutionally suspect, tradition of Reason of State. The contemporary formulation contains elements that were unknown or alien when Guicciardini first used the term in the early sixteenth century: capitalism, free market, global economy, and democracy. What changes did the doctrine of Reason of State undergo that made this accommodation possible? In particular, how did it come about theoretically that "democratic" and "welfare" elements were incorporated into a notion closely identified with absolutism?

The Modernity of the Modern State: The Political Uses of Marginality

During the last half of the nineteenth century, the structure of capitalism changed from an economy of small-scale producers to one dominated by oligopolies of large corporations. This was paralleled by the establishment of governmental bureaucracies, especially of agencies specializing in the regulation and encouragement of business activities, thus signaling the consociation of the political and the economic. It is as an element in this complicated state formation that welfarism emerges.

Welfare is a graft upon the modern state; it is not constitutive of it. Rather, the modern state is constitutive of welfare, setting its terms and assimilating it to certain traditional needs of state action. Accordingly, to think about the welfare state we must first think about the political nature of the modern state.

The modern state, according to Weber, cannot be characterized by its ends, for these are inconstant; it can only be distinguished by its means, which are "physical force." Welfare, then, has to be considered as a function within a state structure that is, in Weber's words, "a relation of men dominating men, a relation supported by means of legitimate, i.e. considered to be legitimate, violence."[3] Weber's formulation may seem excessively stark, but starkness is not, I think, inappropriate when we recall that the evolution of the modern state is a story of an internal form of imperialism that we call centralization of power and of the steady destruction of local power and traditional authorities that we call modernization.[4] The striking connection that Weber posited between the systematic practice of violence, internal and external, and the continuing need for legitimation accurately reflected the peculiar exaggeration of power, which is what is modern about the modern state.

The exaggeration of power is a function both of centralization and of the facileness imparted to power by late modern technologies. Under these conditions, however, the populations deposited by rapid and unceasing social change can only achieve tentative integration. Centralized power, perfected technologies of coercion, disintegrated populations that express their incoherence in a search for lost roots of identity, and the consociation of economy and polity—these are the essential conditions for understanding the meaning of the welfare state and for understanding it politically rather than socially.

A social, or conventional interpretation sees the welfare state as conditioned by the question of human needs or, more precisely, by the needs of the working classes, the poor, the unemployed, the disabled, the handicapped, and, increasingly, women.[5] It does not ask about the political meaning of the choice of these particular categories, which is largely the result of administrative determinations and is importantly arbitrary in nature. For there are no objective criteria by which to settle questions such as, what shall be the period during which unemployed workers or unmarried mothers are eligible for assistance? To be sure, the social interpretation of the welfare state has sensed that there are undesirable consequences of welfare, but the general temptation has been to consider these as side effects. Typically it has meant calling attention to the dependency that welfare programs allegedly create. Dependency is conventionally understood in apolitical terms, as analogous, for example, to drug addiction: welfare recipients become hooked and, like addicts, are unable to function autonomously. But it may be that to describe the recipients as dependent on programs is simply an alternative description of an exploitable relationship to state power.

That relationship is rich in possibilities for state power and its symbolization. Some members of a marginal population (e.g., blacks) may be recruited into the police or military forces, where they are not only disciplined into becoming reliable instruments of social control but their presence is publicized so that they appear as representatives of pluralist democracy whose service validates state power. The economic exploitation of marginalized populations is familiar from Marx's classic account of the role of an industrial reserve army in depressing wages and weakening working-class solidarity. With the emergence of the Economic Polity, however, exploitation is as much political as economic in its objectives. If marginal populations are to be available when the rapidly changing demands of a high-tech economy require them to enter into the commodity relationships of the market, they must first be neutralized politically.[6] Upon beginning his second term, President Reagan most revealingly referred to "the spider's web of dependency," which he claimed had been created by past welfare policies.[7] In fact, the poor are sustained by more than welfare programs. They have frequently developed a defensive culture that is real and political. It includes ties of kinship, neighborhood gangs, underground economies, the political organizations developed by minority politicians, and myriad other relationships from which the poor derive protection and support. Consequently, when the president called for a program to "break the welfare culture," the objective was not simply to free the welfare dependent from the web of governmental power, so that he or she could then be inserted into the disciplinary web of the market, but to break the political culture, and hence the power, of the poor.

The way this works is illustrated by the decision of the Reagan administration to reduce public spending for the revitalization of the older industrial cities and, instead, to initiate a system of voucher payments designed to encourage inner-city inhabitants to search for jobs elsewhere. The vouchers could be used to pay rent anywhere in the United States, thus attracting the poor away from the larger cities, where welfare benefits tend to be higher. At the same time, the Reagan administration sought to reduce "incentives," which of course operate more powerfully upon the powerless, for the poor to remain in their ghettos. Federal housing construction for the inner-city poor has ceased, funds for job programs in the cities have been reduced, and public housing is being sold to private buyers. The importance of place to the political culture of the poor was negatively acknowledged by one of the academic promoters of the urban policy of designed neglect when he noted that previous welfare policies had "encouraged the neediest groups . . . to remain isolated in racially segregated areas."

However, the new policies would "disperse racial concentration by increasing the choices available to racial minorities," yet they "would not focus on the needs of particular cities at all."[8]

In this context, antiwelfare rhetoric actually promotes the goals of state power while appearing to be antistatist. It pounces on incidents of welfare fraud and demagogically incites the taxpayer to indignation at the misuse of his or her taxes. It does this by evoking the contemporary form of folk memory. It appeals to the cinematic myth of the frontier town where, according to the well-worn scenario, the virtuous citizenry is being robbed by the few who prefer a parasitic life to one of hard work. By staging welfare as a confrontation between parasitism and the work ethic, the state is allowed to recede momentarily into the background, thus spotlighting a symbolic moment when the virtuous confront the shiftless, when simple justice demands vigilante action by the resentful citizens. Because in a democracy the state is supposed to be the agent of the citizens, the state intervenes and enforces the law, but it is additionally empowered because it inherits the aura of legitimated arbitrariness created by the frontier scenario. The state is, therefore, allowed to deal arbitrarily with all welfare recipients, not by lynching them but by redefining the conditions and categories of their existence.

A case in point is the periodic review of the 2.6 million people on social security disability rolls. The strategy, which was introduced by the Reagan administration, is intended to determine whether recipients are eligible for benefits. Under procedures that the chief administrator admitted had been "very insensitive" to the rights of recipients, 12 million cases were reviewed, nearly one-half million were told that they would lose benefits, and of these 291,000 were restored upon appeal. The element crucial to the cause of state power is the protracted uncertainty disguised as procedural fairness. Under the changed rules, persons selected for review are instructed to contact a local social security office; they are then required to supply the names and addresses of doctors and hospitals that treated them in the previous year. If the government agent decides that the evidence is not adequate, he or she can ask for additional evidence or another medical examination. If it is determined that the person is sufficiently improved to be stricken from the rolls, the case is reviewed again. Most persons, according to administrators of the program, can expect to be reviewed every three years.[9]

Although the state may sometimes appear vengeful toward welfare recipients, the very same state can also present itself as solicitous: it will ensure that a "safety net" is extended at the right moment to catch the unfortunates who, "through no fault of their own," fall through the spaces created by an economy that is continuously adjusting to new technologies (take-offs) and reorganizations (takeovers).

The thread of contingency that runs through the previous description—arbitrary classifications, a volatile economy, a safety net that is treated as a generous decision by state authorities rather than a right or a claim against the state by a citizen, and the image of recipients either as victims of social forces beyond their control or as criminals whom society should treat harshly—points to the fundamental political characteristic of welfare: its variability.

The Variability of Welfare and State Power

The notion of variability is meant to capture the crucial historical and political characteristics of these programs in America: they are neither consistently cumulative nor stable; nor, when judged by the welfare standards of most advanced industrial societies, are they notably magnanimous—a point of strategic importance, as we shall see shortly. In brief, the variability of welfare programs means that at any political moment they can be expanded, sharply modified, reversed, even revoked altogether. Variability is the condition that makes possible two complementary phenomena: a certain kind of flexible power and a certain kind of pliable citizen. It should be remembered that power depends not simply on the ability to bring about a desired state of affairs; it also depends upon the receptivity of the object, its willingness to support, obey, or, at least, to acquiesce.

The variability of welfare programs produces a paradox about state power: irrespective of whether a programmatic change produces an increase or a reduction in the welfare functions of the state, state power is increased, not necessarily in a sense measurable by budgets or programs but in terms of shaping a reliable citizenry whose responses can be managed in accordance with the needs of the state as perceived by governing elites. State needs reduce to the political neutralization of those whose marginality is essential to the reproduction of state power. Marginal populations are not extraneous to state power but essential. This is because their status of pariah, as defined by the actions and rhetoric of public officials and politicians and disseminated by the media, represents the legitimation of an extension of state power. Marginality is the symbol of political helplessness, of having fewer substantive rights and protections than those enjoyed by the generality of citizens. It signifies the existence of objects that can be handled in a less restrained way by the agents of the state. Thus, marginality is a means of expanding a particular kind of state power, one less hedged by ordinary rules (due process), one freer to respond in accordance with the "objective situation." The "guest worker" and the "wetback," foreigners who cannot find work in their native country, are the symbol of marginality on the plane of the international political economy, the ideal citizens of the Economic Polity: mobile and vulnerable.

A recent reminder of the way in which marginal groups become the occasion for the expansion of state power was the bombing by Philadelphia authorities of a fortified household occupied by a small group of radicals known as MOVE. The incident was particularly striking because it showed how tenuous is the power of social groups struggling to escape marginality. The complaints against the members of MOVE, all of whom were black, were brought by citizens of a predominantly black neighborhood proud of their homes. The operation—which saw police drop a bomb down the chimney of a house containing women and children while firemen allowed both the bombed home and the adjoining ones to burn out of control—was supervised by a black mayor. The net effect was to edge those segments back toward the marginal status they thought they had escaped and to post a sign that marked an expanded boundary of state power.

Marginality is directly related to the incoherence of populations in the face of a rapidly changing society: incoherence means a lack of cultural and social place and of social support systems that enable individuals to resist or to cushion marginalization. The state has capitalized its power by exploiting what its own evolution has importantly helped to create.[10] The Reagan administration, by its antiwelfare rhetoric and its opposition to social spending, succeeded in marginalizing the recipients of welfare and surrounding them with an atmosphere of uncertainty and danger, alternating between threats of new reduction and promises to preserve the "safety net" of a social minimum. The welfare population and the temporarily unemployed, as well as those who are precariously employed, are kept suspended between hope and despair but not plunged into desperation. Marginalization is, in brief, a way of introducing variability: the marginalized groups become the stuff of a form of state power that, as we shall see, finds itself increasingly deprived of flexibility by its own structure.

The power that accrues to the state because of the helplessness of marginal populations has gone unperceived by Reagan's (and now Bush's) right-wing supporters. They continue to charge that the administration lacks the will to implement its threats. Their lament unintentionally exposes the presence of an instrument of power whose utility depends upon there being no solution to the "welfare problem." This is not to suggest that state officials connive at perpetuating welfare in order to increase their power. Rather, the problem presents itself to them as one in which there is no choice. A radical reduction (or increase) in social programs would eliminate the power that accrues to the state by virtue of the uncertainty of a situation in which the question of cuts always appears to hang in the balance, as in the periodic review of welfare rosters. In reality, the Reagan and Bush administrations have had precisely the kind of Damoclean atmosphere surrounding benefits that favors state power.

That the power generated by uncertainty exists is borne out by the fact that when there have been high levels of unemployment, plant closures, and reductions in unemployment benefits, the workers and the poor have remained passive, even docile. "For benefits oblige," Hobbes remarked, "and obligation is thralldome; and unrequited obligation, perpetual thralldome." Such thralldom, Hobbes concluded, was hateful if it concerned equals, but benefits from an acknowledged superior "enclines to love" because the recipient cannot be "depressed" any further.[11]

The governability of the de/oppressed provides a clue as to the proper starting point for a democratic critique of the welfare state. What is at stake in the shrinkage or increase in welfare programs is not ultimately a dispute over spending or conservative stinginess versus liberal compassion but over the necessary conditions for the employment of instruments of statecraft. Those conditions refer to the particular kind of human *materia* of state power. Welfare recipients signify a distinct category, the virtueless citizen. The virtueless citizen has no a priori claim not to be shaped in accordance with the rational requirements of state power. This lack of a claim is registered in the fact that he or she has no control over the conditions of personal empowerment. Or, more strongly, because these conditions may be taken away or even increased, they are not forms of power at all.

Determinations of medical disability, for example, may disqualify citizens from some of the civic obligations that, according to classic theories of republicanism, were essential to nurturing civic virtue. A citizen who is declared disabled may be exempted from military service, jury duty, or standing trial. There may be rational grounds for such exclusions, but the power to determine them belongs to state officials. According to a recent study, the guiding consideration in setting policies has been "flexibility." What begins as a concern for flexible policies usually ends, however, in proliferation of detailed rules governing eligibility requirements that creates a new instrument at the disposal of the discretionary power of the state.[12]

The perfect contemporary expression of the thralldom of the virtueless citizen is the policy of "workfare" now being actively pursued by several state governments, notably California and New York. These programs make aid conditional upon the recipient's accepting some suitable form of work or entering a job program. The effect is usefully ambiguous from the viewpoint of state power: the citizen is neither completely free of the stigma of welfare nor fully sanctified by work but somewhere in between, without the autonomy that work is supposed to make possible yet without the security of an assured minimum that welfare is supposed to afford. The virtueless citizen is the dangling man.

Welfare and Reason of State

The welfare state, I want to suggest, is *Staatsräson,* or Reason of State, in the age of the Economic Polity. To assert that welfare programs are instrumentalities of statecraft is to locate them in this stylized and distinctive mode of political discourse. [13]

Reason of State is a notion that, historically, has provided the justification for a particular type of extraordinary state action. It claims that whenever the vital interests of the state are threatened, rulers should be allowed great latitude in exercising power, even when they violate the legal and moral restraints that ordinarily limit their actions. A maxim of Machiavelli's is usually cited as illustrative of *ragione dello stato:* "To maintain a state, the prince is often forced to do what is not good." [14]

Despite its Machiavellian associations, Reason of State seems a straightforward notion based upon certain identifiable assumptions. One assumption was that Reason of State was virtually inseparable from war and diplomacy because these were matters characterized by contingency, surprise, secrecy, and extreme danger. A second assumption was that Reason of State was only a problem for *Rechtsstaaten,* for states whose rulers were supposed to be constrained by law, tradition, morality, or religion. For tyrannies and despotisms, the dilemmas of Reason of State were less problematic. A third and closely related assumption was that the vital interests of the state were not necessarily identical with the interests of those who happened to be ruling and that, consequently, *Staatsräson* could not be invoked simply because rulers believed that it was in their interest to exercise exceptional powers or ignore recognized norms.

What seems less self-evident is why reason should have been invoked in matters that seem so contingent and variable. In point of fact, Machiavelli did not use the phrase *ragione dello stato*. Giovanni Botero (1544–1617), whose popular *Ragion di Stato* helped to popularize the phrase, employed it to mean the principles, political and moral, that ought to guide the actions of rulers; not only did Botero make no reference to extraordinary state powers, but he insisted upon the observance of religious and moral norms.[15] Although Botero implied that an exalted plane of politics existed where state actors practiced a higher form of rational action,[16] rationality is not a helpful category for understanding Machiavelli's justification for exceptional actions. This is best shown by analyzing a famous passage from Machiavelli's *Discourses* that is widely regarded as the canonical definition of Reason of State: "When the safety of one's country wholly depends on the decision to be taken, no attention should be paid either to justice or injustice, kindness or cruelty, or to its being praiseworthy or ignominious."[17]

The passage was not intended as a license for princes to violate the law or disregard moral conventions. In fact, it was not even addressed to princes but to the "citizen," who in his role as *consigliere* "has to give advice to his country."[18] The advice is offered for a carefully delimited situation, the most extreme of all possible political moments, when the safety of society turns on a single decision. That the bearer of the advice should be a citizen rather than a prince was a crucial piece of republican symbolism. The citizen represents precisely the various social autonomies (e.g., guilds, social ranks, municipal liberties, family, and property) and value formations (custom, common moral and religious beliefs, and legal protections) that would be threatened and breached by the unimpeded application of power required by Reason of State. And precisely because the ruler occupies a more exalted political plane, he is far more likely to be insensitive to the destructive effects of Reason of State.

Machiavelli was most concerned to isolate Reason of State. Thus, he considers the possibility of a constitutional provision that would regularize such extraordinary decisions, only to reject the idea. A republic that relies on "extraordinary measures," he argued, establishes a bad precedent that "sanctions the usage of dispensing with constitutional methods for a good purpose, and thereby makes it possible, on some plausible pretext, to dispense with them for a bad purpose."[19]

The solicitude for institutional practices that is evident throughout the *Discourses* is also present in *The Prince*. In the latter work, his constant advice to the new prince is to found stable practices so as to assure the perpetuation of his power. It is not too much to say that in Machiavelli's political world of rapacious princes, aggressive republics, and class conflicts there is a paucity of regularized processes or institutions as well as a surplus of variability in politics as princes, popes, and condottieri all exchanged places in bewildering "succession." For Machiavelli, Reason of State belongs to a realm of natural forces represented by conquest and domination. Conquest and domination are considered natural phenomena in a double sense: they are inherent in the structure of the world, and they signify life and death, the two most elemental and inescapable human experiences. It is in this naturalistic context that *Fortunà* is located. *Fortunà* represents a form of power that is variable and changing. She symbolizes a threat to the state that is embedded in the order of the world, not merely an exceptional contingency that calls for discretionary power. Machiavelli likened her power to that of a great natural force, a raging stream, or a natural catastrophe such as a flood, earthquake, or plague.[20] The irruptions of *Fortunà* are difficult to anticipate because she seems to have obscure ends that men cannot fully fathom.

The variability of *Fortunà* dictates the distinctively Machiavellian style of action: artifice, cunning, and a strong element of improvisation. This is because the actor is responding to *necessità*, which operates as a natural force in the political world and leaves the actor with no choice if he wishes to survive. He may make preparations that will diminish the impact when *Fortunà* strikes, but Machiavelli does not attempt, as Hobbes would later, to control nature (*physis*) by conventions (*nomoi*). Only skill invested with an element of cunning, *technē* with *virtù*, can avail the actor. The natural dimension of politics requires naturalistic actors, part lion, part fox.[21]

It turns out, then, that *Reason of State* is a revealing term because it is so maladroit when applied to Machiavelli. The variability of natural powers, whether of *Fortunà* or of warfare, is to be countered not by reason (in a strict sense) but by experience, example, and cunning—qualities that lie close to nature and are typically discounted or subordinated by exponents of (philosophical) reason. What Machiavelli taught was not Reason of State, but statecraft. The term *statecraft* does not appear in English usage until the middle of the seventeenth century, when it was associated with the political consolidation of the nation-state begun by the Tudors in the previous century.[22] Machiavelli's statecraft was one part Machiavellism in the popular sense: a sinister, "crafty" quality needed by state-actors if they were to survive the predatory politics commonly practiced by almost all states. But statecraftiness had to be supplemented by another element, statecraftsmanship, or the notion of a skill based largely upon experience combined with applied technical knowledge (e.g., of warfare). Statecraftsmanship was related to what the ancients had called *technē*, or skilled art. The third element of statecraft was implied in the notion of "craft," which by the sixteenth century meant "force" or "power," a meaning still preserved in the German *Kraft*, or strength. This is the element that finds the actor pitting not only skill and cunning against the natural forces of *Fortunà* and of political enemies but also mobilizing the full force of the state to protect its existence or to expand its power.

The Democratization of Staatsräson

The later development of the modern state brought profound changes in each of these elements and prepared the way for the transition from *Staatsräson* to *Wohlfahrtsstaatsräson,* from Reason of State to Welfare-State Reason. An intimation of these changes can be found in a comment by Henry Parker, a spokesman for parliamentary power during the early years of the English civil war. It locates Reason of State in the commonplace distinction between the preservation of the state and its prosperity: "Law secures one subject from another . . . but reason of state goes beyond all particular forms and pacts, and looks rather to the being than well-being of a state."

Parker then adds a further comment that truly exalts Reason of State by transforming it from a naturalistic to a rationalistic subject: "Reason of state is something more sublime and imperial than law . . . when war has silenced law . . . policy is . . . the only true law." [23]

By elevating Reason of State to a "sublime" status above the law and then treating it not as a violation of law but as its substitute, Parker made it possible not only to link Reason of State with rationality but to internalize it, that is, to cease treating Reason of State as preoccupied with external affairs. The crucial word in Parker's formulation was *policy,* a notion that already enjoyed wide usage in the seventeenth century. For my purposes, the only element in its complex etymology that we need to note is that policy is originally derived from the Greek *polis* and that the *polis* signified the exact opposite of bestial and violent nature: it was the locus of reason and culture. Parker's suggestion that "policy" be extended to the anti-polis, antipolitical phenomena of war, invasion, and insurrection signaled an expansion of political reason. Although domination and survival represent themes that are as old as recorded politics, the ideas of rational domination and survival do not. In Thucydides' Melian dialogue, for example, the Athenians do not appeal to reason to persuade the Melians to submit to Athenian might. Instead, they describe their domination as a natural fact, and they try to persuade the Melians to accept it as such and to respond naturally by saving themselves. Rational domination is primarily a seventeenth-century notion stimulated by the Baconian-Cartesian dream of the domination of nature by scientific reasoning.

In the person of Hobbes, the Bacon-Descartes vision was translated into a theory of rational domination of political nature through a science of politics based on the idea of man as matter-in-motion and hence subject to physical laws. Hobbes's famous "state of nature" is simply the idea of *Staatsräson* universalized. In that condition, every person is justified according to the "right of nature" in taking whatever actions he thinks are needed to preserve himself unrestrained by positive laws or moral norms.[24] But contrary to most later interpreters, Hobbes did not eliminate the state of nature by means of a covenant. The state of nature is repressed, not transcended. It exists as a permanent feature of international politics. Domestically it threatens to return every time a law is broken or a promise evaded.[25] Only the fear aroused by the power of an absolute sovereign can preserve peace, but the establishment of absolutism obliterates the traditional distinction underlying Reason of State between exceptional, unbounded power and ordinary, constrained power. *Staatsräson* is normal politics in the Hobbesian commonwealth. Moreover, because each individual is a party to the original covenant, and, as a result, is implicated in all of the sovereign's actions, *Staatsräson* has acquired a "democratic" element previously lacking.

The individualized version of consent, which was consistent with Hobbes's nominalism, was both a reflection and an evisceration of the radical turn taken by Reason of State during the revolutionary upheavals of the era. Among the pamphlets and treatises that justified rebellion against the king, it was commonplace to appeal to the Roman maxim *Salus populi suprema lex est* (the safety of the people is the supreme law).[26] The parliamentary forces, it was argued, were justified in breaking the law, ignoring the religious teachings of the established church, and mobilizing military power without observing the usual constitutional proprieties because the "people," who constituted the realm, were being threatened by the arbitrary actions of the king and his agents. Thus, the survival of society or the people was substituted for the preservation of the state, and revolutionary action for the reason of state authorities. Revolution was, in other words, Reason of State popularized.

These new and "democratic" elements being drawn into Reason of State could not be exploited within the antidemotic framework of Hobbes's theory. In addition and equally important, there was no connection made by Hobbes between reason and state action. Rationality for Hobbes was concerned with the logical structure of consent, obligation, law, and authority; it was silent about action. In fact, when Hobbes turned to the question of policy advice or counsel for the sovereign, he retreated from his usual high doctrine of reason modeled upon geometry and conceded that the best counselors were those with the greatest political experience.[27]

The pivotal figure in the expansion of Reason of State proved to be

Locke rather than Hobbes. Hobbes drew together and exploited the several strands of naturalism, reason, revolution, and the justification for extraordinary state power and its absolution from the ordinary limitations prescribed by law. Locke went even farther. He connected Reason of State to a new idea, modernization, and to a conception of "the people" as a sovereign who were entitled to rebel but not to rule. And he erased Parker's distinction between invoking extralegal powers to defend the state and using them to promote well-being, thus transforming Reason of State from an inherent threat to a constitutional polity, as it had been for Machiavelli, to being its artifact.

Locke's reconstruction of Reason of State in *Two Treatises of Government* begins from a traditional distinction between internal affairs ("the Society within itself") and external affairs ("the security and interest of the publick without") (2.147). The former is designated as the province of the "Executive" power, the latter as that of the "Federative" power. The two powers, Locke notes in a tortured passage, "are always almost united" (2.14), a remark whose casual, unargued quality helps to conceal an important move. Instead of providing a basis for contrasting the broad latitude that must be allowed the federative power with the close containment of the executive power, the internal/external distinction serves to create a domestic domain for *Staatsräson* while lodging it in the same constitutional hands as power over foreign affairs. The federative power, "which," as Locke puts it, "one may call natural" (2.145), follows in the naturalistic tradition of Machiavelli and Hobbes. That power is said by Locke to correspond to "the Power every Man naturally had before he entered Society" (2.145). This means that, literally, the federative power represents alienated power, for it, along with executive power, embodies the precise power that men had to surrender as a condition for civil government to be established. In the state of nature, each man had the rightful power to defend himself and to enforce the law of nature; his natural power was limited by the law of nature. The federative power was defined by Locke so as to preserve the appearance of continuity with man's power in the state of nature: it "contains the Power of War and Peace, Leagues and Alliances, and all the Transactions with all Persons and Communities without the Commonwealth" (2.146). The federative power, he notes, is "much less capable" of being circumscribed by law and "so must necessarily be left to the Prudence and Wisdom of those whose hands [it is] in." This was because the exercise of that power would have to depend upon "the variation of designs and interests" of foreigners (2.47).

In the course of describing the federative power, Locke connects it with the notion of a unified or solidary community that serves not only to strengthen the federative power but to prepare the way for enlarging executive power along the path marked out by the *Staatsrä-son* element in the federative power. When Locke first introduced the notion of a state of nature, and especially when he discussed the origins of private property, he made frequent reference to all mankind forming "one Community of Nature" (2.6, 128). But when men contract to institute a particular society, they "make one Body . . . in reference to the rest of Mankind" so that in controversies with "those that are out of it . . . an injury done to a Member of their Body engages the whole in the reparation of it" (2.145). The cohesive character of the community implied by Locke's language is not accidental, but crucial to the scope of the executive as well as federative power. A solidary community serves as a moral entity that is properly a subject of a common good. Just as the existence of a genuine community justifies the protective function of the federative power, so that community justifies a general guardian power in the domestic domain "within" that allows the executive to do good.

The enlargement of the executive was accomplished by amalgamating the natural power of individuals to enforce the law of nature with the historical power identified with the royal prerogative claimed by English monarchs, thus uniting a restricted power under the law of nature with a notoriously ill-defined power whose limits had been bitterly but inconclusively contested for a century.[28] Prerogative is, according to Locke's definition, the "power to act according to discretion, for the publick good, without the prescription of the Law, and sometimes even against it" (2.160).

Locke's reasoning in justification of such an anomalous power is astonishing because it amounts to a criticism of the political system of his own creation, to a deconstruction of his own theory. He justified exceptional executive power on the grounds that there were inherent shortcomings in the rule of law and parliamentary-based politics, the two main protections against arbitrary power. Legislatures, Locke points out, are not in continuous session, and hence they are "too slow for the dispatch requisite to Execution." But when the legislature does act it acts through the law, and the law cannot foresee "all Accidents and Necessities"; the law is inflexible if applied rigorously under all circumstances (2.160). Thus, the variability of affairs and the need for flexible, prompt action—which had been the hallmarks of *Staatsräson* and the distinctive character of war and invasion, of situations defined by the emphatic presence of force, domination, and survival—are now affixed to domestic concerns, to concerns that, by definition, are farthest removed from the state of nature (which international politics is not) and from the naturalistic grounds of power. Locke accomplishes the change by using the norm of the good (*bonum*) of the community to justify a latitude of power that hitherto had been restricted to its survival (*salus*). To determine whether an exercise of prerogative is justifiable, Locke writes, we need only inquire whether it is for "the good of the Community." A "good Prince," he reassures his reader, "cannot have too much Prerogative, that is Power to do good" (2.164). A ruler pursuing the good in violation of the law will be acting rationally because he will be applying the fundamental principle incorporated into the original contract that "a Society of Rational Creatures entered into a Community for their mutual good" (2.163).

An enlarged *Staatsräson* stands for a broad power to extirpate the irrationalities preserved by "Customs and Priviledges when the reasons of them are ceased." State rationality now has to deal with a new and changing world where "Things . . . are in so constant a Flux that nothing remains long in the same State. Thus People, Riches, Trade, Power change their Stations" (2.157). Change replaces nature as the ground for broad discretionary powers. The new threat that the reason of the state is to combat are the "gross absurdities" that "the following of Custom, when reason has left it, may lead" (2.157). The example Locke uses is the distortion in the system of electoral representation produced by the rotten boroughs. It stands for those "unforeseen and uncertain Occurrences" that could not be anticipated by "certain and unalterable Laws" (2.158). The inability of the legislature to act and the rigidity of the law suddenly reveal that the two main guarantors of men's natural rights are seriously deficient, perhaps because they are so deeply indebted to the element of custom that is now seen to be at odds with the emerging nature of modernity. Because the law is helpless to overcome "the disorders, which succession of time had insensibly, as well as inevitably introduced," the state, in the person of the executive, would be relied upon to overcome "old custom" by "true reason" (2.158).

The Lockean contract thus signifies man's movement from the realm of nature to the realm of history, to that order marked by "succession of time" and "constant Flux." Reason, which Locke declared to be synonymous with the law of nature (1.101, 2.6), now has the task of effecting the values of the law of nature—liberty, protection, preservation, property, and equality—in the realm of history. Reason is no longer directed mainly against nature and the dangers presented in the form of natural powers; this means that unlike Machiavelli and Hobbes, Locke did not conceive of the power that reason must call upon as being defined by the *Kraft* or sheerly physical power associated by his predecessors with nature. Reason is concerned to dominate history, and it takes the form of modernizing "old custom."

Its powers are now directed against the artifacts of man himself: the changes produced not only by the "busy mind of man" but by the decay that time brings to all things so that "the reasons of them are ceased." Reason has to reintroduce reason continually to repair society's "insensible" lapses into irrationality and "gross absurdities" (2.157). The standard according to which reason works is as generous as that formerly available to Reason of State, the good of society. The good of society, as noted previously, has been substituted for security as the *suprema lex*. Lockean rulers inherit the same rights of Reason of State to summon the full power of society, but now it is not for simple defense or domination but for the good of all.

The new Reason of State can call upon a more awesome reservoir of power than anything available to premodern rulers: whereas the latter had to negotiate with partially autonomous centers of power (nobility, church, local estates), the new rulers can apply a power that is awesome because it is constituted indiscriminately. "Men give up all their Natural Power to the Society which they enter into" (2.136). A ruler who "sincerely" takes as his "Rule" the principle of *"Salus Populi Suprema Lex"* (2.158) and makes the domestic well-being of society the basic object of policy need not fear that this will reduce his effectiveness abroad: "The increase of lands and the right imploying of them is the great art of government. And what Prince who shall be so wise·and godlike as by established laws of liberty to secure protection and encouragement to the honest industry of Mankind against the oppression of power and narrowness of Party will quickly be too hard for his neighbors" (2.42).

Thus, statecraftiness has disappeared to be replaced by sincerity in pursuit of the well-being of society, while the *techne* of statescraftsmanship, "the great art of government," will concentrate not on aggrandizement but on the extension and expansion, at home and abroad, of rational productivity or "the right imploying" of resources. The later development of the modern state would bring further changes in the meaning of each of the three elements of statecraftiness, statecraftsmanship, and the *Kraft* of the state. Briefly put, the modern state experienced a crisis expressed in its own increasing rigidification and a consequent deficit in variability. This crisis can be sketched by means of two familiar notions.

Toward Totality

The first is Weber's conception of rationalization. It refers to the spread of instrumental modes of thinking—what Ellul called *"la technique"*—that reduce the world to terms of achieving a given end most effectively and efficiently. Bureaucratic institutions are the formal embodiment of instrumentalism or, more precisely, they embody rationality as modern man has come to understand reason. Rationality has only a tenuous existence independent of the conventions enforced by institutions. By means of bureaucratic institutions, rationality proceeds to set the categories for defining what is officially in the world.[29] Bureaucratic rationality is not confined to governmental arrangements; it has deeply penetrated all modes of social life so that distinctions between "public" and "private" and "state" and "civil society" have lost their salience. The universality of bureaucracy, which exists more as an ideal than as an actuality, signifies nonetheless the determination to reduce the play of contingency and variability. By reducing the world to procedures, bureaucracy hopes to render it calculable.

Science served as the model for the so-called policy sciences that correspond to the second element of "craft," the skilled application of knowledge to the management of affairs of state. Today this means the applied social sciences, primarily the sciences of economics and management. But technical knowledge has a problem: insofar as it acknowledges the need for flexibility, it is closer to being a higher common sense than a body of scientific knowledge; insofar as it is technical or objective, it is less flexible and hence works to build pressures for forms of variable power. Technical knowledge is mainly applied within the rigidified structures that reason has built, and it owes its development to the conditions that administered structures make available. Technical knowledge aims at the reduction of contingency by substituting scientific knowledge. It trades flexibility and uncertainty for predictability.

The second broad development involved what might be called the systematization of the state. This refers to the expansion of the state to include much that had previously been viewed as private, from education to sexual reproduction. It is not merely that the state has "intervened" in numerous domains; it has sought to coordinate the domains themselves.

The state system includes the traditional instruments of governance: first and foremost, military and police power, executive and bureaucracy, courts, legislature, political parties, and those interest groups that adapt their activities to conform with the "rules of the game." To these elements of the state, a new one was added in the twentieth century. Before this century, the relationship of government and economy took the form primarily of clusters of legislation (e.g., railroad legislation), subsidies, and regulations, which, although adding up to a considerable network with a noticeable tilt in favor of business interests, could not be said to have achieved an integrative or organic character. During the present century, however, the state system has evolved from having relationships with large business corporations to becoming inter-related so as to form a system.

This system is huge, for it not only includes the economy and large sectors of civil society (e.g., education) but sees itself as deeply involved in the competition for hegemony in the international economy. Stated differently, the hugeness of the system is not identical with the hugeness of the state. *System,* a term that is widely used and reveal-ingly combines a technical bioengineering meaning with a techno-cratic/bureaucratic one, signifies the transmutation of the state into the Economic Polity. One small sign of the change is the archaic status of the epithets and images once thought to be expressive of the state. *"Majestas," "grandeur," "imperium,"* and "sovereignty" once signified a social totality dominated by a definite, guiding center of volition and ultimate authority, monocratic and monotheistic. Now there is a sys-tem striving to become a totality in which the center is being trans-formed into a mechanism of management and control. Unlike the monocratic structure, in which dominance was the basic political and social fact, the basic fact about power under the regime of the techno-logically advanced Economic Polity is its pervasiveness.

One of the most significant developments in the pervasiveness of power and its totalization is the private colonization of the public sec-tor. For nearly a decade the private sector has steadily acquired func-tions that used to belong to the public sector. These include the expan-sion of private education, private hospitals, the assumption of various welfare programs, corporate subsidies of the arts and of public radio and television, the operation of prisons, and the recruitment of large security forces. Thus, there are now over one million private security guards, but only thirty-six thousand work for a government agency. Or to take another example of what appears on its face to be the pri-vatization of the public domain: in 1962 the Social Security Act was amended to prohibit the use of federal funds to purchase services in the private sector. But beginning with the amendments of 1967 to the same act, these restrictions were loosened, and since then there has been "an enormous expansion of public funds" into the private sector. Then, in 1974, the last major restriction was removed from Title XX of the Social Security Act when private agency donations, such as those represented by the United Fund, could qualify as part of a state's 25 percent local matching share of federal monies, even when the funds were being used to purchase services from the donating agency.[30]

The Political Functions of Civil Society

These developments that find the state slightly decentered but not significantly decentralized have been heralded as marking a new awareness of the limitations of the public sector as well as a new attitude of social responsibility on the part of large corporations. The context in which these developments have been discussed is typically economic: the private sector can "deliver" the social services more efficiently. But this way of presenting the problem helps to obscure the power that will be exercised by agents who appear to be responding to profit motives and market forces but who in reality will be fulfilling the disciplinary needs of the Economic Polity. Those needs are importantly secured, as I have suggested, by uncertainty. The reassignment of social needs to the private sector reintroduces precisely the elements of uncertainty that public guarantees of assistance were supposed to ease. In this setting, the very language of "sectors" is a revealing slip: it reflects the parity of parts in a polity/economy, the suppressed yearning for totality, and the evolution of state-centered power into system power. In that evolution, the power-enhancing role of marginalization is not lost. The courts have ruled, for example, that security guards in the employ of private companies are not subject to the same constitutional constraints that formally inhibit public law enforcement.

The connection between the role of uncertainty and variability in the production of power, on the one hand, and the symbiotic relationship between the polity and the economy and civil society, on the other, are underscored by two recent developments. The first is the extension of the use of lie detectors from the public sector to the private, from the state to civil society and the economy. Businesses now regularly employ the devices as part of their hiring practices as well as for maintaining continuing surveillance over the lives of their employees. The second development is illustrated by the recent recommendations of a presidential commission that called for a sweeping nationwide program of drug testing of private as well as public employees. This step toward the *Gleichschaltung* of state and society was likened to a weapon in the "war against drugs," but the more immediate aim is a method for disciplining a work force that is frequently criticized as being inferior to the Japanese. Thus, the real battleground is the international economy. The disciplinary aims embodied in these proposals, which are already part of the standard practices of some government agencies and business firms, are clearly linked to the uncertainty principle. The tests can be administered at the discretion of employers. The uncertainty becomes nearly exquisite because of the well-known fallibility of drug tests, a political virtue also possessed by lie detectors. The choice confronting the worker is rendered all the more stark by the commission's recommendations of a large increase in the number of prisons and an expanded role of the armed forces in combating the "hostile threat" posed by the drug economy, which, as Washington has frequently insisted, is linked to international terrorism and communism.[31] Clearly, the disciplinary requirements of the Economic Polity are blurring the traditional distinction between prison and society.

Wohlfahrtsstaatsräson

"The essence of the welfare state," according to a standard definition, "is government-protected minimum-standards of income, nutrition, health, housing, and education, assured to every citizen as a political right, not as charity."[32] Or, to cite another formulation, the welfare state is "the predictable delivery of public-funded benefits to people in need without imposing systematic degradations and restrictions upon them."[33]

These statements convey the ambivalence that is to be found among those writers who are broadly sympathetic to the extension of services associated with the welfare state but who are also apprehensive about the expansion of state power implicit in welfare functions. One student of the welfare state has formalized the ambivalence by proposing a distinction between the "repressive" functions of the state and its "welfare" functions. He has then shown that these are simultaneously present in the contemporary state, not only in the simple sense of, say, the co-presence of the Department of Justice operating alongside the Department of Health and Human Services, but of the intermingling of both functions in the same department. Thus, the "repressive" agency may have responsibility to protect the legal rights of dependent children, while the "welfare" agency polices welfare rolls in order to ferret out those whom President Reagan once labeled "welfare chiselers."

Many social democrats have chosen to ignore the repressive nature of state power, its Weberian nature, even though socialist theory was once renowned for its view of the state as the instrument of class rule and the guarantor of the system of private ownership of the means of production as well as of the unequal power relationships that that form of ownership presumes and reproduces.[34] Today there is a marked tendency among social democrats to modify their former conception of the state as the mere extension of capitalist power in favor of some version of state "autonomy," that is, the state seems at times able to pursue policies that, on their face, are opposed to the "logic" of capitalist power—for example, to enact legislation recognizing and protecting the rights of trade unions.[35]

Clearly, if socialists are to favor the extension of welfare programs, they must assume that the state can be used; or, stated differently, that the state is not encapsulated in the Economic Polity. Without that assumption, social democracy has no *raison d'être*. Further, social democracy assumes the perpetuation rather than the abolition of capitalist forms of ownership. In focusing upon benefits, the origin of the benefits in a particular form of ownership of the means of production comes to matter less than their abundance. Some Swedish social democrats have argued straightforwardly for a policy of helping to fatten the capitalist calf rather than slaughtering it. Social democracy is thus ironically the means of resolving the so-called motivation crisis of mature capitalism.[36]

Briefly stated, the "motivation crisis" refers to the claim of socialist critics that the liberal capitalist state is threatened because, first, the work ethic has deteriorated, with a consequent decline in productivity and capital accumulation; and, second, due to structural changes in the economy, there has been a marked shrinkage in the sector from which welfare benefits were financed. The resulting shrinkage of welfare programs, it is claimed, leads to a withdrawal of political loyalty and support by ordinary citizens. Although this theory was intended to demonstrate that capitalism was approaching an impasse, its actual and unintended effect has been to expose the way in which new social democratic strategies are helping to avert the crisis of capitalism. For if capitalism is to be exploited by socialist pressures, then socialists have a direct interest in increasing the productivity and efficiency of capitalism. Accordingly, socialists should concentrate upon restoring worker motivation. They should educate workers to see that their self-interest lies in making capitalism more efficient and productive. If they succeed, then the capitalist economy will take its place alongside the capitalist state: both will then be sufficiently autonomous to be exploited. Then all that is needed politically is a strong trade union movement and a mass political party organized around the cause of social Keynesianism.[37] Unfortunately, the likely effect of the strategy will be to resolve the legitimation crisis at the expense of democratic possibilities. Democracy will have been reduced essentially to a means for mobilizing electoral pressures to extract welfare. It will have been sacrificed to the "higher" synthesis of socialism and capitalism symbolized by the welfare state.

The consequence of the socialist discovery of state autonomy is to produce a convergence between social democracy and what might be called neo-Bismarckism. The latter is represented in American political science by Huntington, Krasner, and Nordlinger.[38] They have argued for state autonomy, both as an actual fact and as a normative desideratum. The Bismarckian element in their writings is their concern for a strong state, one sufficiently removed from domestic political pressures to be able to respond vigorously, promptly, and effectively to the Soviet threat and to the changing tactical map of international *Realpolitik*. In this context, the idea of state autonomy is in large part contemporary jargon for *Staatsräson*. Bismarck was also among the first nineteenth-century statesmen to enact social legislation not as a remedy for social injustice but as a way of scotching discontent and increasing state power. The neo-Bismarckians have also perceived this connection between social discontent and state power.[39] But they face, as Bismarck was not required to, the full tide of rising expectations of the lower classes that capitalism unavoidably arouses in the course of shaping consumer consciousness. Huntington, in particular, is alarmed by the way that "modernization" has stirred the political consciousness of the poorer strata of society, made them susceptible to the appeals of politicians in search of votes, and produced an "overload" of social demands upon limited national resources at a critical moment when the national interest requires that defense spending be given priority.[40] Expectations have to be lowered without, however, creating pessimism among the general citizenry of consumers; this requires that state officials be allowed considerable flexibility. This situation is viewed as endemic to any highly integrated and complex economy, and, therefore, it is urgent that governments have the necessary authority to act quickly and even to flaunt orthodoxy, as in the recent crisis involving Continental Bank or, before that, the Chrysler bailout. In other words, the discretionary power that the state is able to legitimate vis-à-vis welfare functions is symptomatic of a need for unconstrained state power in virtually all social and economic sectors.

Thus, we are in the presence of a new form of *Staatsräson*. It is the fate of our times that the German language, rather than ancient Greek, allows me to coin an appropriate word for this new power: *Wohlfahrtsstaatsräson*. As I have contended, the new *Staatsräson*, like the old, is a response to unpredictability, but the forms of unpredictability are not symbolic of a naturalistic politics or of the incomplete politicization of the world, as they were in Machiavelli's image of a raging stream that sweeps all before it. Instead, they are represented in the interplay between a volatile international political economy and a rigidified bureaucratic structure of decision making. As that international economy has become more interdependent, it has also become more intensely competitive. Innovations then become a condition of survival, but they also produce consequences that no one nation can control. As a result, Machiavellism, or statecraftiness, reappears in different forms: over the control of scientific discoveries and their publicization; over export quotas, tariffs, currency exchange, and interest rates. In short, the international political economy is as much an order that demands *Realpolitik* as was the older order of nation-state rivalries. The new order demands ad hoc solutions as much as the old, and those demands are reflected back into the domestic political economy. Thus, if the governing elites find that current definitions of employment result in payment systems that ultimately place U.S. firms at a competitive disadvantage, then the Bureau of Labor Statistics simply redefines what it means to be employed or unemployed. Or the meaning of the term *class* can be redefined: the relation of class to the organization of production can be ignored in favor of a conception of class defined by welfare standards for demarcating a "poverty line."

Indeed, the substitution of bureaucratic for sociological conceptions of class reveals the essence of *Wohlfahrtsstaatsräson*. A bureaucratic class is a classification, a category defined by the application of abstract criteria that are designed to accentuate attributes deemed systematically useful rather than to accommodate the differences created by historical practices, institutions, and values. Contrary to Weber's myth, in which growing bureaucratization meant the spread of rationality, order, rule-bound decisions, and predictability, bureaucracy introduces arbitrariness into the constitution of its classifications and then disguises that initial move with an overlay of procedural rules.[41] Bureaucracy signifies, not as Weber thought, the antithesis of *Staatsräson*, but its ritualization.

The impulse that guides the *Räson* of the *Wohlfahrtsstaat* is the yearning for totality that has been such a prominent element in the ideologies and politics of this century. All economic, military, political, and revolutionary thinking and practice have been shaped by the urge for complete coordination and systematization. What remains of pluralism, which had flourished early in this century, is mostly the eccentricities and rage of separatism. The distance traversed by political development from the early modern beginnings of *Staatsräson* to the postmodern *Wohlfahrtsstaatsräson* can be measured by recalling that earlier, when the state first appealed to reasons of high policy as a justification for extraordinary powers, it was not simply a matter of lawbreaking that was involved but an incursion into private spheres that possessed their own sources of power, structures of authority, and systems of norms. *Staatsräson* had to confront ecclesiastical authorities of sacred origin, private property protected by custom and sanctioned by natural law, family and kinship structures whose ultimate origins were believed to be biblical, and elaborate charters of communal and municipal liberties. These autonomies were crippled in the course of the complex history of political and legal centralization, the growth of urbanization, and the dislocations caused by industrial and technological changes. The most extreme suppression of pluralism was accomplished by twentieth-century totalitarianism. The extinction of political difference is also implicit, however, in the yearning for totality of which systems-talk is the ideological expression. System thinking extinguishes difference not by suppression but by a combination of translation and abandonment: social phenomena are renamed "inputs" or treated as "costs" and "benefits" and absorbed into these categories. What cannot be accommodated or co-opted doesn't "count" and can be ignored.

The nonsuppressive extinction of difference is powerfully illustrated in the completely inverted picture of reality created by the Reagan regime. On the one hand, presidential rhetoric extolled the values of localism, voluntarism, and decentralization and strenuously attacked the idea of state power and state intervention. However, the reality is that the power of the national state has demonstrably increased, not only in military and diplomatic interventionism abroad, but in control, surveillance, and the promotion of moral and religious orthodoxy. State power is now so assured that it can be attacked with impunity by those who preside over its use. The state is now so unchallenged internally, either by a vigorous system of opposition parties and movements or by independent local authorities, that it can appear to reverse nearly two hundred years of aggrandizement at the expense of local self-government. Instead of encroaching on lesser autonomies, it proclaims its surplus of power and "returns" functions and monies to state and local officials, thereby propping up a system that it needs both to obscure its own increasing power and to render it more efficient by converting local government into essentially administrative units in a national system of management. Localism is that state-sponsored Potemkin Village in the age of *Wohlfahrtsstaatsräson*.

Ten / Democracy without the Citizen

> It seems to have been reserved to the
> people of this country, by their conduct
> and example, to decide the important
> question, whether societies of men are
> really capable or not, of establishing good
> government from reflection and choice, or
> whether they are forever destined to de-
> pend, for their political constitutions, on
> accident and force.
> — THE FEDERALIST, NUMBER I

These words of Alexander Hamilton from the first of *The Federalist Papers* set a framework by which he hoped to persuade the citizens of New York State of the positive value of the proposed constitution, which they were being asked to ratify. He seemed to be linking two points together, the merits of the proposed constitution and the fact that it was being presented as a matter of "reflection and choice." In the remaining *Federalist Papers*, Hamilton and his co-authors, Jay and Madison, would hammer endlessly on the nature of that choice. It was between the order promised by a new system of central government and the existing state of anarchy, as *The Federalist* saw it, in which the former colonies mostly governed themselves. In a later number of *The Federalist*, the choice was further sharpened when Madison contrasted the republican system embodied in the Constitution with the idea of a pure democracy. The former stood for a highly restricted system of citizen participation associated with representative government, the latter for direct and continuous participation. Thus, the choice was twofold, between centralized power and decentered power and be-tween two conceptions of the citizen. I shall return to the choice posed by *The Federalist* because it is, I shall suggest, crucial to an understanding of our present situation.

Standing where we do now, two hundred years later, Hamilton's challenge invites a far more equivocal response than would have seemed possible, say, a quarter century ago. Then we would have known nothing of the Vietnam War, of the political assassination of the Kennedy brothers and Martin Luther King, of the Watergate scandal, and of the near-impeachment of President Nixon.

1987 proved to be a bad year for the Constitution. The Irangate scandal exposed a tangled web of intrigues that stretched from Washington to Nicaragua via the Middle East, with frequent side trips to Swiss banks, but there remained at its center a simple point: constitutional processes were consistently violated and, as a result, broke down. The question posed by these events does not primarily concern whether various individuals, including the president of the United States, were guilty of wrongdoing. Such a formulation implies that government is normally contained within a system of legal and institutional restraints and that the Iran-contra affair involved a question of whether or not certain illegal acts were committed. The further implication is that if the illegal acts were performed, and if they are subsequently punished, then the affair will have been satisfactorily resolved.

What is missed by that formulation is the question of power. The constitutional way of talking about power is to treat illegal acts as an attempt to grasp at more power than the office entitles the holder to claim or to misuse a power that the holder can rightfully claim. To state the point slightly differently, constitutional systems typically presuppose that public officials are chronically short of power, that power is akin to a scarce commodity because the material ingredients of power as signified, for example, by taxes upon the wealth of private citizens or corporations are themselves limited. But as soon as we consider some of the revelations of the Iran-contra case, the first thing we encounter is the tremendous sums of money and resources (e.g., armaments) being exchanged or transferred. Thus, unlike the classic situation of unconstitutional actions originating in a power shortage, the current example seems to involve surplus power, more power than the individuals knew how to handle effectively. So much so that at times the actors seemed to be throwing armaments after hostages long after it became apparent that the hostage holders were engaged in a hoax of extracting arms for hostages they never intended to deliver.

But to understand the full nature of the problem of power it is necessary to note that the Constitution presupposed that political power was to be a governmental monopoly. This was the point of the Preamble to the Constitution and its assertion of the sovereignty of the people. The formula "We, the People, in order to form a more perfect Union . . ." proclaims that the only legitimate source of power is to be derived from the people and entrusted to their elected representatives. If there is one lesson that became unmistakably clear during the Reagan era, it is that political power is not the monopoly of government. The most spectacular instance was the remarkable network of public and private relationships which Colonel North and his associates had created to deal with arms transfers to Iran, Israel, and Nicaragua. So complex were these relationships that it is virtually impossible to say, for example, whether the contras should be described as an arm of the CIA or as a private army financed by American conservative foundations. What one can say with reasonable confidence is that public and private power have become entangled so as to create a different version of power than that defined and controlled by the Constitution.

There are many other examples of this form of power. Consider the phenomenon commonly described as "the privatization of public functions." It appears in the increasing numbers of private schools as well as in private operation of public hospitals, private assumption of public transportation, and private absorption of public welfare functions, to mention only the most obvious. The natural reaction is to assume that because a public function has been transferred to private hands the power of the government has been reduced—and even that power itself has disappeared because what was formerly an exercise of public power has now become a mere matter of management and economics. What in fact occurs through privatization is not the elimination of power but the elimination of politics, that is, the public discussion and argument over how power is to be used, for what ends, and who is responsible.

The Constitution, then, is in trouble because it is no longer the best description of the kind of power that is sovereign. The main reason for the demotion of the Constitution is that political institutions do not represent the principal power-generating sources or the principal mechanisms of control. Stated simply, the forms of power which have been developed in this country far exceed the power capacity envisioned by the Constitution. The symbolic moment when that fact was publicly solemnized was in John Kennedy's famous inaugural address of 1961. He set out a vision of a society committed to bearing any burden or sacrifice anywhere in the world. Clearly, that vision presupposed sufficient power to carry out that challenge. The challenge itself carried a radical revision of the traditional understanding of the field, or scope, of power. The previous understanding had been that war and military interventions were the exceptional moments when power had to be projected abroad. Such moments represented an emergency, an abnormal condition when society had to be temporarily mobilized in order to protect itself or its perceived interests abroad; when power had to be, as it were, unnaturally expanded.

The new understanding represented an enlarged conception of power and a disguised state of limited but permanent mobilization that would shortly be tested and bloodied in the so-called Vietnam experience. This shift from a constitutional conception of power to a conception of potentially unlimited power was made possible by the experience of near-total mobilization during World War II, including the mobilization of science, universities, and private industry which made possible the manufacture of the atomic bomb, the first universal form of destructive power in the history of mankind.

During the four decades since the end of World War II, the momentum of wartime has been perpetuated by systematic policies aimed at creating forms and magnitudes of power hitherto unknown. The most dramatic expression of this proliferation of power forms is the launching of spaceflights for both commercial and military exploitation and the emergence of space as the new location of international rivalries as well as the potential battleground of the future.

I shall label this new power system that has come into existence the megastate. That term is intended to capture not only the expansion of power made possible by science and technology but also the pervasiveness of power encouraged by the new mix of public and private elements. The dynamics of the megastate, the search for ever larger forms of power and the tacit assumption that, in principle, there are no limits to the power potentially available, come from two sources. One is the dynamic of imperialism, which takes the form that American security depends upon projecting a powerful presence everywhere on the globe and beyond. The other is the intense competitive pressure arising from the international economy, which makes the power of the megastate an important counter in that competition.

The major instrument of the megastate is bureaucracy, whether public or private. There are certain conditions that maximize the effectiveness of bureaucratic power. These were described long ago by Max Weber as the "rationalization" of the world. Bureaucratic power operates most effectively under conditions of calculability—that is, conditions that power holders can count on to remain stable so that their actions do not have to be constantly changed and so that outcomes can be predicted. When conditions are stable, a governmental bureaucracy can govern by uniform regulations and can apply the same decision rules; similarly, stable conditions allow business corporations to plan operations more confidently and to achieve a greater degree of consist-ency in their products. The dream of public bureaucracies is a uniform, mass society; the dream of private bureaucracies is a mass market of consumers with roughly the same tastes.

The problem of the megastate lies behind the Iran–contra affair, but what is so important is not the misplaced emphasis but rather that the way in which the affair has been publicly handled unintentionally reveals some of the conditions which make the megastate possible. For the emergence of the megastate not only renders constitutional understandings of power problematic but makes conceptions of democracy, and especially of the democratic citizen, anachronistic.

Initially the mass media and many politicians wanted to trivialize the Iran–contra events so as to promote general acceptance of the notion that, at worst, President Reagan and his advisers were negligent and overzealous in a "good cause." This fact is itself a symptom of a megastate mentality that, in many ways, is as alarming as the specific violations. It is a bad kind of consensus that has as its condition that, if we are to function as a society, we shall all have to become political amnesiacs who agree to forget violations of the Constitution or of traditional political practices. Was President Reagan's notorious forgetfulness, therefore, not only a personal failing but the metaphor for a collective failing, for a collective disinclination to grasp what has been going on and to delegate responsibility to powerful individuals who, like the admirals and colonels and bankers surrounding the president, are trained to take charge rather than to be responsive to the public? A forgetful president is as likely to be victimized as a memoryless public.

A politics without memory is the precise definition of the media-constituted politics which forms such an essential element in the structure of megastate power and of the structure of passivity which sustains it. Media politics consists of a succession of images designed to make the present moment the definition of reality dissociated from the past and hence a reality dominated by the present. The present becomes merely an arbitrary arrest of sound, motion, and fashion, while the future has no organic connection to past or present and is simply the next successful image. Media politics isolates the present moment and invites us to respond with "common sense" because common sense can be relied upon to say, "Why make a big fuss? Life goes on, so let us put this behind us and get on with the problems we have to deal with and can."

The crucial point is, however, that common sense thus conspires unwittingly with media politics to sever the image from power and to present it as something else, such as "cowboys" running loose in the NSC or as an "aberration," in John Tower's words. Why, however, is common sense so obliging to power? Why should common sense not feel that it has suffered a common insult when public officials violate the constitutional norms that "we the people" are said to have ordained? Is the fact that we do not sense a common violation related to the fact that the choice posed by Hamilton, between republicanism and democracy, has worked out in ways that exceed even Hamilton's fondest hopes?

Media politics signifies a certain kind of focus, not upon action—to which media cannot do justice because, inherently, the media are impatient—but upon allegations, which it then images. The image then stands for or represents the allegation. But what the media cannot convey are, first, the historical depths of events and, second, the broadly political implications of those same events. Neither historicity nor the political can be represented. For example, consider a previous point: one of the most striking features of contemporary politics over the past several years is that the distinction between public life and private enterprise has become deeply compromised. Such a claim would be ignored by the media because it cannot be imaged or succinctly represented. This is because the distinction depends upon an understanding of what is at stake in the difference between, say, the political and the merely managerial; that understanding, in turn, is unintelligible without some knowledge of the historical experiences encapsulated in the notion of the political.

What its dependence upon media politics served to conceal from common sense was that the Irangate scandal was not an isolated episode but the deep-running problem of a megastate that is continuously seeking to override or to nullify various restraints on its power. The severity as well as the complexity of the problem lies in the paradox that state power was dramatically expanded under an administration that publicly professed a deep abhorrence of state power. Yet under that antistate administration, hardly a day went by without some action or proposal for the enlargement of state power. Sometimes it took the form of a proposal to relax a restraint, such as the one that led to the revision of the Freedom of Information Act, or the more recent call for reducing the procedural safeguards embodied in the so-called Miranda Doctrine. Other times the government declared that it wanted government employees to submit to mandatory but random drug tests, or still other times it suggested that the threat of an AIDS epidemic justifies mandatory testing of various segments of the population.

But expanded power is not limited to exercising control over individuals. Toward the end of its second term, the Reagan administration waged a determined fight to establish a broadened interpretation of the 1972 Anti-Ballistic Missile Treaty with the hope of evading the treaty's limitations on the testing and deployment of defense systems which the Senate thought it had imposed when it originally ratified the treaty. At the same time that the discretionary power of the state is being pressed past previous legal limitations, that same state power is being exerted more circuitously, even benignly, by creating new relationships of dependency. It is estimated that anywhere from 20 to 40 percent of the physicists in the United States are now working on research closely related to Star Wars.

Whether the dream be of an entire society subjected to periodic urinalysis or one protected by an enormous shield of Star Wars defenses—a kind of huge national contraceptive which will do for incoming missiles what smaller versions will do for nonmonogamous sex—the point is the same: state power increases.

These examples are recent, but they do not represent a departure from the earlier practice of the Reagan administration or from its campaign promises. The problem is that Americans are unable to recognize the nature of state power because they have been taught a certain common sense that identifies state power exclusively with government regulation of business practices, taxation, and the particular redistributive programs for the poor, unemployed, or disadvantaged. Subsidies to corporations, aid to small business, and scholarship assistance to middle-class youngsters are normally regarded as "public spending" rather than as exercises of state power. Common sense recognizes dependency when it appears as "welfare mothers" but not as astrophysicists.

The use of the term "government" rather than "state" is not a question of mere linguistic preferences but the difference between the limited power implications of the one and the more extended power implications of the other. If we say, for example, that "the government has just set standards for controlling drug abuse among government employees," the image evoked is of an agency, such as the Department of Justice, issuing a regulation. It is a very spare image of power, confined and identifiable. But if we say, "The state is now engaged in using the issue of dangerous drugs to impose greater control over the population generally," we are pointing to a more extended entity than "the government" and to a wider purpose, as well as to a more extensive exercise of power. The fact that many corporations and schools, especially in athletic programs, have adopted a similar policy has the net effect of unifying governmental and private power to produce a wider and deeper effect than if either had operated singly. It also means that an objective ordinarily denied to governmental power can be achieved. For the Constitution prohibits governmental power from entering into the internal life of schools and private corporations for the purpose of regulating the private morals of students or employees. But because we have been taught to think of governmental action as operating in the public sector and corporations acting in the private sector and of their relationship as adversarial, we remain ignorant of crucial interconnections that are shaping our lives.

THE REEDUCATION OF common sense begins with the critical notion of the megastate. For common sense must become sensitized to a form of consociated power in which governmental and nongovernmental powers are suspected of being complementary and conjoined rather than antagonistic and differentiated.

Because of the limitations built into their political education, Americans usually fail to recognize the expansion of state power. Hence, even when increased power is announced openly it is typically disguised in a different form, commonly one to which it is difficult to take exception. Thus, even before taking office Reaganites had made it clear that they intended to increase the power of the state. They did not use that precise language. Instead, they spoke of a promise to increase American military strength and to make it second to none; to conduct an aggressive foreign policy, intervening where necessary and striving to undo Soviet control rather than merely responding belatedly to Soviet initiatives. They pledged a strong build-up of what might be called the structure of internal pacification: police forces would be increased; new technologies of law enforcement and surveillance would be introduced; more prisons would be constructed and a war on drugs unleashed; legal protections for the accused would be weakened or eliminated; and discipline would be restored in the schools.

The current crisis, like those that have preceded it, is centered upon the presidency. The Reagan presidency—and now the Bush presidency—is not an aberration but the latest instance of a deep-seated problem that has produced three constitutional crises in less than a quarter century. The first of these was the unconstitutional expansion of presidential power during Lyndon Johnson's conduct of the Vietnam War. The second was the various violations of law by President Nixon that culminated in his near-impeachment and actual resignation—the first in the history of the Republic; and the third was the violations of law and disregard for the powers of Congress revealed in the Irangate scandal. Each has centered in the presidency, and each has involved the breach or evasion of legal constraints by the president or his agents.

The natural impulse is to look more closely at the character of those who have been president during these dark moments. Although character is not to be discounted, and although each of the presidents may be said to have displayed a blunted sensibility for constitutional proprieties, such an inquiry misunderstands the nature of the problem and, as a consequence, mistakes the remedy. The constitutional excesses of recent presidents should be looked upon as the expression of more impersonal forces and tendencies which cannot be contained within the limits set by our constitutional traditions and legal norms. The reason for this lies partly with the nature of power as conceived throughout much of our constitutional history and, partly, with the nature of power as it has come to be constituted at the present time.

The original constitution embodied two competing notions of power. One was staked out by Madison and Jefferson. It insisted upon binding the powers of the national government by the literal language of the Constitution. The government's powers were limited by the specific objects set out in the Constitution; only those means could be employed that were absolutely essential to the achievement of the specified ends. Or, in Jefferson's words, the point of the Constitution was "to lace up straitly within the enumerated powers" the powers assigned to the national government.[1] This position viewed power with increasing suspicion the more it was removed from the influence of state governments and the citizens. Its basic assumption was that power was less trustworthy the more it was dissociated from the participatory practices of local politics. Its unstated assumption could be put this way: it could not conceive of a national politics in terms that could be reconciled with the politics of citizens.

The other position was associated with Hamilton. While it accepted the idea that a constitution stood for a conception of limited governmental powers, it did not believe that this restrictive conception formed the starting point for understanding the kind of power society needed. Rather, the starting point was that colonial society desperately lacked a strong central power, a national government that could act assertively and decisively. To be able to do that, the government would have to possess sources of power independent of the individual states. The powers to wage war, establish armed forces of its own, levy taxes without having to depend on the states, regulate commerce, establish national standards of money, and control final interpretation of the Constitution all signified an attempt to establish a new power base independent of the states.

But Hamilton was also to make an argument for an expanded conception of power, one that did not depend so closely upon specific provisions of the Constitution but rather was to be determined by the nature of the objects that the new constitution set for the government.

Thus, the Constitution authorizes Congress to declare war. According to Hamilton's view, the national government could lay claim to any amount of power that would enable it to wage war successfully as long as it did not violate specific constitutional provisions: "The government ought to be cloathed with all the powers requisite to the complete execution of its trust."[2] Thus, the nature of war, rather than the nature of the Constitution, initially defined the magnitude of power which government could justifiably claim.

But in order to legitimate that broad notion of power it had to be accompanied by an appropriate conception of the citizen. How much civic involvement was needed for this new kind of power? What did this kind of power need from the citizen? What had this kind of power to fear from the citizen? Because the Constitution proposed to establish a centered system of power, a national government, it had to create a new type of citizen, one who would accept the attenuated relationship with power implied if voting and elections were to serve as the main link between citizens and those in power. At the same time, if the attenuated relationship were to work, if it were to succeed in conveying enthusiasm as well as material support to the center, it needed a citizen who could identify himself with a power that was remote, abstract, and so distant that, for the most part, it would operate unseen. In other words, because the project involved establishing a form of power which bore certain unfortunate resemblances to the kind of power which the colonists had rejected less than two decades earlier when they had rebelled against the authority of the British Crown and Parliament, the Constitution had to reject the idea of the citizen which the colonists had themselves assumed when they had defended local participatory politics against the distant authority of the British Crown and Parliament.

These earlier controversies left Americans with a conception of citizenship divided within itself and, for that reason, unable to evolve in ways that would meet the challenge of modern power. The civic self was divided between national citizenship, which the original constitution had restricted to the act of voting and had ingeniously prevented from organizing a majority purpose, and local citizenship, which had a busy and active life of frequent elections, officeholding in state legislatures, town councils, and local committees, jury duty, and militia service. In contrast, the civic self designed by the Constitution was not a design of citizenship but of a legitimation process.

Further, it was, as *The Federalist Papers* made clear, a political structure whose purpose was to elevate the presidency as the center of a centralized system and, by the same token, to demote the legislature. The implicit task set by that presidential form was to develop a citizenry that would look at the president in a new and depoliticized way: as a monarch above politics, as a father figure, as an easily accessible symbol of unity (as contrasted with the diversity represented in Congress). In short, a citizenry was conceived in terms that allowed the American political animal to evolve into the domesticated creature of media politics.

But the Constitution also had to contend with a rival form of civic life and a rival conception of the citizen. For there existed in the colonies at that time a flourishing political life that did not depend upon the Constitution but preceded it. The political life-forms of state and local governments and of the voluntary and spontaneous associations of citizens to which Tocqueville later drew attention presented a sharp contrast to the formalistic and abstract politics centering upon the national government. It was a different kind of politics, immediate, direct, and recurrent. It was a politics of experience and based on substance rather than image.

Thus, the actual politics of the country was, as it were, different from and larger than the constitutional definition of it. The actuality of American life then, as well as now, is that American politics in all of its ramifications requires a multiple civic self, one who is required to act the citizen in diverse settings: national, state, city or town, neighborhood, and voluntary association. It is perhaps the most complex conception of citizenship ever devised, and yet we have no coherent conception of it. Instead, we have assumed that the issue could be defined in terms of a simple confrontation between two opposing conceptions: the republican or representative conception of the citizen as an occasional participant through the single act of voting, on the one hand, and the democratic one, which conceived citizenship as direct participation in self-government, on the other.

These notions are inadequate, but in different ways. The republican model is the most dangerous because it wants the citizen to be a loyal subject; that is, to provide a stable basis of support and legitimacy so that those in power can undistractedly concentrate upon exercising power in a dangerous, complex, and changing world. If it didn't need the legitimacy that at the present is primarily supplied by elections, a legitimacy that enables it to extract resources and human labor and skills from society, it would happily dispense with the whole business of electoral politics. For its ideal is a politics of management, not a politics of citizens. Its notion of public politics is what can be distilled through the media. It wants a citizen adapted to the megastate.

It is clearly impossible to impose a democratic conception of the citizen upon the political realities of the megastate. But the democratic conception is also inappropriate because participation in megastate power is difficult. If the politics of the megastate is to be even minimally democratized, however, it will require a citizen who fulfills his or her civic role by doing something other than passively supporting those in authority. It demands a critical, thoughtful citizen who can participate in the form in which megastate politics presents itself: it is abstract, remote, and often technical in character. It demands a citizen who can participate intellectually and passionately in the controversies that surround the megastate, such as nuclear weapons, ecological problems, the actions of public men and women, foreign policy, and much else. The task of the citizen is to insist upon a widened debate in these vital matters: to reclaim public space as a space for deliberation, criticism, and alternatives and to prevent important political matters from being depoliticized and turned into in-house discussions.

The democratic conception of the citizen must be preserved as an ideal form, the measuring rod of what it means to be a citizen. It must be kept alive and reinvigorated at all of the political levels which have not been fully incorporated into the politics of the megastate. Democracy stands for an alternative conception of politics, even a standing criticism of and a living opposition to the megastate and to media politics. The political forms accessible to the democratic citizen are, as suggested earlier, diverse, not only in their substance but also in the degree of active participation they allow. The citizen of a state cannot be as directly involved as the citizen of a town; and the latter cannot be as concerned as the citizen of a neighborhood school district. The value of each of these involvements lies in their coexistence, the fact that they place different demands and offer different experiences. For what democratic politics is about is not simply discussion and cooperation among friends and neighbors but deliberation about differences, not just differences of opinion and interest, but the different modes of being represented in race, culture, ethnicity, religion, gender, and class. The encounter with difference is becoming the most important experience in contemporary America as new populations make their homes here. For difference presents a potential anomaly to the politics of the megastate: it upsets the passivity that is the essential condition of bureaucratic rule and the imaged politics of the mass media.

Eleven / Democracy and
Operation Democracy

Ever since World War I, when Woodrow Wilson justified America's entrance into the war under the slogan of "making the world safe for democracy," it has been commonplace for American presidents and political leaders to claim democracy both as an objective or end that justifies the use of state power and as a subject or agent whose will—because it is a democratic will—legitimates that end. The unstated assumption has been that it is "natural" for democracy to promote democracy abroad. A further assumption has been an equation, that the United States equals democracy. This cluster of assumptions and objectives I call Operation Democracy. Its essence is to use democracy to promote the ends of Americn foreign policy and, ostensibly, to use foreign policy to promote democracy.

How, then, must we think about using the state to promote democracy? "Democracy," historically, has not been a statist term. The authors of *The Federalist Papers* regarded it as an antistatist conception of politics, one that threatened to make effective state power impossible. Something, then, has to be done to democracy to permit its use by the state. What must we do to the idea and practices of democracy, so that they can become reincarnated as Operation Democracy? What operations must be performed upon democracy before it can become operational as policy? A first clue is provided by examining how democracy is used by politicians and publicists.

In the public rhetoric of our day, one often encounters the statement that democracy is a "value," or that democracy "represents" certain values (e.g., individual rights or freedom). This mode of speech has become so familiar that it has dulled public sensibility about the political implications of what seems an innocent usage.

To conceive of democracy as "values" is not a mere matter of "saying something" but a political move with profound consequences. It is part of a strategy for dissociating democracy from the specific and historical context that gives it concrete meaning. When values are dissociated from context, they retain only an innocuous or formal meaning, e.g., "freedom is the absence of coercion." That emptiness allows the value to be used for almost any political purpose, including purposes that are diametrically opposed to the value when it exists in its historical context. Thus, Soviet dictators used to laud the Soviet Constitution as "democratic," thereby trading on the honorific associations of democracy while contradicting virtually all of the principles and practices identified with democracy in its "home" context.

Dissociation from context, then, should be understood as a political strategy, a move that prepares values to be used to promote state power and the interests embodied in state power. Decontextualization represents an inversion of the usual role of values. The political values most typically invoked in the United States—freedom of speech and religion, property rights, due process and equal protection, the right to vote, and the responsibility of public officials to the electorate—are predicated on a lively suspicion of state power. They are, in this regard, democratic elements, intended either to protect the individual against arbitrary state action or to enable him or her to control it.

That these values have acquired these particular meanings is, however, owing to the role that political culture has played in interpreting the American experience of collectivity. The categories that the culture has supplied to interpret the collective experience have disposed Americans to be suspicious of state power and distrustful of state authority. Due process, for example, does not inherently imply distrust of state power. One can easily imagine a political society where due process would be understood and used to expedite state power, to make it more efficient. Due process has come to mean protection against arbitrary state power because for nearly three centuries Americans have interpreted it in the light of the English common law and an inherited political language emphasizing individual rights, constitutional limitations on power, and suspicion of officeholders.

When values are removed from their context, they are, in effect, dehistoricized: they retain their formal properties but surrender their specific, situational meanings for a universal status. Universal or dehistoricized values appear as naturally global, that is, as good for every people. And in the abstract they are. The difficulty is that no people or society is abstract. For every society has a history, and that history embodies various ideas and practices that that society has fashioned to articulate its conceptions of social, political, moral, and religious relationships. This poses a fundamental antagonism between universal values and local contexts. A superpower that stakes out the entire globe and surrounding space as its field of operations will be drawn toward universal values—the more universal, the better, because the more formal and empty the values the easier it is to define them in ways advantageous to the interests of the megastate, the easier to override local contexts on the grounds of "justice, necessity and democratic tradition," to quote Charles Krauthammer's phrase.[1]

An illustration of the point is provided by Ronald Reagan's secretary of state, George P. Shultz, in his attempt to missionize African nations about the virtues of a free market. Speaking of societies which the *New York Times* correspondent described as suffering "from deep poverty, illness and malnutrition," the secretary said, "I don't want to be knocking generosity but I think . . . that it is in our interest to see countries become market-oriented in their economic system. It relates itself to openness and democracy, a form of government that we think is not only good for the people involved but basically good for us."[2] Dehistoricized values are thus values redesigned to become objects that can be manipulated according to whatever purpose the manipulator has in mind. And, as the example just cited demonstrates, the contexts to which the values are applied are also treated ahistorically so that local facts become blurred. Thus, Secretary Shultz discovered, to virtually everyone's astonishment, freedom of the press and no political prisoners in Liberia.

The function of these strategies is to mystify the inherently antidemocratic power relationships of Operation Democracy. When Secretary Shultz declares that democracy "is not only good for the people involved but basically good for us," the paternalism of the formula assumes a dominator-dominated relationship. The United States is telling others what is good for them. The consequences are as corrupting to the democratic pretensions of the one as they are to the (possibly) democratic aspirations of the other. The reason why a megastate must pervert the democratic possibilities of any society that it is attempting to convert is because no megastate will ever knowingly encourage a political system in a client state that is potentially subversive of the power of the megastate.

Yet that is precisely the threat that a democratic politics possesses. The whole point of a democratic political structure is to be responsive to the local needs, grievances, and aspirations of ordinary people. Its point is not to provide a stable basis for multinational corporations or stations for U.S. military satellites. Nowhere is democracy's potential for instability greater than in Central America, the area of most concern to our present policy makers. The history of all the countries in that area is an almost unrelieved record of domestic oppression and exploitation and of American support for those who have been most responsible for the brutalization of their own populations. The rhapsody about El Salvador being sung in Washington is not, as some believe, a song about the promotion of democracy. The fact that the United States finally encouraged some reduction in the free enterprise of death squads is, of course, welcome, but that does not mean—any more than Duarte's election meant—that democracy has come to El Salvador. The decline of death squads is not proof of democratization, only of a minimal respect for human life, a value neither invented by the United States nor monopolized by it. Power remains an elite monopoly in Salvador, and the United States far prefers to deal with the uncertainties accompanying elite rivalries than with those generated by populist discontents.

A megastate must impose itself because it must have conditions suitable to the exercise of its peculiar kind of power, power that is distilled from science, technology, corporate interests, and public contributions (taxes, etc.). The thrust of that power can be described, following Max Weber, as "rationalizing," that is, it seeks to establish the most efficient relationship between the means (the use of available resources) and the ends (e.g., restoring America to a competitive position within the international economy). Rationalization works best when it can ignore local peculiarities and apply a strictly economic conception of efficiency (the most cost-efficient and productive use of resources). The notion that the United States should follow a policy that "proclaims overt and unashamed American support for anti-Communist revolution" wherever feasible in the world, as Krauthammer has urged,[3] merely conceals imposition under the guise of revolution and thus slides over the inherent antagonism between free politics and imposition under the tutelage of the megastate.

THIS MAY STRIKE the reader as an overly academic or abstract way of approaching the question of whether democratic values can or should be promoted by American foreign policy. But the point being made has serious implications. Abstraction from context describes precisely the kind of operation that takes place when or if democracy becomes an object of foreign policy. Abstraction is a reminder of how values are inevitably transformed when they are redesigned as weapons in the rivalries between great powers. A transformation necessarily results because of the change in context—from a setting in which the values have been historically interwoven with and adapted to practices and beliefs, molded and mellowed, contested and defended, refined so as to compose a distinctive political life-form, a democratic political society—to a setting where those values now operate as counters in a strategy whose context is a global cold war.

To describe democracy as a political life-form means that it is a historically specific way of structuring and exercising power, of conducting common affairs, and of defining an appropriate political culture for nourishing the habits, behavior, and outlook that sustain and distinguish the democratic way. The severance of so-called democratic values from democratic structures, processes, and culture permits government officials to promote a "democratic value," such as respect for human dignity, by secretly and illegally selling arms to secure the release of hostages, that is, by circumventing the established political processes of consultation and public deliberation and by violating the political sensibilities nurtured by the political culture (e.g., making arms available to governments that support terrorism abroad and stifle dissent at home).

Is such an action an aberration, or is there some basic contradiction between caring for a democratic political culture at home and promoting democratic values abroad along with the interests embodied in state power? Are democratic values and practices really a constitutive element of state power, or are the elements that constitute state power antithetical to democracy?

The relationship between power, interests, and values in the context of international rivalry has been a topic discussed by political theorists ever since Thucydides first posed the problem in his so-called Melian Dialogue. After World War II the topic was set in a particular framework, that of "realism" versus "idealism" or "utopianism." Stated broadly, the realists maintained that foreign policies had to be based squarely upon "the national interests," of which the interest in national power was fundamental and overriding. Moral considerations, in this view, presented a danger because they inhibited the statesman from making clear-eyed judgments about what is to be done under conditions of bewildering complexity, urgency, and intense competition with rivals who are ever vigilant to take advantage of the slightest misstep and rarely hesitant to resort to morally reprehensible means if these will enable them to gain their self-interested ends.

The idealists insisted that if states were not bound by moral constraints or did not actively seek to inject moral values into their decisions, relations between states would degenerate into the "state of nature" depicted by Hobbes. In the absence of right, every state would pursue its ends by whatever means it deemed useful.

The debate, which was especially heated in the years immediately after World War II, engaged some of the most famous scholars, publicists, and statesmen of that era, such as Hans Morgenthau, George Kennan, Walter Lippmann, and Reinhold Niebuhr. One of the many dubious achievements of the Reagan administration was to have provided several occasions for reconsidering the problem. From the inauguration of Ronald Reagan to his departure from office, his administration presented the remarkable spectacle of a foreign policy that declared its intention of "having it all," of being both realist and idealist, both aggressive and aggressively moral. It promised a morally positive, interventionist foreign policy and it boasted that it had made good on that promise in Grenada and Central America.

The so-called Reagan Doctrine, which was outlined by the president in a speech of 14 March 1986, announced that American policy would actively promote democracy throughout the world, It would, he declared, throw its weight on the side of the "democratic revolution" new sweeping the world, not only in the Philippines, Argentina, Haiti, and El Salvador, but among the Afghan rebels and the Nicaraguan contras. As a token of its seriousness the government established a special agency, the National Endowment for Democracy, to funnel money abroad to support the forces of democracy. But intertwined with this "idealistic" agency, whose name was obviously selected to exploit the soft and sweet cultural resonance of the National Endowment for the Humanities and the National Foundation for the Arts, was a promise of force. The United States, the president insisted, would continue to send not only "humanitarian" assistance but also weapons and American troops to support "freedom fighters"—although the operation was promised to be so finely calibrated as to stop just short of involving this country in a full-blooded war. However, his speech also carried a veiled threat, that if these measures proved insufficient, there was always the possibility of an American invasion.

The Reagan Doctrine thus represents a combination of the realist's zest for exercising power without apologies and the idealist's conviction that moral responsibility requires that power be used selflessly for moral purposes. This combination has been developed at greater length by Charles Krauthammer in a series of articles published in the mid–1980s in the *New Republic*. As a context for considering his arguments and exploring their implications, I want to turn briefly to the postwar controversy between realists and idealists in order to draw attention to one crucial area of agreement that existed among some of the adversaries because it is significantly missing both from the official formulation of the Reagan Doctrine and from Krauthammer's gloss of it.

The older debate was mostly conducted before the proliferation of nuclear weapons had occurred; before the development of nonnuclear weapons of unprecedented destructive power; before the emergence of terrorism as an accepted instrument of foreign policy; before the appearance of a huge international market in the manufacture and sale of armaments; and before international rivalries had reached interstellar dimensions. The debate of the late 1940s and early 1950s occurred at a moment when the possibilities of the military exploitation of science and technology had just begun. Accordingly, one would expect the notions of power entertained by both realists and idealists of those pre-Apollo days to be exuberant and expansive, since they had probably not fully absorbed the fearsome meaning of Hiroshima and had certainly not anticipated the rapid militarization of space.

The fact is, however, that the most prominent realists and idealists shared a common concern to restrain American power rather than expand its uses. Parsimonious rather than profligate, they looked upon power as a scarce, not as an indefinitely renewable, resource. This was the attitude of George Kennan, whose early attacks upon "moralism" were inspired by a conviction that highmindedness helped to promote exaggerated and improbable goals for foreign policy makers and encouraged them to pursue objectives that would severely strain American resources. Kennan's famous articles advocating a policy of "containment" of the Soviet Union were a case in point. They argued that American power should be used to block Soviet expansion, not to enlarge American *imperium*.

At the other end of the spectrum, the idealists argued in a similarly restrictive vein. They advocated a strong United Nations as a means of curbing Great Power rivalries, and they often defended large foreign aid programs in the belief that by promoting economic recovery in Europe and elsewhere a bloc of independent nations would come into existence and serve as buffers between the superpowers. Thus, neither side was hospitable to notions of unlimited power or of a state committed to continuous intervention in the internal life of other states. It is worth noting that three of the most visible participants in the debate,

Kennan, Morgenthau, and Lippmann, would all oppose the Vietnam War.

The symbolic moment when that tacit agreement about the necessary limits of power was challenged came with John Kennedy's inaugural address of 1961. Its vision of a mobilized society committed to bearing any burden or sacrifice in the cause of freedom anywhere in the world foreshadowed the replacement of the cautionary counsels of the 1940s and 1950s by the more expansive conception of power which produced the so-called Vietnam experience and is still accepted as dogma by policy makers. The shift was made possible by the intensive cultivation of American power which took place in the postwar years. For almost half a century there has been a vigorous and systematic state policy aimed at creating forms and magnitudes of power hitherto unknown. The launching of spaceflights for both military and commercial exploitation and the development of space as a battleground served as hard proof that the unlimited objectives enunciated in the Kennedy inaugural were the ideological correlative of the actuality of limitless power.

Because there seemed to be no predetermined limits to U.S. power, decision makers were not forced to choose between the advancement of national interest (power) and the promotion of American values abroad. To those who would be exercising power it promised a perfect world where self-interest, power, and values could be synergetically intertwined. The pursuit of self-interest would automatically produce the good of all if those who were about to be benefited could be induced to buy our two goods, American values and American products. Power could thus have what free market capitalism seemed unable to supply by itself: a good conscience, not just an easy one.

The hold that that vision had over Reagan's foreign policy was illustrated once more by Secretary Shultz. "There is," he averred, "a sense in which everything has a strategic dimension to it. We want to see a way of thinking [in Africa] that's congenial to us flourish. Beyond that, of course, a very heavy proportion of our exports go to the developing countries, something like 40 percent. So, as these economies develop, it is good for our economy."[4] Now the development of power depends not only upon the cultivation of scientific knowledge and technical skills. It also depends upon a certain kind of society, one whose members are willing to hand over their labor to the state in the form of trillion-dollar defense budgets and multibillion-dollar foreign assistance programs, both benevolent and military.

One question that naturally arises at this point is, Does this enlarged conception of power and its uses require a citizenry which, in supporting state power in the ways being asked of it, would be undermining democratic values? Some decades ago John Dewey wrote a book, *The Public and Its Problems*. The text of today's self-styled neo-interventionists could be more aptly titled, *The Public Is the Problem*. For, as we shall see shortly, the proponents of the Reagan Doctrine have identified the American public as the greatest stumbling block to the pursuit of a heroic foreign policy. The Reagan Doctrine was, then, not solely a rationale for an expansionist foreign policy but the expression of an inherent antagonism between the interests that have become unified in the state and the traditional political and constitutional values that have constituted the American political identity. Or, more strongly, Operation Democracy signifies that a form of state power has evolved which can only develop if it de-democratizes its "home base," that is, if it alters American political or collective identity to render it more congenial to the perceived requirements of American power. Operation Democracy, then, requires nothing less than the reconstitution of American power at home by measures that diminish and weaken the democratic elements of the American polity. Further, the megastate cannot promote democracy abroad because it itself is not the extension of democracy at home but a projection of other forces.

KRAUTHAMMER'S ATTEMPT TO create an intellectual apology for the Reagan Doctrine and for the enlarged concept of power which inspired that doctrine can best be examined against the backdrop of the new forms and conceptions of power that I have been sketching. His starting point, as stated in his articles in *The New Republic*, is revealing. The United States needs, he claims, "an assertive, activist, interventionist foreign policy." Why does the United States need such a policy? Because, according to Krauthammer, it is a "great power" and, by definition, it has "interests beyond the security of its borders."[5] Thus, the starting point is not American democracy as such but the peculiar needs of a transcending form of power, the Great Power or megastate, whose nature is such that it cannot remain inside its own borders.

This starting point is, by nature, antidemocratic. Democracy is, as I suggested earlier, the political form that is inherently distrustful of large-scale politics because such politics is inevitably accompanied by bureaucratic administration, centralization of power, the elevation of elites, the passivity of the citizenry, and the erosion of participatory politics. When democracy is stretched to fit the needs of global empire, its substance is thinned to the vanishing point. It is reduced to being formalistic and formulaic. It can then inspire pronouncements like Secretary Shultz's when he said of Liberia, "There is freedom of the press here, there is an opposition, there are no political prisoners."[6]

But why does the megastate become discontented and seek *Lebens-raum?* Why is it unnatural for such a state to act as if its identity cannot be preserved and cultivated in the traditional manner, that is, by observing the limits represented by the notion of boundaries?

In the past, political theorists have tried to answer these questions in various ways. One way has been to say that a Great Power does not transcend its boundaries simply because it is a great power, which, like an overfull bottle, suffers from surplus power and hence must spill over neighboring societies. Rather, they become Great Powers because they seek to go beyond their historical boundaries. Or in Krauthammer's somewhat euphemistic formula, "a great power does not find its interests. It chooses them."[7] This formulation, which we might label "decisionism" in order to underscore its emphasis upon what Nietzsche called "the will to power," inevitably ends up extolling the notion of "strong will" and heroic action as the test of moral seriousness that separates real political men from moist-eyed romantics. It is, however, the victim of an illusion that it desperately embraces, the illusion of an unconstrained or undetermined state. The illusion is maintained by refusing to ask, What are the forms of power that make the Great Power great? Once that question is asked, once we are compelled to inquire about the nature of the interests which constitute state power, then it begins to appear that perhaps Krauthammer has gotten things exactly backwards. The megastate does not choose its interests; the interests choose the megastate. The American megastate was no more free to choose, say, a reasonable *modus vivendi* with Castro's Cuba than it was to throw its full, long-term support to the Sandinistas. For the decision makers to have made those choices would have meant that the state would have been in opposition to the interests whose dynamics constituted its power.

In order, therefore, to explain the nature of the megastate's power we must look for forms of power which are inherently expansionist rather than asserting that great power is at the command of the state and that it is an arbitrary matter as to how that power will be used. A starting point in the megastate's conception of power was foreshadowed by Hobbes: "[Man] cannot be content with a moderate power . . . because he cannot assure the power and means to live well, which he hath present, without the acquisition of more."[8]

The virtue of Hobbes's formulation is that it calls attention to a certain kind of power that is immoderate by nature, that cannot rest content because the kind of power it is is rendered insecure by its very possession. The power that answers to that name is power based upon competition and comparative advantage. Not all forms of power answer to that name. Democratic power, for example, requires a very different approach to power, one that emphasizes cooperation, public deliberation, and diffused and shared power rather than centralized and monopolized power. Until recently, too, the power represented by scientific knowledge made appeal to an international community of science, to the mostly unhampered exchange of information, and to the right to conduct research without first obtaining a governmental imprimatur.

This suggests that it is important to go behind slogans about using American power to promote the values of democracy abroad and to see what sleight-of-hand is taking place concerning power. Whenever the word "power" is used, either euphemistically or explicitly, in connection with state action, as when it is said that "the U.S. government is using its power to influence the leaders of Mexico," the impression is created that power is something homogeneous that our government "possesses," like gold deposited in standardized bars. Power is not like that, however. It is acquired mainly through money and the resources that money commands. What money buys, politically, is control over the institutions and processes that represent legitimacy. Power is the complex outcome of unending competition among those who are able to command organized resources. It is a struggle in which elections, voters, legislatures, and politicians express the power of organized resources, such as are represented by corporations and governmental bureaucracies, rather than being the primary sources of power.

Legitimacy works two ways. It enables those who have gained control over the authoritative institutions (e.g., the presidency or the Congress) to extract resources from the general membership, as in taxes or by military conscription. But legitimacy also means affording access to the seals of legitimacy on certain terms while denying it on others; for example, it is legitimate to raise huge funds to win elections but illegitimate to bribe public officials.

State power, then, is a story of how forms of power are translated from one form, say, corporate wealth, into another, say, friendly members of the Federal Reserve Board or assistant secretaries of defense in charge of defense contracts. It is also a story with a subtext of defeat and powerlessness, of groups with sociologically defined existence— race, ethnicity, income, education—but few or no resources to organize. Yet their lives are part of the story. For there is no power over without a power under, no dominator without a dominated, no winners without losers.

In order to give expression to this subtext, two notions have been widely used over the last century to describe the dynamics that cause state power to exceed historical boundaries. One is imperialism, the other capitalism. Neither of these notions figured importantly or at all in Krauthammer's early version of his doctrine of neo-internationalism, although more recently he has acknowledged the existence of an "American *imperium*." However, the acknowledgment is made only to dismiss the point of imperialism. "True," Mr. Krauthammer writes, "the American *imperium* is about power, but power in the service of certain values. These values we hold, domestically, to be not only good but self-evidently good. And as we have gone abroad, we have spread them."[9]

The unexamined "we" that figures so confidently and unproblematically in Mr. Krauthammer's claims serves to attach "us" complicitly to the state. At the same time, the idea of power with which "we" are identified is remarkably indifferent to power's genealogy. For it is power without the stigmata of domestic conflict, power immaculately conceived, unmarred by the sufferings and frustrations of those who are unincorporated in "we." It is power that does not know that it has been washed in the blood of lambs.

What is striking about Mr. Krauthammer's conception of power is that it never occurs to him that there could be a vision of *Realpolitik* that would be just as tough-minded, just as intent upon self-interest, and just as illusionless as he sometimes professes to be. The objections of Third World countries to American intervention and domination as well the protests of critics of American capitalism at home are typically dismissed by Krauthammer as "vulgar Marxism" or sentimental anticolonialism, never as critiques of power that strive to be realistic. In fact, it is he that proves most romantic in his understanding of power. One would never guess from his articles that American capitalism is in any way bound up with state power, or that the advancement of capitalism, which Secretary Shultz was never shy about, is a prime object of foreign policy. Although he refers to "interests," he never pauses to analyze that term, or to break down its constituent elements so that a reader might see which are the preponderant interests, which the excluded, and so on. A more straightforward assertion of the nature of American power and its projection abroad can be found in the presidential speech elaborating the Reagan Doctrine. The "aim" of our "global foreign policy," the president asserted, was to create a "free, open, and expanding market-oriented global economy."

Like Edmund Burke, who did not want "the state . . . to be considered as nothing better than a partnership agreement in a trade of pepper and calico . . . or some other such low concern,"[10] Krauthammer does not want American intervention sullied by vulgar motives of the sort that the Reagan administration openly reveled in. "Once a great power defines national interest beyond the terms of its own safety," Krauthammer solemnly declares, "it necessarily enters the realm of

values."[11] The "realm of values" has a peculiar status in Krauthammer's eyes. Values are not so much objects of choice, an option that a
state might be able to promote if the occasion allowed; for him, values
are "musts" rather than "oughts." "Power," he tells us, "must be in the
service of some higher value. And that value is freedom, or more generally the spread of Western political norms: pluralism, [human]
rights, and democracy." These are "higher" values for Krauthammer
because they appear to him to be purely political or moral, presumably
in a way that Shultz's beloved icon of the free market or the protection
of private property would not. The purpose of higher values is not
difficult to ascertain. Krauthammer sees them as redeeming what
would otherwise be a meaningless struggle between rival imperial-
isms. Where there is "a moral meaning and a moral purpose" present
in the conflict with the USSR, somehow the consequences of an imperialist struggle, indeed of imperialism itself, become praiseworthy
rather than blameworthy. "The cry of a bereaved mother," in Krauthammer's remarkable imagery, "is not an argument against war. It is
an argument against an unjust war."[12]

As I have previously noted, neo-internationalism approaches the
problem of power and values in the confident belief that the things of
Caesar's and the things of the spirit are inherently compatible. "The
spread of these values supports American power" just as "American
power is needed to support the spread of these values." But if this is
the serendipitous case, what explains the urgent tone of Krauthammer's brief? What is the problem that he seeks to solve by insisting on
the moral character of interventionism?

The answer was suggested earlier when I noted that the text of interventionism could be entitled *The Public Is the Problem*. "The problem is American popular will, which is deeply divided on whether to
accept the responsibilities of a great power."[13] Krauthammer is convinced that what is blocking the moral imperialism of Operation Democracy is a "native American instinct against intervention." Americans, it seems, will not support interventionism for reasons of
"interest" alone, according to Krauthammer.[14]

Although this diagnosis has a distinguished academic lineage,
which includes Henry Kissinger and Samuel Huntington, it also gives
the show away. It reveals a profoundly antidemocratic assumption,
that the citizenry is opposed to interventionism. Instead of accepting
that judgment, however, which is what would be presumed in a democracy, apologists for interventionism resort to the ideological sub-
terfuge of justifying intervention in the name of democratic values;
that is, they will, in effect, impose a policy which contradicts what the
people want. The shallowness of the democratic convictions of those

peddling Operation Democracy can be gauged by Krauthammer's treatment of the arms-for-Iran and money-for-the-contras scandal.

"The problem" posed by Irangate, according to Krauthammer, "is not democracy"—which must come as a relief to the nonexistent constituency that believed that it was. "Democracy is instrumental. Its role is faithfully to transmit the popular will." The real problem is that many Americans do not want "to accept the responsibilities of a great power."[15]

Krauthammer notwithstanding, Irangate does involve democracy because democracy is not simply a matter of expressing a popular will—a function that arguably has become, at best, highly attenuated—but a method of ordering political accountability to a superior authority, the citizenry. And that is what Irangate is about. President Reagan's directive of 17 January 1986 not only authorized sales of weapons and spare parts to Iran but directed that the operation should be kept secret from Congress, that is, from the only constitutional body that represents "the people."

The problem raised by Irangate is fundamental because it is merely a perpetuation of the problem posed by the Vietnam War, Watergate, Grenada, and aid to the contras. The megastate is not simply in tension with democracy, as Krauthammer suggests. That formulation implies that the condition of democracy at home is satisfactory and that the only question is whether democracy is sufficiently mature to be able to give the megastate the support it requires. My claim is, however, that the megastate is the enemy of democracy at home and that the same pressures that drive it abroad and cause it to reshape foreign societies in certain ways are at work domestically.

A convenient starting point is provided by the same presidential address of 14 March 1986 reaffirming America's commitment to "a global foreign policy" and to promoting the "democratic revolution" occurring throughout the world. That speech openly asserted that for this commitment to be effective the nation would have to reduce public debate. American support for "resistant forces fighting against Communist tyranny" could succeed only if it was extended "without publicity." "American interests," the president declared, "will be served best if we can keep the details of our help, how it is provided—out of view." He explained that to "hobble ourselves" by ordinary constitutional procedures "makes it harder to shape events while problems are still manageable." The price of open politics, he suggested, was an ineffectual state. "We are certain to face starker choices down the road"—meaning, presumably, that American troops would invade Nicaragua—unless the American people consented to clandestine politics that would allow greater leeway to the president.

The same pattern of seeking to insulate state decisions from public scrutiny had already begun in the president's directive of 17 January 1986. The latter had eliminated Congress from the policy process; now, under the guise of promoting democracy abroad, the president would eliminate the citizenry at home.

These de-democratizing moves are not an aberration, the misjudgments of a drowsy president, but inherent in the role of the externally oriented megastate. A revealing example is the establishment of the National Foundation for Democracy, mentioned earlier. The aim of the NFD is to use public funds to assist the growth of democracy abroad. The main conduits for the program would be private organizations, especially American trade unions, which would assist their counterparts abroad. Leaving aside some embarrassing incidents in which the NFD was found to be subsidizing far-right groups, and even ignoring the difficulties of holding private groups politically accountable, the greatest danger posed by the NFD is to the independence of the trade unions. A cozy relationship between union leaders and government was the hallmark of fascism and remains typical of communist regimes. The further question is one that embroiders a theme we have already encountered: is it in the interest of the megastate operating abroad that at home it has a docile rather than a militant trade union movement?

An administration that is impatient with democratic politics at home is not, on the face of it, the most likely promoter of democracy abroad. A brief review of how democratic values fared under the Reagan administration should persuade all but the most inveterate Reagan adulator not only of the hypocrisy in its democratic pretensions but of its dangerous tendencies.

The Reagan administration deliberately sought to roll back the civil rights gains of the 1960s, and by its coded demagoguery it succeeded in reviving a level of racial hostility and tension unlike anything experienced in this country since the urban upheavals of the 1960s. From the moment early in the first Reagan administration when the air traffic controllers' union was broken, no opportunity was lost to weaken the power of unions. Its record on the question of women's rights was nearly as bad. Its support for public education, a crucial matter in any society purporting to be democratic, was weak, except for the secretary of education's fervent crusade on behalf of morality and virginity. It consistently favored a variety of measures which would restrict public access to information and extend the powers of governmental surveillance. Its proposals for subjecting public employees to compulsory urinalysis represented a profound invasion of privacy, as did various attempts to use state power to impose an element of religious uniformity in schools and to inject its presence into the abortion question. When these policies were—and are—combined with a running attack upon the courts, a systematic effort to staff the courts with ideological zealots, and a persistent campaign for reducing the legal protections enjoyed by the accused, it is clear that the country is in the midst of a profound antidemocratic thrust.

The dimensions of that reaction have not been faced because, in part, the public has been misled into believing the antistate rhetoric of the Reagan and Bush administrations. Except for some measures of economic deregulation and a lack of enthusiasm for enforcing civil rights legislation, the present and past administrations have performed prodigies in strengthening the power of the state. Trillion-dollar defense budgets not only increase the military power of the state but create a large sector of the economy dependent upon governmental contracts and subject to governmental supervision. Government-sponsored research has worked a similar result in extending state influence over universities and academic life generally. Welfare programs, although they are roundly criticized in the rhetoric of the administration, have not been significantly reduced for the simple reason that they represent an important mechanism of control over the poor and working classes.

Thus, democracy at home is being reduced to the same status as the democracy purportedly being promoted in Nicaragua, El Salvador, Guatemala, Honduras, and Afghanistan: the status of being a serviceable condition for the generation, expansion, and application of state power. Democracy can be invoked to gain legitimation from a citizenry for whom democracy still retains a valid resonance, but the actual political conditions being fostered are undercutting the possibilities of democracy. In recent years, American society has grown more inegalitarian, more divided by extremes of wealth and poverty and of education and ignorance, more openly ruled by elites, more systematically dominated by corporate power, more retarded by a mass media that ensures political and cultural immaturity, and, in its politics, more systematically corrupted by money.

Operation Democracy can be summed up: In response to the needs of the megastate, democracy is made safe for the world by being radically transformed at home.

Notes

1: Collective Identity and Constitutional Power

1. Carl J. Friedrich, *Constitutional Government and Democracy: Theory and Practice in Europe and America* (Boston: Little, Brown, 1941), p. 21; Jacob E. Cooke, ed., *The Federalist* (Middletown, Conn.: Wesleyan University Press, 1961), no. 22, p. 146.

2. For a further discussion of myth, see Sheldon S. Wolin, "Postmodern Politics and the Absence of Myth," *Social Research* 52 (Summer 1985): 217–39.

3. On the antifederalists generally, see Jackson Turner Main, *The Anti-Federalists: Critics of the Constitution* (Chapel Hill: University of North Carolina Press, 1961). See, more recently, Herbert J. Storing, *What the Anti-Federalists Were For* (Chicago: University of Chicago Press, 1981); Sheldon S. Wolin, "The People's Two Bodies," *Democracy* 1 (January 1981): 9–24.

4. For Montesquieu's views, see *De l'esprit des lois,* especially bks. 11–12. Hume's position is most accessible in his *Essays Moral and Political* (various editions). See, in particular, "Of the Original Contract," "Of Civil Liberty," and "Of the Origins of Justice and Property." Recent discussions of Hume include Duncan Forbes, *Hume's Philosophical Politics* (Cambridge: Cambridge University Press, 1975); David Miller, *Philosophy and Ideology in Hume's Political Thought* (Oxford: Oxford University Press, 1981); and earlier, Sheldon S.

Wolin, "Hume and Conservatism," in D. W. Livingston and J. T. King, eds., *Hume: A Re-Evaluation* (New York: Fordham University Press, 1976).

5. *New York Times,* 6 September 1986.

6. Ibid.

7. See E. James Ferguson, *The Power of the Purse* (Chapel Hill: University of North Carolina Press, 1961), esp. pt. 4; Forrest McDonald, *Alexander Hamilton* (New York: Norton, 1979), chaps. 6–10.

8. See Robert Harrison, "The Weakened Spring of Government Revisited: The Growth of Federal Power in the Late Nineteenth Century," in Rhodri Jeffreys-Jones and Bruce Collins, eds., *The Growth of Federal Power in American History* (DeKalb: Northern Illinois University Press, 1983), pp. 62–67; Morton Keller, *Affairs of State: Public Life in Late Nineteenth-Century America* (Cambridge, Mass.: Harvard University Press, Belknap Press, 1977).

9. Harry N. Scheiber, "American Federalism and the Diffusion of Power," *University of Toledo Law Review* 9 (1978): 619.

10. See Harrison, "Weakened Spring of Government Revisited," 63.

11. Paul A. C. Koistinen, "The Industrial-Military Complex in Historical Perspective: World War I," *Business History Review* 41 (Winter 1967): 378–403.

12. See, generally, Jürgen Habermas, *Legitimation Crisis,* trans. Thomas McCarthy (Boston: Beacon Press, 1975).

13. James Sundquist, "The Crisis of Competence in Government," in Joseph A. Pechman, ed., *Setting National Priorities for the 1980s* (Washington, D.C.: Brookings Institution, 1980), p. 531.

14. Speech to Joint Session of Congress, *New York Times,* 5 February 1986, sec. A–20.

15. President's Budget Message, *New York Times,* 6 February 1986, sec. B–12.

16. Speech to Joint Session of Congress, *New York Times,* 5 February 1986, sec. A–20.

17. See Lester M. Salamon, "Non-Profit Organizations: The Lost Opportunity," in John L. Palmer and Isabel V. Sawhill, eds., *The Reagan Record* (Cambridge, Mass.: Ballinger, 1984), pp. 2612–85.

18. For various statements championing private takeovers of public functions, see Harvey Brooks, Lance Liebman, and Corrine S. Schelling, eds., *Public-Private Partnership: New Opportunities for Meeting Social Needs* (Cambridge, Mass.: Ballinger, 1984).

19. On the widespread use of private security police, see the article on the subject in the *New York Times,* 29 November 1985, sec. A–1. For the sale of governmental services and installations, see Martin Tolchin, "New Momentum in the Selling of Government," *New York Times,* 18 December 1985.

20. "El Salvador is Fertile Ground for Protestant Sects," *New York Times,* 20 January 1986, sec. A–2.

21. The concept of the economic polity is developed at some length in Chapter 9.

22. *New York Times,* 19 December 1985, sec. A–14.

2: Injustice and Collective Memory

1. Ernest Renan, "Qu'est-ce qu'une nation?" *Oeuvres complètes* (Paris: Calmann-Lévy, 1947–61), 1: 887–906, at p. 892.

2. Benedict Anderson, *Imagined Communities: Reflections on the Origin and Spread of Nationalism* (London: Verso/New Left Books, 1983).

3. Saint-Augustine, *Confessions,* trans. W. Piney-Coffin (Harmondsworth: Penguin Books, 1976), 10.8, 17 (pp. 214–16, 224).

4. *Leviathan,* ed. C. B. Macpherson (Harmondsworth: Penguin Books, 1968), chap. 15, p. 210.

5. Ibid., p. 209.

6. John Rawls, "A Well-Ordered Society," *Philosophy, Politics, and Society,* fifth series, ed. P. Laslett and J. Fishkin (New Haven: Yale University Press, 1979), pp. 10, 11, 15.

7. Hobbes, *Leviathan,* chap. 15, p. 211.

8. *Two Treatises of Government,* ed. P. Laslett (New York: Mentor Books, 1965), 2:54.

9. Hobbes, *Leviathan,* chap. 15, p. 202.

10. Locke, *Two Treatises,* 2:6–8.

11. Hobbes, *Leviathan,* chap. 15, p. 216.

12. Ibid., chap. 10, p. 152.

13. Paul Hazard, *Crisis of the European Conscience, 1680–1715,* trans. J. Lewis May (Cleveland: World, 1963), p. 284.

14. Locke, *Two Treatises,* 2:94.

15. Ibid., 2:87.

16. *The Wealth of Nations,* ed. A. Skinner, 2 vols.(Oxford: Oxford University Press, 1976), 2:910.

17. John Rawls, *A Theory of Justice* (Cambridge, Mass.: Harvard University Press, 1971), p. 75.

18. See Frances Fox Piven and Richard A. Cloward, *Regulating the Poor* (New York: Pantheon Books, 1971).

19. Lawrence M. Mead, *Beyond Entitlement: The Social Obligations of Citizenship* (New York: Free Press, 1986), pp. 2, 3, 15.

3: Elitism and the Rage against Postmodernity

1. New York: Simon and Schuster, 1987. The page numbers in parentheses refer to page numbers in Bloom's book.

2. Robert Paul Wolff, "The Closing of the American Mind," *Academe* 73 (September–October 1987): 64–65.

3. In this Pynchonesque world of ours, military contractors, like Olin, lavishly endow centers of the humanities which are more reactionary than their donors but advertise themselves as though they represent the political opposite of what they or their benefactors are.

4: Archaism, Modernity, and Democracy in America

1. *De la Démocratie en Amérique,* ed. J.-P. Mayer, 2 vols. (Paris: Gallimard, 1961), I(1), p. 5. I have used the edition of *Démocratie en Amérique* in the *Oeuvres complètes,* ed. J.-P. Mayer, André Jardin, and others (Paris: Gallimard, 1961–). *Démocratie* appeared as the first two volumes in the Mayer edition, but the editor labeled them as I(1) and I(2). The same system is followed here. Hereafter I shall refer simply to *Démocratie* and to the complete works as OC. Unless otherwise specified, all translations are my own.

2. Letter to Reeve, 22 March 1837 (OC, vol. 6(1), pp. 37–38). Also see Tocqueville's letter to Beaumont of 3 March 1853 (ibid., vol. 8(3)).

3. Letter to Reeve, 22 March 1837, p. 38

4. *Démocratie,* 1:12.

5. *The Old Regime* was published in 1856 in the incomplete form in which Tocqueville had left it; a second volume had been promised.

6. It is important to note that before Tocqueville completed *Democracy* he had written an essay on "France before the Revolution," which was published in *Westminster Review* in 1836. In that essay he foreshadows much of *The Old Regime.*

7. *L'Ancien régime et la révolution,* p. 73. This work is volume 2 of the complete works.

8. Ibid., p. 74.

9. The richest source of Tocqueville's views on the newness of America can be found in his travel diaries. These are collected in OC, vol. 5.

10. *Démocratie,* I(1), p. 4.

11. Ibid., p. 1.

12. Ibid., pp. 1–4.

13. Ibid., p. 11.

14. To Kergolay, 18 October 1847, OC, vol. 13(2), p. 209; see also the letter to Reeve of 9 September 1839, OC, vol. 6, p. 47.

15. The French neglect of Tocqueville has been remedied in recent years by several important studies: Jean-Claude Lamberti, *La notion d'individualisme chez Tocqueville* (Paris: PUF, 1983) and *Tocqueville et les deux démocraties* (Paris: PUF, 1983); Pierre Manent, *Tocqueville et la nature de la démocratie* (Paris: Julliard, 1982); Françoise Furet, *Workshop of the Historian* (Chicago: University of Chicago Press, 1985), which contains two essays on Tocqueville, and the same author's *Interpreting the French Revolution* (Cambridge: Cambridge University Press, 1981), which has a long analysis of *The Old Regime;* and the fine biography by the late André Jardin, *Alexis de Tocqueville, 1805–1859* (Paris: Hachette, 1984).

16. In the history of political theory there was a continuous tradition of books of counsel, the most famous of which was, of course, Machiavelli's *Prince.* Curiously, Henry Reeve, Tocqueville's translator, thought that *Democracy* was "the people's *Prince.*" Letter to Reeve, 22 February 1840, OC, vol. 6, p. 55.

17. Cited in Jack Lively, *The Social and Political Thought of Alexis de Tocqueville* (Oxford: Clarendon Press, 1962), p. 8.

18. See Letter 9 (Hamilton) of *The Federalist.*

19. J. T. Schleifer, *The Making of Tocqueville's "Democracy in America"* (Chapel Hill: University of North Carolina Press, 1982).

20. *Démocratie,* I(1), pp. 257 ff.

21. See *The Federalist,* No. 10.

22. *Démocratie,* I(1), p. 25.

23. Ibid., I(1), pp. 65–67.

24. See, for example, the comments of Melvin Richter, ed., *The Political Theory of Montesquieu* (Cambridge: Cambridge University Press, 1977), pp. 7 ff., and Richter's article "The Uses of Theory: Tocqueville's Adaptation of Montesquieu," in Melvin Richter, ed., *Essays in Theory and History* (Cambridge, Mass.: Harvard University Press, 1970), pp. 74–102.

25. *De l'esprit des lois,* ed. Roger Caillois, 2 vols. in the Pléiade edition of Montesquieu's *Oeuvres complètes* (Paris: Gallimard, 1951), 1:405.

26. Ibid., bk. 2, chap. 4; bk. 4, chap. 9.

27. In general see François Jean Marie Olivier-Martin, *L'Organisation corporative de la France d'ancien régime* (Paris: Recueil Sirey, 1938), especially chap. 8.

28. Louis Hartz, *The Liberal Tradition in America* (New York: Harcourt, Brace, 1955).

29. The importance of the theme of "nature" in Tocqueville's writings has been neglected. Chapter 1 of *Démocratie* attempts a physical description, much as a Montesquieuan might, as the starting point for understanding America. There is also much material in the travel sketches referred to in note 9.

30. *The Complete Writings of Thomas Paine,* ed. P. Foner, 2 vols. (New York: Citadel Press, 1945), 1:376. The quotation is from *The Rights of Man.*

31. *Démocratie,* I(1), chap. 6.

32. Franklin Ford, *Robe and Sword* (Cambridge, Mass.: Harvard University Press, 1970).

33. See Howell A. Lloyd, *The State, France, and the Sixteenth Century* London: Allen & Unwin, 1983); Claude Frédéric Lévy, *Capitalistes et pouvoir au siècle des lumières,* 3 vols. (Paris: Mouton, 1969), especially vol. 3.

34. *Démocratie,* I(1), chap. 2.

35. Ibid., bk. 2, chap. 2.

36. Ibid., I(1), pp. 214–15, 273–74.

5: Tending and Intending a Constitution

1. On the highly organized effort of the Framers to promote ratification, see Merrill Jensen, *The Articles of Confederation* (Madison: University of Wisconsin Press, 1940). See also Linda G. DePauw, *The Eleventh Pillar: New York State and the Federal Constitution* (Ithaca: Cornell University Press, 1966); Jackson Turner Main, *The Anti-Federalists, Critics of the Constitution, 1781–1788* (Chapel Hill: University of North Carolina Press, 1961); and Herbert J. Storing, *What the Anti-Federalists Were For* (Chicago: University of Chicago Press, 1981).

2. For discussions of *The Federalist,* see Trevor Colbourn, ed., *Fame and the*

Founding Fathers: Essays by Douglass Adair (New York: Norton, 1974); David W. Epstein, *The Political Theory of "The Federalist"* (Chicago: University of Chicago Press, 1984); Albert Furtwangler, *The Authority of Publius* (Ithaca: Cornell University Press, 1984); Morton White, *Philosophy, "The Federalist," and the Constitution* (New York: Oxford University Press, 1987); Martin Diamond, "The Federalist," in Leo Strauss et al., *History of Political Philosophy* (Chicago: University of Chicago Press, 1963), pp. 573–93; and Forrest McDonald, *Novus Ordo Seclorum: The Intellectual Origins of the Constitution* (Lawrence: University Press of Kansas, 1985).

3. *The Federalist,* ed. Jacob E. Cooke (Middletown, Conn.: Wesleyan University Press, 1961), no. 33, p. 207.

4. See Chapter 8, "Contract and Birthright."

5. The letter is reproduced in Max Farrand, ed., *The Records of the Federal Convention,* 3 vols. (New Haven, Conn.: Yale University Press, 1911), 2:666–67.

6. Ibid., p. 666.

7. Ibid., 1:48–49.

8. Alexis de Tocqueville, *Democracy in America,* trans. George Lawrence, ed. J.-P. Mayer (Garden City, N.Y.: Doubleday, 1969), p. 287.

9. Ibid., p. 44.

10. Ibid.

11. Ibid., p. 522.

12. Ibid., p. 524.

13. Farrand, *Records,* 3:401.

14. On the political changes introduced by the states following the rupture with Britain, see Jensen, *Articles of Confederation,* pp. 16ff. See also Jack P. Greene, "The Role of the Lower House of Assembly in Eighteenth-Century Politics," *The Reinterpretation of the American Revolution, 1763–1789,* ed. Jack P. Greene (New York: Harper and Row, 1968), pp. 86–109.

15. Farrand, *Records,* 2:125. See also the comments of Rutledge at ibid., p. 452.

16. *The Federalist,* no. 37, p. 233. Madison modified this outburst in a later number. There he asserted that the proposed constitution would be simply an "expansion of principles" already in the Articles. No. 40, p. 263.

17. Farrand, *Records,* 2:53; also pp. 89–90 and Madison's letter to Jefferson, 24 October 1787, in ibid., 3:133.

18. *The Federalist,* no. 1, p. 105.

19. Ibid., no. 11, p. 70.

20. Samuel Bryan, "The Letters of 'Centinel'" *The Anti-Federalists,* ed. Cecilia M. Kenyon (Indianapolis: Bobbs-Merrill, 1966), p. 4.

21. *The Federalist,* no. 1, p. 3.

22. Farrand, *Records,* 1:552.

23. James Winthrop (?), "Agrippa," in Kenyon, *Anti-Federalists,* p. 134.

24. *The Federalist,* no. 2, p. 9.

25. Ibid., no. 10, pp. 56–57, 61.

26. Ibid., no. 9, pp. 50–51.

27. Ibid., no. 16, p. 102; no. 9, pp. 52–54; no. 10, pp. 61ff.

28. Ibid., no. 1, p. 6.
29. Ibid., no. 3, p. 15; no. 4, p. 22; no. 70, p. 471.
30. Ibid., no. 27, p. 172.
31. Ibid., no. 4, pp. 20–21.
32. Ibid., no. 9, p. 51.
33. See ibid., no. 40, pp. 258ff., where Madison tries to defend the convention against the charge that it had exceeded its mandate.
34. Ibid., no. 14, p. 88.
35. Ibid., no. 4, p. 22.
36. Ibid., no. 14, p. 84.
37. Ibid., no. 31, p. 194.
38. Ibid., pp. 195–96.
39. Ibid., no. 17, p. 107; no. 27, p. 173.
40. Farrand, *Records*, 3:143.
41. *The Federalist*, no. 16, p. 103.
42. Ibid., no. 39, p. 255.
43. Ibid., no. 17, p. 107.
44. Ibid.
45. Ibid., no. 70, p. 472; no. 74, p. 500.

6: Montesquieu and Publius

1. Jefferson to T. M. Randolph, Jr., 30 May 1790, *Papers of Thomas Jefferson*, vol. 16, ed. Julian P. Boyd (Princeton: Princeton University Press, 1950), p. 449.

2. Alexis de Tocqueville, *De la Démocratie en Amerique*, ed. J.-P. Mayer, 2 vols. (Paris: Gallimard, 1961), I(2), pt. 1, chap. 10. These volumes constitute the first two in Tocqueville's *Oeuvres complètes*, edited by Mayer and subsequently by André Jardin. For the influence of *The Federalist* upon Tocqueville, see James T. Schleifer, *The Making of Tocqueville's "Democracy in America"* (Chapel Hill: University of North Carolina Press, 1980). Also Charles Beard, ed., *The Enduring Federalist* (New York: Viking, 1948) and Morton White, *Philosophy, "The Federalist," and the Constitution* (New York: Oxford University Press, 1987).

3. See Douglas Adair, *Fame and the Founding Fathers,* ed. Trevor Colbourn (New York: Norton, 1974), especially the essay "That Politics May Be Reduced to a Science: David Hume, James Madison, and the Tenth 'Federalist'"; David Epstein, *The Political Theory of "The Federalist"* (Chicago: University of Chicago Press, 1984); Albert Furtwangler, *The Authority of Publius* (Ithaca: Cornell University Press, 1984); Gordon Wood, *The Creation of the American Republic, 1776–1787* (New York: Norton, 1972), pp. 469–564; Garry Wills, *Explaining America: The Federalist* (New York: Doubleday, 1981); John P. Diggins, *The Lost Soul of American Politics: Virtue, Self-interest, and the Foundations of Liberalism* (New York: Basic Books, 1984), chaps. 1–4.

4. For recent studies that emphasize Montesquieu's "scientific" approach, see the stimulating essay by Louis Althusser in *Montesquieu, Rousseau, Marx*

(London: Verso/New Left Books, 1982, 1972), pp. 13–107. For a critique of Althusser from a more conventional view of science, see Georges C. Vlachos, *La Politique de Montesquieu* (Paris: Editions Montchrétien, 1974).

5. Montesquieu, *De l'esprit des lois,* in *Oeuvres complètes,* ed. Roger Caillois, Pleiade edition, 2 vols. (Paris: Gallimard, 1958), bk. 1, chap. 3 (vol. 2, p. 237). Hereafter *Esprit.*

6. "Essay on the Constitution and Function of the Provincial Assemblies," *Condorcet, Selected Writings,* ed. Keith Baker (Indianapolis: Bobbs-Merrill, 1976), p. 86.

7. *Esprit,* preface, vol. 2, pp. 229–30.

8. For Montesquieu's emphasis upon "the political" see *Esprit,* Avertissement (vol. 2, pp. 227, 228) and bk. 24, chap. 1 (vol. 2, p. 714). In his *Defense de l'esprit des lois,* Montesquieu described *Esprit* as "a work of pure politics and pure jurisprudence" (vol. 2, p. 1121).

9. Ibid., bk. l, chap. 1 (vol. 2, p. 232).

10. Ibid., bk. 1, chap. 1 (vol. 2, pp. 232–34).

11. Ibid., bk. 26, chap. 1 (vol. 2, pp. 750–51).

12. Ibid., vol. 2, p. 1138.

13. Ibid., bk. 11, chap. 6 (vol. 2, p. 407).

14. Ibid., bk. 24, chap. 19 (vol. 2, p. 407).

15. Ibid., preface (vol. 2, p. 231). On the concept of "system" among eighteenth-century writers, see Otto Mayr, *Authority, Liberty, and Automatic Machinery in Early Modern Europe* (Baltimore: Johns Hopkins University Press, 1986), p. 117.

16. *Esprit,* bk. 5, chap. 14 (vol. 2, p. 297).

17. Ibid., bk. 2, chap. 4 (vol. 2, p. 247).

18. Ibid., bk. 3, chap. 7 (vol. 2, p. 257).

19. Ibid., bk. 5, chap. 13 (vol. 2, p. 292).

20. Ibid., bk. 2, chap. 1 (vol. 2, p. 239).

21. *Lettres Persanes,* no. 63 (vol. 1, p. 223).

22. *Esprit,* bk. 6, chap. 1 (vol. 2, p. 309).

23. Ibid., bk. 5, chap. 14 (vol. 2, p. 297).

24. *The Federalist,* ed. Jacob E. Cooke (Middletown, Conn.: Wesleyan University Press, 1961), no. 43, p. 297.

25. Art. 1.8.18: "The Congress shall have the power: . . . To make all laws which shall be necessary and proper for carrying into execution the foregoing powers, and all other powers vested by this Constitution in the government of the United States, or in any department or officer thereof."

Art. 6.2: "This Constitution and the laws of the United States which shall be made in pursuance thereof; and all treaties made, or which shall be made under the authority of the United States, shall be the supreme law of this land; and the Judges in every State shall be bound thereby, any thing in the Constitution or laws of any State to the contrary notwithstanding."

26. *The Federalist,* no. 33, p. 204.

27. Ibid., no. 1, p. 3.

28. Ibid., no. 85, p. 594.

29. Ibid., no. 9, p. 50.

30. Ibid., p. 51.

31. Thomas Hobbes, "De Corpore," 7.2. Vol. 1 of *English Works,* ed. Sir William Molesworth (London, 1839).

32. *The Federalist,* no. 14, p. 88.

33. See "Letters of Cato," III, *The Complete Anti-Federalist,* ed. Herbert J. Storing, 7 vols. (Chicago: University of Chicago Press, 1981), 2:110–11. One prominent supporter of the Constitution, Thomas McKean of Pennsylvania, did argue that "despotism," if wisely administered, "is the best form of government invented by the ingenuity of man." Speech of 23 November 1787, *Documentary History of the Ratification of the Constitution,* ed. John P. Kaminski and Gaspare J. Saladino (Madison: State Historical Society of Wisconsin, 1984), 15:71. On the antifederalists, see Herbert J. Storing, *What the Anti-Federalists Were For* (Chicago: University of Chicago Press, 1981); Wood, *Creation of the American Republic* (see n. 3), pp. 519ff.

34. *The Federalist,* no. 23, p. 151.

35. Ibid., no. 37, p. 233.

36. Ibid., no. 9, pp. 52–53; see also no. 23, p. 148.

37. Ibid., no. 85, p. 594.

38. Ibid., no. 15, p. 97.

39. Ibid., no. 4, pp. 20–21.

40. For references to the science of politics, see ibid., pp. 51–52, 193ff., 324, 594.

41. Ibid., no. 23, p. 151; no. 68, p. 461.

42. Ibid., no. 85, pp. 591, 594.

43. Ibid., no. 6, p. 28; no. 8, p. 47.

44. Ibid., no. 31, p. 193.

45. Ibid., no. 31, p. 194.

46. Ibid., no. 31, p. 195.

47. Ibid., no. 23, p. 150.

48. Ibid., no. 37, pp. 232–33.

49. Ibid., no. 37, pp. 233–34.

50. Ibid., no. 37, pp. 235–37.

51. Ibid., no. 37, p. 238.

52. Ibid., no. 10, pp. 63–64; no. 51, pp. 351–52.

53. Ibid., no. 48, p. 333.

54. Ibid., no. 47, p. 324.

55. Ibid., no. 10, p. 59.

56. Ibid., no. 51, p. 352.

57. Ibid., no. 44, pp. 304–5.

58. Ibid., no. 23, p. 147.

59. Ibid., no. 15, p. 97; no. 12, p. 79; no. 34, p. 211.

60. In the constitution that he brought to Philadelphia, Hamilton favored a lifetime executive and Senate.

61. *The Federalist,* no. 68, p. 461.

7: E Pluribus Unum

1. "The Address and Reasons for Dissent of the Minority of the Convention of the State of Pennsylvania to their Constituents," *The Anti-Federalists,* ed. Cecilia M. Kenyon (Indianapolis: Bobbs-Merrill, 1966), p. 46.

2. John Locke, *Two Treatises of Government,* ed. Peter Laslett (New York: Mentor Books, 1965), 2:96.

3. *The Federalist,* ed. Jacob E. Cooke (Middletown, Conn.: Wesleyan University Press, 1961), no. 14, p. 84.

4. Thomas Hobbes, *Leviathan,* ed. C. B. Macpherson (Harmondsworth: Penguin Books, 1968), chap. 16, p. 220.

5. Etymologically, "ordain" means both to sanctify and to arrange, to legitimate and to constitute.

6. See H. C. Baldry, *The Unity of Mankind in Greek Thought* (Cambridge: Cambridge University Press, 1965).

7. *The Federalist,* no. 2, p. 9.

8. See Sheldon S. Wolin, "Postmodern Politics and the Absence of Myth," *Social Research* 52 (Summer 1985): 217–39.

9. Genesis 11:1 ff.

10. See Francis Oakley, *Omnipotence, Covenant, and Order* (Ithaca: Cornell University Press, 1984).

11. *The Federalist,* no. 31, p. 195.

12. Ibid., no. 23, p. 146.

13. Ibid., p. 147.

14. Ibid.

15. Ibid., p. 149.

16. Ibid., no. 10, pp. 58–59.

17. Ibid., p. 58.

18. Ibid.

19. Ibid., p. 62.

20. Alexis de Tocqueville, *De la Démocratie en Amérique,* 2 vols. in *Oeuvres complètes,* ed. J.-P. Mayer (Paris: Gallimard, 1961), I(2), p. 108.

21. Ibid.

22. Louis Hartz, *The Liberal Tradition in America* (New York: Harcourt, Brace, 1955), pp. 6, 20.

23. See Madison's discussion of the controversy surrounding the meaning of "consolidated power" of the national government in Max Farrand, ed., *The Records of the Federal Convention of 1787,* 3 vols. (New Haven: Yale University Press, 1911), 3:464, 473.

24. *The Federalist,* no. 17, p. 108.

25. Ibid., p. 107.

26. Ibid., pp. 105, 107.

27. Ibid., p. 105.

28. Stephen Hopkins, "An Essay on the Trade of the Northern Colonies" (1764), *Tracts of the American Revolution, 1763–1776,* ed. Merrill Jensen (Indianapolis: Bobbs-Merrill, 1967), p. 50.

29. Cited in Richard Koebner, *Empire* (Cambridge: Cambridge University Press, 1961), pp. 85–86.

30. "The Rights of Colonies Examined," *Tracts of the American Revolution,* p. 57.

31. F. L. Ganshof, *Feudalism,* 4th ed. (New York: Harper and Row Torchbooks, n.d.), p. 6.

32. See the suggestive article by Rowland Berthoff and John M. Murrin, "Feudalism, Communalism, and the Yeoman Freeholder: The American Revolution Considered as a Social Accident," *Essays on the American Revolution,* ed. Stephen G. Kurtz and James H. Hutson (New York: Norton, 1973), pp. 256–88.

33. On the *thèse nobilaire,* see Nannerl Keohane, *Philosophy and the State in France* (Princeton: Princeton University Press, 1980); and the older study by Carcassonne, *Montesquieu et le Problème de la Constitution Française au XVIIIe Siècle* (Paris, 1927).

34. Montesquieu, *De l'esprit des lois,* bk. 30, chap. 1.

35. As contained in Richard Hofstadter, ed., *Great Issues in American History from the Revolution to the Civil War, 1765–1865* (New York: Vintage Books, 1958), pp. 28, 29.

36. *The Federalist,* no. 17, pp. 108, 109; also no. 19, p. 118.

37. Ibid., no. 17, pp. 110, 111.

38. Ibid., no. 15, p. 93; no. 44, p. 305.

39. Ibid., no. 9, p. 53.

40. Ibid., no. 17, pp. 109, 110; no. 45, pp. 318–19.

41. Ibid., no. 17, p. 109.

42. James Winthrop (?), "Agrippa," in Kenyon, *The Anti-Federalists,* p. 134.

43. *The Federalist,* no. 27, pp. 173–74.

44. Ibid., no. 21, pp. 133, 134; no. 9, p. 5 (new science), p. 55 (imbecility).

45. Ibid., no. 17, p. 209.

46. Ibid., no. 21, pp. 133–34.

47. Ibid., no. 22, p. 141.

48. Ibid., no. 9, p. 50.

8: Contract and Birthright

1. See Sheldon S. Wolin, "Postmodern Politics and the Absence of Myth," *Social Research* 52 (Summer 1985): 217–39.

2. Richard Hooker, *Of the Laws of Ecclesiastical Polity,* bk. 1, chap 10, sec. 8.

9: Democracy and the Welfare State

1. Max Weber, "Religious Rejections of the World and Their Directions," *From Max Weber: Essays in Sociology,* trans. H. H. Gerth and C. Wright Mills (New York: Oxford University Press, 1946), p. 334.

2. One of the most important exceptions would be Claus Offe. See his essays "Political Culture and Social Democratic Administration" and "Euro-

pean Socialism and the Role of the State" in Offe, *Contradictions of the Welfare State,* ed. and trans. John Keane (Cambridge, Mass.: MIT Press, 1984).

3. "Politics as a Vocation," *From Max Weber,* p. 78.

4. For a quantitative analysis of the growth of centralization in the United States, see Marshall Meyer, *Change in Public Bureaucracies* (Cambridge: Cambridge University Press, 1979). Note also Wilensky's remark that "political elites who embrace the welfare state in centralized polities can better overcome resistance to the necessary taxes and expenditures than in decentralized polities" (David Wilensky, *The Welfare State and Equality: Structural and Ideological Roots of Public Expenditures* [Berkeley and Los Angeles: University of California Press, 1975], p. 52).

5. On the arbitrariness attending determinations regarding the disabled, see Deborah A. Stone, *The Disabled State* (Philadelphia: Temple University Press, 1984).

6. See, on this topic, Claus Offe, "Social Policy and the Theory of the State," in *Contradictions of the Welfare State,* pp. 88ff.

7. "State of the Union Message," 4 February 1986.

8. John Herbers, "Mobility for the Poor Sought in Housing Plan," *New York Times,* 1 June 1985, sec. A–1.

9. Robert Pear, "U.S. Will Resume Review of Rolls," *New York Times,* 6 December 1985, sec. A–1.

10. For the development of the modern state as side effects, see Marc Raeff, *The Well-Ordered Police State: Social and Institutional Change through Law in the Germanies and Russia, 1600–1800* (New Haven: Yale University Press, 1983). The classic study in this genre is Tocqueville's *Ancien régime.*

11. Thomas Hobbes, *Leviathan,* ed. C. B. Macpherson (Harmondsworth: Penguin Books, 1968), chap. 11, p. 162.

12. Stone, *The Disabled State,,* p. 11.

13. The standard work on Reason of State is Friedrich Meinecke, *Machiavellism,* trans. Douglas Scott (London: Routledge & Kegan Paul, 1957). A number of useful essays can be found in Roman Schnur, ed., *Staatsräson: Studien zur Geschichte eines Politischen Begriffs* (Berlin: Duncker and Humblot, 1975). More specialized studies include William Church, *Richelieu and Reason of State* (Princeton: Princeton University Press, 1971), and Etienne Thau, *Raison d'état et pensée politique à l'époque de Richelieu* (Paris: Armand Colins, n.d.).

14. Niccolò Machiavelli, *Il Principe (The Prince),* ed. L. Arthur Burd (Oxford: Clarendon Press, 1891), chap. 19, p. 318 (my translation).

15. Giovanni Botero, Dedication, *The Reason of State,* trans. P. J. Waley and D. P. Waley (New Haven: Yale University Press, 1956), pp. xiii-iv.

16. Botero remarked that "all that is done" regarding the foundation and extension of state power "is said to be done for Reasons of State, yet this is said rather of such actions that cannot be considered in the light of ordinary reason" (*The Reason of State,* bk. 1, sec. 1, p. 3).

17. Niccolò Machiavelli, *The Discourses,* ed. B. Crick, trans. L. J. Walter and B. Richardson (Harmondsworth: Penguin Books, 1970), 3.41, p. 515.

18. Ibid.

19. *The Discourses*, 1.34, p. 195. Machiavelli continued, "No republic is ever perfect unless by its laws it has provided for all contingencies, and for every eventuality has provided a remedy and determined the method of applying it."

20. *The Prince*, chap. 25.

21. *The Prince*, chap. 19.

22. OED lists the first English use by Fuller in 1642.

23. Cited in Margaret Judson, *The Crisis of the Constitution* (New Brunswick, N.J.: Rutgers University Press, 1946), p. 432.

24. *Leviathan*, chap. 14, pp. 189–90.

25. *Leviathan*, chap. 13, pp. 186–88; chap. 26, pp. 201–2.

26. Strictly, the maxim should read *esto* rather than *est*, as C. H. McIlwain used to insist. It was invoked at Rome when the institution of the constitutional dictatorship was brought into force, but it applied to the consul responsible for external affairs.

27. *Leviathan*, chap. 25, p. 307.

28. The essential background of Locke's views lies in *Bate's Case* (1606) and the opinion of Chief Baron Fleming. The latter argued that the king possessed an "absolute power" that applied "only" to the "general benefit of the people and is *salus populi*." This power, Fleming continued, was not restricted to exceptional occasions but fell under "rules of policy" that applied to all "matters of state" (*A Complete Collection of State Trials*, ed. T. B. Howell [London, 1816], 2:389. See also the useful survey by David S. Berkowitz, "Reason of State in England and the Petition of Right, 1603–1629," in Schnur, *Staatsräson*, pp. 164–212.

29. On the subject of rationalization, see the fundamental essay by Karl Löwith now translated as *Max Weber and Karl Marx*, ed. Tom Bottomore and William Outhwaite (London: Allen & Unwin, 1982); also Wolfgang Mommsen, *The Age of Bureaucracy: Perspectives on the Political Sociology of Max Weber* (Oxford: Blackwell, 1974); and Wolfgang Schluchter, *The Rise of Western Rationalism: Max Weber's Developmental History*, trans. Guenther Roth (Berkeley and Los Angeles: University of California Press, 1981).

30. Neil Gilbert, *Capitalism and the Welfare State: Dilemmas of Social Benevolence* (New Haven: Yale University Press, 1983), pp. 7–8. On the widespread use of private security police, see the article on the subject in the *New York Times*, 29 November 1985, sec. A–1.

31. *New York Times*, 3 March 1986, sec. A–1.

32. Wilensky, *The Welfare State and Equality*, p. 1.

33. Theda Skocpol and John Ikenberry, "The Political Formation of the American Welfare State in Historical and Comparative Perspective," in *The Welfare State, 1883–1983*, vol. 6, *Comparative Social Research*, ed. Richard F. Tomasson (Greenwich, Conn.: JAI Press, 1983), p. 89.

34. On the Marxist conception of the state, see Bob Jessop, *The Capitalist State* (New York: New York University Press, 1982), chap. 1; and Nicos Poulantzas, *Political Power and Social Classes*, trans. Timothy O'Hagan (London: New Left Books and Sheed and Ward, 1973), p. 2.

35. See, for example, Theda Skocpol, *States and Social Revolutions: A Comparative Analysis of France, Russia, and China* (Cambridge: Cambridge University Press, 1979), pp. 24ff.

36. Jürgen Habermas, *Legitimation Crisis,* trans. Thomas McCarthy (Boston: Beacon Press, 1975); James O'Connor, *The Fiscal Crisis of the State* (New York: St. Martin's Press, 1973).

37. Walter Korpi, *The Working Class in Welfare Capitalism: Work, Unions and Politics in Sweden* (London: Routledge & Kegan Paul, 1978); see Ian Gough, *The Political Economy of the Welfare State* (London: Macmillan, 1979), for a somewhat tougher Marxist view.

38. Samuel Huntington, *Political Order in Changing Societies* (New Haven: Yale University Press, 1968); Stephen D. Krasner, *Defending the National Interest: Raw Materials, Investments, and U.S. Foreign Policy* (Princeton, N.J.: Princeton University Press, 1978); Eric A. Nordlinger, *The Autonomy of the Democratic State* (Cambridge, Mass.: Harvard University Press, 1981).

39. Hugh Heclo, *Modern Social Politics in Britain and Sweden* (New Haven: Yale University Press, 1974), p. 303.

40. Samuel Huntington, "United States," in *The Crisis of Democracy: Report on the Governability of Democracies to the Trilateral Commission* (New York: New York University Press, 1975), pp. 59–74.

41. One should add, contrary also to Niklas Luhmann, *Politische Theorie in Wohlfahrtsstaat* (Munich: Olzog Verlag, 1981).

10: Democracy without the Citizen

1. *The Writings of Thomas Jefferson,* 10 vols., ed. Paul L. Ford (New York: Putnam, 1892–99), 5:286.

2. *The Federalist,* ed. Jacob E. Cooke (Middletown, Conn.: Wesleyan University Press, 1961), no. 23, p. 147.

11: Democracy and Operation Democracy

1. Charles Krauthammer, "The Reagan Doctrine." This appeared originally in *Time* magazine. I have used the version published by the Council on Religion and International Affairs carrying the title *Intervention and the Reagan Doctrine* by Robert W. Tucker, Charles Krauthammer, and Kenneth Thompson (New York, 1985), p. 20.

2. *New York Times,* 18 January 1987, sec. E–3.

3. Krauthammer, "The Reagan Doctrine," p. 20.

4. *New York Times,* 18 January 1987, sec. E–3.

5. "The Poverty of Realism," *New Republic,* 17 February 1986, pp. 14, 16.

6. *New York Times,* 16 January 1987, sec. A–1.

7. Krauthammer, "The Poverty of Realism," p. 17.

8. Thomas Hobbes, *Leviathan,* ed. C. B. Macpherson (Harmondsworth: Penguin Books, 1968), chap. 11, p. 161.

9. Krauthammer, "Morality and the Reagan Doctrine," *New Republic,* 8 September 1986, p. 18.

10. Edmund Burke, *Reflections on the Revolution in France*, Everyman Ed. (London: Dent, 1910), p. 93.

11. "The Poverty of Realism," p. 17.

12. "Morality and the Reagan Doctrine," p. 24.

13. "Divided Superpower," *New Republic*, 22 December 1986, pp. 14–17.

14. "The Poverty of Realism," p. 18.

15. "Divided Superpower," pp. 14–17.

Index

Sheldon S. Wolin, noted political theorist, is professor emeritus at Princeton University and has held appointments at the University of California, Berkeley and Santa Cruz; Oxford; and Cornell. Among his books are *Politics and Vision: Continuity and Innovation in Western Political Thought; The Berkeley Student Rebellion* (with S. M. Lipset); *Hobbes;* and *The Berkeley Rebellion and Beyond* (with John Schaar).

Designed by Chris L. Hotvedt
Composed by Graphic Composition, Inc., in Bembo text and display
Printed by Edwards Brothers on 50-lb. Glatfelter Natural, B-16 paper.

Made in the USA
San Bernardino, CA
28 October 2015